Automating and Orchestrating Networks with NetDevOps

Ivo Pinto, CCIE No. 57162

Faisal Chaudhry, CCIE No. 2706

Cisco Press

Automating and Orchestrating Networks with NetDevOps

Ivo Pinto
Faisal Chaudhry

1 2023

Library of Congress Control Number: 2023905787

ISBN-13: 978-0-13-799728-2

ISBN-10: 0-13-799728-0

Warning and Disclaimer

Trademark Acknowledgments

Special Sales

For information about buying this title in bulk quantities, or for special sales opportunities (which may include electronic versions; custom cover designs; and content particular to your business, training goals, marketing focus, or branding interests), please contact our corporate sales department at corpsales@pearsoned.com or (800) 382-3419.

For government sales inquiries, please contact governmentsales@pearsoned.com.

For questions about sales outside the U.S., please contact intlcs@pearson.com.

Feedback Information

At Cisco Press, our goal is to create in-depth technical books of the highest quality and value. Each book is crafted with care and precision, undergoing rigorous development that involves the unique expertise of members from the professional technical community.

Readers' feedback is a natural continuation of this process. If you have any comments regarding how we could improve the quality of this book or otherwise alter it to better suit your needs, you can contact us through email at feedback@ciscopress.com. Please make sure to include the book title and ISBN in your message.

We greatly appreciate your assistance.

Vice President, IT Professional: Mark Taub

Alliances Manager, Cisco Press: Arezou Gol

Director, ITP Product Management: Brett Bartow

Managing Editor: Sandra Schroeder

Development Editor: Ellie C. Bru

Senior Project Editor: Mandie Frank

Copy Editor: Bart Reed

Technical Editor: Asier Arlegui Lacunza

Editorial Assistant: Cindy Teeters

Designer: Chuti Prasertsith

Composition: codeMantra

Indexer: Erika Millen

Proofreader: Barbara Mack

Americas Headquarters
Cisco Systems, Inc.
San Jose, CA

Asia Pacific Headquarters
Cisco Systems (USA) Pte. Ltd.
Singapore

Europe Headquarters
Cisco Systems International BV Amsterdam,
The Netherlands

Cisco has more than 200 offices worldwide. Addresses, phone numbers, and fax numbers are listed on the Cisco Website at www.cisco.com/go/offices.

Cisco and the Cisco logo are trademarks or registered trademarks of Cisco and/or its affiliates in the U.S. and other countries. To view a list of Cisco trademarks, go to this URL: www.cisco.com/go/trademarks. Third party trademarks mentioned are the property of their respective owners. The use of the word partner does not imply a partnership relationship between Cisco and any other company. (1110R)

Pearson's Commitment to Diversity, Equity, and Inclusion

Pearson is dedicated to creating bias-free content that reflects the diversity of all learners. We embrace the many dimensions of diversity, including but not limited to race, ethnicity, gender, socioeconomic status, ability, age, sexual orientation, and religious or political beliefs.

Education is a powerful force for equity and change in our world. It has the potential to deliver opportunities that improve lives and enable economic mobility. As we work with authors to create content for every product and service, we acknowledge our responsibility to demonstrate inclusivity and incorporate diverse scholarship so that everyone can achieve their potential through learning. As the world's leading learning company, we have a duty to help drive change and live up to our purpose to help more people create a better life for themselves and to create a better world.

Our ambition is to purposefully contribute to a world where

- Everyone has an equitable and lifelong opportunity to succeed through learning

- Our educational products and services are inclusive and represent the rich diversity of learners

- Our educational content accurately reflects the histories and experiences of the learners we serve

- Our educational content prompts deeper discussions with learners and motivates them to expand their own learning (and worldview)

While we work hard to present unbiased content, we want to hear from you about any concerns or needs with this Pearson product so that we can investigate and address them.

Please contact us with concerns about any potential bias at https://www.pearson.com/report-bias.html.

Figure Credits

Figure 3.3: Amazon Web Services, Inc

Figures 3.4-3.7, 3.9, 3.11-3.13, 3.15, 3.17, 4.1-4.3, 6.3: Jenkins project

Figures 5.2, 5.3: Google LLC

Figures 5.4, 5.6-5.10, 5.12: EVE-NG Ltd

Figures 6.1, 6.2: GitHub Inc

Figure 6.4: Slack Technologies, LLC

About the Authors

Ivo Pinto, CCIE No. 57162 (R&S, Security, and Data Center), CISSP, is a Solutions Architect with many years of experience in the fields of cloud, automation, and enterprise and data center networking. Ivo has worked at Cisco in different roles and different geographies, and he has led the architecture and deployment of many automated global-scale solutions for Fortune 50 companies that are in production today. In his latest role, he is responsible for the architecture of multiple ISV products at Amazon Web Services (AWS). Ivo has authored multiple white papers, blogs, and the book *Network Automation Made Easy*.

You can follow Ivo on LinkedIn @ivopinto01.

Faisal Chaudhry, CCIE No. 2706 (R&S and Voice), is a Distinguished Engineer in Cisco Customer Experience (CX). In his current role, Faisal works with Cisco customers and industry on cloud automation and orchestration, software-defined networking (SDN) solutions, and network function virtualization (NFV). He is a frequent speaker at key industry events and customer seminars. Faisal started his Cisco career in 1996 in San Jose, California. He has worked in various roles, including technical leader, manager, and consulting systems engineer in different geographies. He holds a bachelor's degree in electrical engineering. Faisal is among the Hall of Fame Distinguished Speakers at Cisco Live.

About the Technical Reviewer

Asier Arlegui Lacunza, CCIE No. 5921, has been with Cisco since 1998 and currently works as a Principal Architect in the Cisco Customer Experience organization. In the past 20+ years of his career at Cisco, he has worked as a technical architect on a wide range of enterprise (data center, campus, and enterprise WAN) and service provider (access and core networking) technology projects, with a focus on network automation. He holds a master's degree in telecommunications engineering from Public University of Navarra, Spain.

Dedications

Ivo:

I would like to dedicate this book to Celia; she is the only reason I decided to take on the writing journey for a second time. To all others, unnamed in this dedication, thank you—you know who you are.

Faisal:

This book is dedicated to my *parents* and *family* for their unconditional love and support.

Also, to *couple* of inspirational *leaders* at work for their immeasurable encouragement during the phase of writing this book. Thank you! this book would not have been possible without your support!

And to my *co-author*, who came up with the idea to write this book. You can thank me for all the good reviews ;-)

Acknowledgments

We would like to thank and acknowledge several people who have helped us directly or indirectly with the necessary skills that enabled us to write this book.

Special thanks to the technical reviewer, Asier Arlegui Lacunza, who contributed to a substantial increase in quality, not only with corrections but also with suggestions to the content of this book.

This book wouldn't have been possible without the support of many people on the Cisco Press team. Brett Bartow, director of the Pearson IT Professional Group, was instrumental in sponsoring the book and driving it to execution. Eleanor Bru, development editor, has done an amazing job in the technical review cycle, and it has been an absolute pleasure working with her. Also, many thanks to the numerous Cisco Press unknown soldiers working behind the scenes to make this book happen.

Contents at a Glance

Reader Services

Register your copy at www.ciscopress.com/title/ISBN for convenient access to downloads, updates, and corrections as they become available. To start the registration process, go to www.ciscopress.com/register and log in or create an account*. Enter the product ISBN 9780137997282 and click Submit. When the process is complete, you will find any available bonus content under Registered Products.

*Be sure to check the box that you would like to hear from us to receive exclusive discounts on future editions of this product.

Contents

Chapter 4   How to Implement NetDevOps Pipelines with Jenkins   157

Chapter 5   How to Implement Virtual Networks with EVE-NG   197

Icons Used in This Book

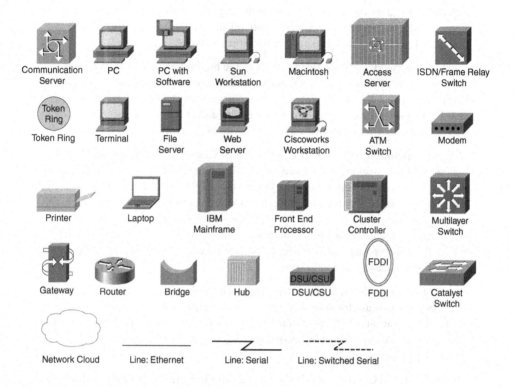

Command Syntax Conventions

The conventions used to present command syntax in this book are the same conventions used in Cisco's Command Reference. The Command Reference describes these conventions as follows:

- **Boldface** indicates commands and keywords that are entered literally as shown. In actual configuration examples and output (not general command syntax), boldface indicates commands that are manually input by the user (such as a **show** command).

- *Italics* indicate arguments for which you supply actual values.

- Vertical bars (|) separate alternative, mutually exclusive elements.

- Square brackets [ ] indicate optional elements.

- Braces { } indicate a required choice.

- Braces within brackets [{ }] indicate a required choice within an optional element.

Introduction

Businesses are growing in size and complexity, trying to deliver value to their customers at unprecedented speeds. This puts pressure on all components of a business to match this delivery velocity—networking infrastructure included.

Traditional networking is not able to adapt to the high velocity of today's businesses. Some have turned to network automation, but automation alone still falls short of the businesses' velocity goals. IT professionals are now, more than ever before, challenged by their businesses to meet a level of network agility and elasticity that only adopting software DevOps practices, automation together with orchestration, can solve.

This book approaches the topic from the point of view of an IT professional who is well-versed in networking and related topics—including cloud, compute, and other components in today's networks—and is trying to take both physical and virtual infrastructure to a semi- or fully automated state. Because automation alone is not enough, this book explains the fundamentals of NetDevOps, starting from its origins, to use cases, to advantages and disadvantages. It dives deep into specific components, such as CI/CD with Jenkins and testing with EVE-NG. However, it covers the topics holistically, always focused on use cases and architectures.

A key aspect of the book is its practical approach to the topic. It is filled with code snippets you can reuse for your own use cases, as well as real case studies that show practical applications of all you will learn. The book includes a tutorial-style approach to two use cases, that guide you, from start to finish, in the implementation of a NetDevOps pipeline.

Although this is a Cisco Press book, it takes a vendor-neutral approach to automation and orchestration tools and techniques. It will give you the knowledge you need to make informed decisions when tackling your own use cases.

Goals and Methods

The goal of this book is to help you understand what NetDevOps is and how traditional network engineering can benefit from adopting DevOps software practices.

You will learn practical applications of NetDevOps, in the form of case studies, and how they address common traditional network engineering gaps. Furthermore, through code snippets, you will be able to quickly take advantage of these practices and tackle challenges in your own environment.

To implement some snippets, you will need tools. In this book you will find descriptions of state-of-the-art tools, guides on how to install and use them, as well as alternatives, as the authors take a vendor-neutral approach.

Who Should Read This Book?

Network automation and orchestration touches several network components, such as routers, switches, firewalls, virtual machines, and cloud infrastructure. In general, IT professionals are divided in their areas of expertise. Individuals are spread into focus areas such as the following, which in some cases overlap:

- Servers and virtualization

- Storage

- Switching and routing

- Security

- Software applications

- Cloud

As the focus of this book is network automation and orchestration, the audience is the sum of all system administrators, storage administrators, networking engineers, software virtualization engineers, and network management engineers.

DevOps and software engineers can also benefit from this book to understand how their skills can be applied to infrastructure (for example, network infrastructure).

How This Book Is Organized

This book is set up to help you understand and replicate the use cases on your own. It is recommended that you read through the chapters in order to get the full benefit of the book.

This book explains the fundamentals of NetDevOps practices, but applied to common use cases the typical engineer job needs. This approach helps show the value automation and orchestration bring to any technology domain.

This book offers a number of advantages:

- An easy reading style with no marketing

- Comprehensive coverage of the topic, from fundamentals to advanced techniques

- Practical approach to network automation and orchestration focused on use cases

- Real case studies, instead of hypothetical situations, of projects the authors have led

- Reusable code snippets

- End-to-end tutorial style guides

- Explanations of tools and their applications, with vendor-neutrality

Book Structure

The book is organized into six chapters:

- **Chapter 1, "Why Do We Need NetDevOps?":** This first chapter highlights the need for more robust and automated network operations. It describes the origins of NetDevOps, highlighting advantages and drawbacks, and finishes with a description of the components that make up its practical implementations.

- **Chapter 2, "Getting Started with NetDevOps":** This chapter describes the main use cases where NetDevOps excels—and how to tackle them. It also details the challenges expected during the adoption of NetDevOps practices as well as common decision pitfalls and investments like tooling or upskilling.

- **Chapter 3, "How to Implement CI/CD Pipelines with Jenkins":** This chapter deep dives into a specific CI/CD tool, Jenkins, from installation to architecture to syntax. This end-to-end chapter covers all aspects of Jenkins, including other CI/CD alternatives.

- **Chapter 4, "How to Implement NetDevOps Pipelines with Jenkins":** This chapter ties together the previous two chapters in a practical manner. It takes the use cases introduced in Chapter 2 and implements them with examples of tooling and code snippets from Chapter 3. This chapter also describes common NetDevOps pipeline actions (for example, linting) that are present in most production-level implementations.

- **Chapter 5, "How to Implement Virtual Networks with EVE-NG":** This chapter describes the network testing tool EVE-NG. It walks you through a step-by-step guide on how to install EVE-NG as well as how to create, use, and configure virtual topologies and how to approach common network testing challenges. The chapter finishes with a comparison between EVE-NG and other vendor alternatives.

- **Chapter 6, "How to Build Your Own NetDevOps Architecture":** This is a highly practical chapter. It guides you through the steps required to implement a minimally viable NetDevOps pipeline in a tutorial-like fashion. This chapter covers two use cases: a configuration change and a compliance verification. It puts to practice most of the tools and concepts shown throughout the book. Lastly, this chapter introduces the concept of ChatOps and shows how to interact with your network using Webex, a chat application.

Chapter 1

Why Do We Need NetDevOps?

Agility to deliver new capabilities and features quickly, improved reliability, enhanced quality in the delivery of new features, reduced human error in network operations, and cost optimizations are just some of the characteristics often desired by IT operations and development teams. The traditional mode of deployment and operating networks has often been characterized as slow in nature due to no or limited use of automation and lack of use of newer software delivery techniques.

This chapter introduces the concept of NetDevOps, along with why we need it, what its benefits are, and some of the tools used for NetDevOps. In particular, we cover the following topics:

- Drivers for NetDevOps
- What NetDevOps is and its advantages
- Modern networking product characteristics
- The tools and components involved in NetDevOps

Note This is an introductory chapter that presents NetDevOps and its components. This chapter lays the foundation for detailed technical information for some of the components covered in subsequent chapters.

Market Trends

Business growth and increased profitability are common goals for an organization. The senior management of an organization will always be looking at ways to grow their core business, be profitable, and improve the way they deliver capabilities and services to their internal users, customers, and/or partners. Digitalization is a fundamental strategy to achieve these goals. Such digital transformations are a journey and allow the organization to innovate at speeds never seen before. Organizations are developing new and innovative ways to develop cloud-native applications for multicloud environments, with the goal of delivering services to their consumers (that is, customers and internal employees) at any location with great speed and agility. Organizations are adopting agile principles to work quickly and continuously improve the experience of users consuming the services they deliver by continuously collecting and measuring the feedback from their consumers.

Networks and associated networking products play a critical function in helping organizations to achieve such vision and goals. Networking functions include the capability to provide connectivity for users and devices to consume applications and services on local area networks, wide area networks, and multiclouds (private and public). The networking functions, such as routers and switches, include both physical and virtual networking functions (VNFs).

Importantly, the business owners are looking for the ability to perform changes and roll out new capabilities on the network in a quick, reliable manner and at scale rather than waiting for hours, days, weeks, or months. In other words, network operations must be like the cloud operating model, where agility, flexibility, reliability, and lower cost of operations are just a few of the benefits. Hence, networks must be enablers rather than inhibitors for the organization and underpin the growth for the business. All these factors serve as the drivers for using automation on the networks.

Advanced data insight capabilities from networks, end-user observability, and application performance also enable advanced functions such as closed-loop automation and help to move from reactive to self-driven and self-optimizing behavior. The networks also provide the telemetry for insights and visibility into the network consumption, enabling fault management. Hence, these capabilities have now become an integral part of network solutions that help to drive digital transformation of the organization.

Networks also provide security capabilities that now commonly utilize the zero-trust principle of "never trust, always verify" (https://en.wikipedia.org/wiki/Zero_trust_security_model). Security is no longer confined to the perimeter of the enterprise network; instead, with the adoption of public cloud services (IaaS, SaaS, PaaS, and so on), the security threat landscape and attack surface are rapidly evolving. The network and application security market itself has shifted toward the cloud delivery model. Network security solutions also cater to and protect applications and the end users accessing those applications in the cloud. The dynamics in network security itself utilize automation and orchestration capabilities—for speed, agility, and scalability—to detect malicious behavior and enforce policies to protect the users and services running on the networks against threats.

Simplifying network operations and reducing the overall operating costs are other key goals that business owners within an organization desire. If deeper analysis into network operations is done, the reasons for high operating costs are normally associated with the way networking products are consumed and run by IT operations. A study conducted by

McKinsey for Cisco provided the following insights into the reasons behind higher network operating costs:

- Ninety-five percent of network changes are performed manually via a command-line interface (CLI).

- Seventy percent of policy violations on the networks are due to human error.

- Seventy-five percent of operating expenses (OpEx) are spent on network changes and troubleshooting.

From these statistics, we can clearly see that the use of automation in deploying and operating networking products is limited. These statistics also show that manual network operations aggravate the overall situation and contribute to higher operations costs; in other words, the more network operations are performed manually, the more policy violations may occur, and the more time is spent troubleshooting. The goals to overcome such challenges have contributed to the way the open-source standards bodies and vendors are developing new features, protocols, and capabilities in modern networking products and architectures. We look at some capabilities of modern networking products in the next section.

Modern Networking Products

At a high level, at least two capabilities are required for deploying, managing, and operating devices in a network: configuration management and network management. There is also a need for administrating devices by admin users, which may include initial deployment and provisioning of the devices and, subsequently, performing day-to-day configuration changes of devices and the network as whole to enable newer capabilities and such. These capabilities are referred to as "configuration management" in this book.

To get insights into the health of the networks, there is need to retrieve the state of each individual device (such as CPU and memory), the device's external links, the routing protocols (such as BGP), and the features (such as routes in routing table) enabled on the device. This operational state information helps to build the overall health and operational view of the network and is referred to as "operation or network management" in this book.

As covered previously, the demands from the business owners and the industry trends have resulted in the development of newer techniques and capabilities in networking products. Speed, agility, reliability, and lower operating costs are just a few motivations for the development of these new features, techniques, and capabilities.

Traditionally, networking products use a command-line interface (CLI) for configuration and viewing operational data. Use of a CLI has benefits because the interface uses text-based syntax that's human-readable; therefore, it's easy to read and understand the commands. The drawbacks are that the CLI syntax of various networking products from a single vendor, let alone products from multiple vendors, can be different from each other.

Also, parsing the text-based responses from the CLI can be a tedious and challenging process, especially since the responses from CLI execution produce unstructured data. It has become evident that the CLI is not an optimal solution for managing configurations of networks, and alternate capabilities continue to be developed. These capabilities are discussed further in this section.

Limitations with device-by-device management led to development of software-defined networking (SDN) solutions that provide centralized configuration and network management capabilities using SDN controllers. SDN controller-based solutions for campus, WAN, and data center (DC) networks are widely adopted in the market now since these solutions provide centralization management as well as offer automation, flexibility, and efficiency. Cisco DNA Center (DNAC), Cisco vManage, and Cisco Application Policy Infrastructure Controller (APIC) are examples of SDN controllers in campus, WAN, and DC networks, respectively. Keep in mind that even in SDN controller-based solutions, the CLI continues to be made available on network devices and used by network administrators for many valid reasons such as troubleshooting and viewing operational data by executing a few CLI commands on a small scale.

Conventionally, fault management of networking products is done by using Simple Network Management Protocol (SNMP). It is a poll-based mechanism that has been used for decades for collecting information from devices for network management.

In the case of SNMP, a network management system (NMS) pulls the operational data frequently from devices. Frequent polling of network devices allows for reactive behavior; that is, the NMS must first poll the data from the devices, correlate the events, and subsequently allow corrective actions to be taken. These measures are taken on events that may have occurred minutes, hours, or even days earlier on the devices and network. Therefore, the time lag is huge. Instead of relying on the reactive nature of SNMP's fault management, a shift toward proactive and even predictive behavior on the networks can provide many benefits, such as a reduction in network downtime, improved network quality, a higher quality experience, and lower cost of operations.

The shift to a proactive and predictive network requires detailed data from the network devices, thus enabling analytics-ready data for the applications and NMS that consume that data. Additionally, the data from networking devices should be generated and made available as and when events occur; in other words, a move to near real-time event collection must be done. Both capabilities—extracting detailed data and extracting it as quickly as possible from the network devices—are important characteristics and considerations for newer protocols and network management techniques such as streaming telemetry. Both allow the shift in networking architectures toward self-healing mechanisms.

These mechanisms naturally enable the utilization and development of machine learning (ML) and artificial intelligence (AI) applications to improve the efficiency, security, and reliability of the networks by helping to make more intelligent and better-informed decisions. What's more, these mechanisms help to optimize the overall network operations aligned with the business objectives of the organization. ML and AI applications could be offered and developed natively on networking products such as centralized controllers in software-defined networks or offered separately as a service. The benefit of such capabilities is that human intervention for identifying and resolving trivial network issues is reduced (or even removed all together). Hence, the engineers and architects can be freed up to focus on enhancing the bottom line and improving the revenue of the core business of the organization.

These trends have resulted in development of capabilities in networking devices that expose their operational and configuration data in a way that applications can ingest and then push the data via a consistent mechanism and at a scale. Work within standards bodies (such as IETF) and open-source communities has led to the development of newer protocols, such as NETCONF, RESTCONF, gNMI, YANG data models, and so on, for the networking products.

Refer to Figure 1-1, which provides a high-level overview of how modern networking products expose their configuration and operational capabilities via a consistent mechanism. Let's review this figure further, starting at the bottom:

- A router with many features, including the BGP routing protocol, interfaces for connectivity to LANs or WANs, and quality of service (QoS) capabilities, is shown at the bottom of the figure. These capabilities are exposed both for configuration purposes and for retrieving operational data from the router using a consistent and well-defined hierarchical data structure. This is referred to as the data model.

- YANG is data modeling language used for both configuration and state data (aka operational data) in modern networking products, and it lays a strong foundation for the automation of these products. More details about YANG data models are provided in the following section.

- The actual data, which is expressed in a structure defined by the YANG data model, can be encoded via a method such as JSON, XML, or Google Protocol Buffer (aka GBP or protobuf). The amount of operational data produced by products can be huge. To transport the large amount of data efficiently to monitoring systems for analysis in a consistent manner, Google Protocol Buffer can be used.

- This encoded data produced by the router or any network device, as shown in Figure 1-1, can be transported using a variety of transport protocols. The choice of transport layer depends on the upper layer protocol used. For example, NETCONF uses Transport Layer Security (TLS) or SSH for establishing sessions between a network device and the external client.

- NETCONF, RESTCONF, and gNMI are some of the protocols commonly available on modern networking platforms for programmability and telemetry.

The use of a YANG model as the basis for configuration and operational data is commonly referred to as "model-driven programmability" and "model-driven telemetry," respectively.

We will investigate the details of configuration and network management in the following sections.

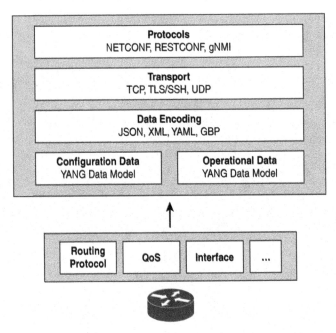

Figure 1-1 *Modern Networking Products' Capabilities*

Configuration Management Overview

Modern networking products—both individual network devices and SDN controllers—are now designed and built with an "application programing interface (API) first" mindset. These modern platforms expose configuration management capabilities using protocols such as NETCONF, RESTCONF, gNMI, and so on. These protocols provide a mechanism for machine-to-machine communications and hence allow for automated configuration of a single networking device as well as large-scale configurations of multiple devices.

NETCONF and RESTCONF are two such protocols developed within the IETF standard body and predominantly focused on configuration management. gNMI stands for gRPC Network Management Interface and is a protocol that can be used for configuration management and for extracting operational data (the latter of which is more focused on telemetry from networking devices). As the name indicates, gNMI is built on the open-source gRPC (Remote Procedure Call) framework. gRPC, which stands for Google Remote Procedure Call, was initially developed by Google for interprocess or intersystem communications. It provides many benefits such as support of TLS for security, support of HTTP/2 to reduce latency, high performance, and efficient transport. Note that NETCONF provides the capability for retrieving operational data from the networking devices using the polling mechanism as well.

Regardless of the type of protocol used, the data sent to (or from) a networking device needs to be formatted in a way that allows the networking device and remote configuration management server to understand it properly. As indicated earlier, the data modeling language provides the specification for communication to the networking device, resulting in consistent and robust communication. The data modeling language provides the structure for the actual data (that is, what's allowed, what's disallowed, and so on). Hence, use of a data model helps to validate the data being transported, resulting in error-free transport of data to or from a networking product. YANG (Yet Another Next Generation) is a data model language mostly used in modern networking products. In simpler terms, YANG only defines the schema and provides the blueprint for data, while the actual data may be encoded in a format such as JSON, XML, or GBP. For example, the YANG data model for the IPv4 address of an interface should allow four octets separated by decimal points, and each octet should allow a decimal value between 0 and 255.

The data format allows communication of structured data between networking devices and an external system via the previously mentioned protocols and hence is also utilized in automation activities.

Initiatives within industry such as IETF and OpenConfig utilize YANG models for configuration management purposes. As shared earlier, the term "model driven programmability" is commonly used to describe this. Further details about the data model language (YANG) and encoding formats are beyond the scope of this book.

For the purposes of automating configuration management, various commercial and open-source tools are available for use. Ansible, Terraform, Chef, Puppet, and Cisco Network Services Orchestrator (NSO) are a few examples of configuration management tools used extensively in the industry.

Depending on the network architecture and capabilities supported by network devices, there are multiple possible scenarios for the use of modern configuration management solutions. Let's look at a couple of common scenarios.

Scenario: SDN-Based Networks

When SDN controller-based solutions are used, configuration management tools perform network automation activities via SDN controllers. The automation scripts on tools execute tasks or control the resources by communicating directly with SDN controllers. In such cases, the execution of tasks via configuration management tools reduces the overhead and dependency of navigating through the graphical user interface (GUI) of SDN controllers.

For example, consider a scenario where Ansible is used as the configuration management tool for Cisco Application Centric Infrastructure (ACI) within a data center (DC). Cisco ACI uses Cisco APIC as the SDN controller. Ansible provides modules that interact with APIC directly using the APIs that are exposed by APIC. Hence, Ansible can perform configuration management tasks as per automation scripts developed in Ansible.

Scenario: Non-SDN-Based Networks

In case the network devices are deployed and managed directly (that is, without any SDN controller), these tools can hide the complexity of developing CLI scripts for configuration management and abstract the configuration of networking devices.

As stated earlier, the configuration management tools utilize adapters or plugins to communicate to the network devices. The plugins or adapters on these tools also provide support for both modern protocols (NETCONF, gNMI, RESTCONF, and content in a YANG model format) as well as traditional CLI methods for communicating and pushing configurations in the network devices.

For example, Ansible supports many modules that can send Cisco IOS, IOS-XE, IOS-XR, and Cisco Nexus OS CLI commands to the respective network devices. Similarly, Ansible supports modules that use the NETCONF protocol and YANG data model–based content to configure Cisco network devices. The use of NETCONF and the YANG model for automation has additional benefits. For example, if a certain feature is supported by NETCONF and the YANG model on devices from multiple vendors, then a single task or command on an automation tool can be used to configure all those devices. However, support for NETCONF and YANG on network devices is prerequisite for this.

Cisco NSO, as an example, also uses a YANG-based modeling language to manage devices and services. Additional examples and details about Ansible and Terraform are covered in this book.

Network Management Overview

For the monitoring of network products, SNMP is traditionally used as a pull-based mechanism that monitors tools to retrieve operational data regularly from the target devices. Additionally, such polling, when done frequently, could result in higher CPU utilization on the target devices. This sort of polling is an inefficient use of resources for both monitoring tools and the target networking devices. To overcome SNMP's limitations, streaming telemetry capabilities are used in modern products. Streaming telemetry allows you to retrieve as much data as possible, as quickly as possible, with minimal impact to the CPU processing on networking products.

SNMP is a pull-based mechanism, whereas streaming telemetry implementations use push-based technique. In the case of SNMP, the network management server must poll the network devices frequently to get the operational data. In the case of streaming telemetry, the network device pushes the operational data to the network management server. The device may push data at regular intervals, as required by the network management server, or at specific intervals, as per its configuration. Hence, streaming telemetry is a lot more efficient and allows almost real-time access to events happening on the network devices.

Streaming telemetry is also referred to as "model-driven telemetry" since it uses YANG data models to define the structure of operational data. As stated in the "Configuration

Management Overview" section, a YANG data model provides a consistent and reliable mechanism to retrieve operational data from the target networking devices.

YANG data models can also be enhanced or extended, allowing vendors to insert vendor-specific data. There are multiple ongoing initiatives within the industry, such as IETF, native, and OpenConfig, to develop and utilize YANG models. In these initiatives, using model-driven telemetry to extract operational data from networking devices is one of the sources of inspiration, in addition to using YANG models for model-driven programmability. Here are some key points:

- Within IETF, the Networking Modeling (netmod) working group has the charter to maintain the guidelines for developing and maintaining a conceptual framework for YANG models. (See https://datatracker.ietf.org/group/netmod/about/ for more details.)

- While IETF is working toward the goal of developing and standardizing YANG models, vendors also develop their own YANG models for the specific features and capabilities of their platforms at the demand of customers and for time-to-market reasons. The term "native data models" refers to YANG data models that are developed and supported by vendors.

- OpenConfig is an initiative and consortium initiated by multiple network operators with the common goal of defining vendor-neutral YANG data models, based on the actual needs and use cases of these operators (see https://www.openconfig.net/). Network management using streaming telemetry is one of the use cases for this initiative. The models developed by these operators are kept at https://github.com/openconfig/public.

In summary, network and configuration management functions of the modern platform help in automation and smoother operational management capabilities that enable the NetDevOps framework. Let's look more into NetDevOps and its advantages.

NetDevOps and Its Advantages

To understand NetDevOps, we'll start by exploring DevOps. Traditionally, the development and operations departments within the IT software development environment have different goals and typically are segregated from each other organizationally. Development teams are tasked with developing new applications or enhancing existing applications, while operations teams are tasked with maintaining the IT environment. The former targets introduce new applications as quickly as possible, while the latter is focused on providing an error-free and no-downtime environment to their users.

As the IT department within an organization expands, the development and operations teams could end up working with each other in a limited fashion. There could be a disconnect between the two departments, and the handover of new applications or new capabilities might not be seamless. This results in conflicts and inefficiencies. To overcome some of these challenges, the concept of DevOps was conceived somewhere around 2007 or 2008. "Dev" refers to development, and "Ops" stands for operations. As the name indicates, the goal is to combine the two teams into one coherent function.

DevOps is a framework and set of practices. The goal of DevOps is to provide smooth, quick, and high-quality products using automation and collaboration between the development and operations teams. The core principle is to add business value to an organization. The DevOps framework goes through the complete process of developing, building, testing, and releasing software (or any product) to the target users as quickly as possible. The following definition comes from Wikipedia (https://en.wikipedia.org/wiki/DevOps):

> "DevOps is a set of practices that combines software development (Dev) and IT operations (Ops). It aims to shorten the systems development life cycle and provide continuous delivery with high software quality."

The DevOps framework encompasses various phases—from the prioritization of ideas by working with business owners, to taking those ideas forward in the development cycle, to validating and finally moving it into production. DevOps does not specify any tools as prerequisites to achieve the previously mentioned goals. However, for automating, collaborating, developing, and releasing software, multiple tools are used during the development and operationalization phases.

Agile software development principles/practices are commonly used in DevOps to provide continuous delivery of software (products, features, or capabilities) by breaking down the delivery into smaller steps. It helps to break down the boundaries between development and operations by developing and releasing features in smaller chunks rather than using the big-bang "waterfall" approach, where every detail is scoped out before developing and releasing a feature in one go. Faster time-to-market is one of the benefits achieved with this approach to DevOps.

High-quality products are only delivered if the feedback from the end users or intended customers of the product is solicited. Hence, incorporating feedback continuously into product updates and delivering iteratively is a key part of the DevOps strategy. Optimization of products and the delivery of capabilities based on the end user input, accommodating changing market needs, is another benefit of DevOps.

Automated building and testing, continuous integration, and continuous delivery are used during the various phases of software development and delivery using agile practices. Continuous integration (CI) is the capability that merges the new code, frequently authored by developers, into the main code. Validation and readiness testing of the new code is then performed. Continuous delivery (CD) then takes the process forward by performing further integration testing on environments such as staging and pre-production. Once successfully tested, the code can be deployed into production. This last step can be done manually or automatically and is called "continuous deployment." Additional details about CI and CD are provided later in this chapter.

Applying the previously mentioned DevOps principles and strategies for software development to network operations is called NetDevOps. Just like DevOps, NetDevOps is focused on providing the following benefits and advantages to the organization:

- Adding value to the business through the optimization of network operations by using automation. Instead of managing networks using the CLI, you can utilize tools and machine-readable techniques for automation. Using automation techniques for the initial configuration and day-to-day operations of the networking devices through software development techniques or via code is also referred to as infrastructure as code (IaC).

- Delivering new features and capabilities on the network faster. Agile software development methodologies are used for network deployment and operation. This provides speed, agility, scalability, and flexibility in adding network features.

- Reducing the risks of network outages by making frequent and small updates to the networks. Iterative updates to the networks reduce the risks normally associated with the introduction of large changes on the network. The introduction of smaller changes also helps in isolating network issues quicker.

- Enhancing the end-user experience through a feedback loop mechanism by measuring the end users' experience of the applications running on the network and the actual value delivered. The iterative feedback process allows you to tweak and improve their network experience. It also allows you to amend the strategy based on their actual network experience.

- Providing enhanced collaboration by breaking down the silos between business owners and the development and operations teams.

- Providing reliability as the solution is developed and tested before releasing and deploying it to production.

Team Roles in NetDevOps

Assembling a team with the required skills is an initial step in NetDevOps. However, the technical skills are only one piece of the puzzle—teamwork, collaboration, and time management are other attributes required by everyone to deliver on their assigned commitments and are essential for success. The team structure includes multiple roles and must have representation from development, operations, and other teams. The overall NetDevOps operational structure for an organization is beyond the scope of this book.

As organizations embark on their NetDevOps journey, they may assemble the NetDevOps team for specific projects within a silo, isolated from existing teams and then allow the team to execute on those projects, learning from their initial delivery experience, before slowly expanding to other parts of the organization in a phased and systematic approach (basically, the crawl, walk, then run approach).

The NetDevOps teams in any two organizations could be different from one another. There is no correct or incorrect team structure. The selection of roles depends on the types of activities performed. The following list provides some commonly used roles in NetDevOps projects:

- **Product owner:** As the name implies, this role is responsible for defining the project requirements by working with the rest of the team and organization, assigning and prioritizing the required activities.

- **Team lead:** This is a technical, skilled role with hands-on experience in developing within the build and release management lifecycle. Further, the team lead is responsible for managing the team that is developing, testing, and delivering the tasks.

- **Architect:** Depending on the type of NetDevOps engagement, architects are required with design and implementation skills related to technologies such as security, cloud, and SDN.

- **Developer and/or automation expert:** This team member has programming and configuration management skills. Examples include Python developers and those with experience in Ansible or Terraform for automating the configuration and lifecycle management of networking, cloud, and other products used in the network environments. Depending on the nature of the required activities, developers with user interface (UI) and backend application development skills may also be required for a project. Additionally, test engineers from Q&A teams may be involved in the project. All these resources are expected to be fully skilled in CI/CD pipeline development and delivery methodologies using tools such as Jenkins.

Stages of NetDevOps

Figure 1-2 provides an overview of the various stages applicable to NetDevOps.

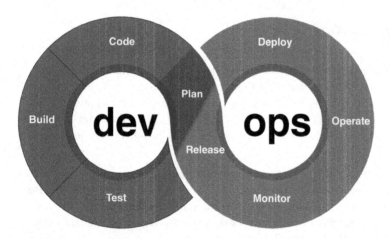

Figure 1-2   *Net DevOps Stages*

Let's look at these stages and some of the tools that can be used in them. Keep in mind that it is not necessary to have a one-to-one relationship between a tool and a stage. Some tools may be applicable to multiple stages. Examples of uses for a few of these tools are provided in the following sections.

Plan

Setting a goal and proper planning are critical parts of the success of any project. Multiple steps are performed as part of the Plan phase. This includes gathering requirements, soliciting feedback from other relevant stakeholders, and then developing a product roadmap. A project normally starts by capturing the high-level goals (that is, epics). An epic basically provides the high-level description of the business initiative (for example, increase efficiency in the data center by automating day-to-day operations).

The epics are broken down into smaller "user stories," which are high-level descriptions of the requirements captured in a way that NetDevOps team members can understand clearly. The user stories are expected to be short descriptions and should articulate the value they deliver to the end users or consumers of the feature (for example, use Ansible to automate configuration changes for Nexus switches in the data center).

Each user story is normally further broken down into more granular "tasks." There can be many tasks within a user story. The tasks may include items related to the development of new features, modifications to existing products, design changes to existing capabilities, software defects, and so on. Each task is expected to be completed by one of the NetDevOps team members, although multiple resources can work on a task due to high complexity of a task or for learning and education purposes. "Create an Ansible script to add new VLANs on Nexus switches" is an example of a task.

The product owner is expected to lead the Plan stage and work with team members from different departments such as business, development, and operations. The product owner, by working with the team, prioritizes the tasks and puts them in a backlog, which is the foundation for the planning of development activities. The tasks from the backlog are assigned to team members in weekly or bi-weekly sprints.

All these steps in the Plan stage are performed before embarking on the actual development of the product. Unlike the waterfall approach, the iterations (or sprints) are shorter in duration, thus allowing you to incorporate feedback and to change direction within a short span of time.

Jira, Rally, and Trac are examples of a few tools that keep track of all the activities—documenting the requirements in the form of epics, user stories, tasks, backlog, and so on. Because many team members are involved in the Plan and subsequent stages, tools such as Confluence, Slack, and Cisco Webex are normally used for collaboration and documentation purposes.

Code

The development phase starts with the Code stage. The tasks from the backlog being assigned to NetDevOps team members leads to the actual execution during this stage. The nature of the execution activity depends on the actual task. For example, it could be Ansible code for automating network configuration created by a developer, a design activity by an architect, a software defect fixed by a developer, and so on.

In the context of NetDevOps, the code could be scripts for the initial deployment, day-to-day management, and maintenance activities of networking devices. Files for running configurations and backup configurations of networking devices could also be generated and kept as code. The syntax for the scripts or code depends on the tool used, such as Ansible or Terraform. Configuration management scripts in Ansible are referred to as playbooks. These files are written in YAML format and are human readable. Terraform scripts are written in HashiCorp Configuration Language (HCL) format and are human readable as well. Network automation scripts could also be written in Python and other programming or interpreted languages.

Machine-readable and structured data files typically complement the scripts by adding the actual data values into networking devices. JSON, YAML, and XML are commonly used formats for such structured data files. The choice of format depends on factors such as the knowledge of the engineer, the format support by the tool, and the type supported by the protocol used to push the data to the networking device.

To author code, each developer must consider the operating system, the tools, and their dependencies (that is, the working environment). Once the code (scripts, data files, and so on) is produced by a developer, peers can then review, amend, or validate that code. Tracking and managing the code changes by multiple peers need to be done as well. These steps help to repeatedly produce high-quality code during an iterative process. The process for collaboration should be easy and seamless; thus, the NetDevOps team members can focus on their work and deliverables rather than spending time sharing updates and communicating with each other.

In the following sections, we will review the working environment and managing modifications to the code in more detail, as well as the associated tools for such activities.

Development Environment

To produce high-quality code, the developers may use multiple tools and software applications during the software development phase. Each of these software applications or tools can have multiple dependencies to operate properly. Hence, a stable working environment for developers is required. Such a working environment is sometimes referred to as the "development environment."

Standardizing the development environment provides consistency and ease of use in terms of sharing information among developers. It also reduces the risk of surprises since the code is authored and compiled by multiple developers using the same tools. Additionally, enforcing best practices and providing recommendations for a consistent coding style can assist in producing high-quality code.

The selection of specific tools by developers and enforcing their use is an important choice for an organization. The development environment can be a hosted desktop using applications such as Virtual Desktop Infrastructure. It could also be installed locally on developers' workstations (Windows, macOS, or Linux) with all the required software tools and applications, with or without the ability for developers to make any customizations.

The list of tools developers require depends on the actual products and activities involved in the NetDevOps project. However, a baseline set of tools can be created. Here's an example:

- An integrated development environment (IDE) is one of the commonly used applications by developers. An IDE provides an editor that offers syntax checks, code completion, debugging, integration with other tools, and more, for programming or interpreted languages such as Python and configuration management tools such as Ansible and Terraform.

    Atom, Visual Studio Code, and Sublime are examples of IDEs that either come with specific versions of Python, Ansible, and Terraform applications or allow easy integration of such applications.

- Git is the most popular version control system and is covered in detail later in this chapter and throughout the book. Using the CLI is the most popular way of performing git operations.

- Python is an interpreted language that is commonly used for network automation.

This list of tools is shown as reference and can be part of the development environment baseline. Additional tools for compiling the source code and to produce the compiled binary code may also be required for use by the developers.

Version Control and Collaboration During Software Development

The software code created by developers normally encompasses many files. Multiple developers may also need to collaborate and contribute to these files. As part of their activities, these developers need the ability to share the code with their peers for various activities such as code review, soliciting and sharing comments, managing any code conflicts, going through the code approval process, making amendments to the code, and so on.

Furthermore, creating new features or making changes to an existing version of code may not go as planned. Issues may be discovered during the testing of a code version within the staging, pre-production, or production environment. Hence, the capability to use the previous version of the complete software product or to roll back the newly developed software code to one of the prior versions is required. This can be possible only if tracking and managing of prior changes to software code have been performed.

There may also be regulatory requirements, as per the organization own's policies, government laws enforced by regulatory agencies, and so on, that regulate version control capabilities as a necessity.

To meet the requirements for managing changes and to help manage code revision, version control systems are used. Git is the most well-known and popular distributed version control system used for maintenance during the Code phase and is commonly used as the tool of choice in NetDevOps. Git is an open-source distributed system released under GNU General Public License version 2.0 (GPLv2), thus allowing the flexibility to share and change it.

Git provides distributed model - which is one of it's powerful capability. Code is commonly shared via public hosted repository services. GitHub, GitLab, and Bitbucket are a few examples of such cloud-hosted services that use git and allow users to create their public or private repositories. Developers save their code on these centralized repositories, which allow multiple developers to collaborate in real time. In the case of GitHub and GitLab, these centralized repositories are hosted in the cloud and offered as a service.

For NetDevOps use cases, the shared repositories on GitHub or GitLab host the configuration files, automation scripts, and so on. Also, NetDevOps team members use git to collaborate with each other on that content. Examples of and more detail on git workflows are provided later in this chapter.

A version control system is also called "source control," and the two names are used interchangeably.

Build

After the development of the code, the next step is to produce executable software and to perform initial tests on the code. This executable software can then be made available for solution testing. The process of compiling the software is done by an automated build process.

Tests on specific, small portions of the code are done as part of the build process. This concept in software development, where a chunk of newly produced code is validated and tested, is called unit testing. These unit test cases are normally written by the same developers who authored the code since they are most familiar with the actual additions or changes made to it. These tests help in catching any issues as early as possible and hence make the final product more reliable. These unit tests during the Build phase also save time and money by not advancing to higher-effort, complex, and time-consuming phases of solution integration testing, deployment, and so on.

Depending on the type of programming language used, there may or may not be any executable or compiled code as an outcome of the Build phase. Ansible playbooks and Python scripts are a couple of scenarios where no compiled code is generated. In the case of Java or C++, the compiled code in the form of binary files is produced. In such cases, additional tools are normally used by software developers to help with the build process for these programming languages. For example, Java tools such as Maven and Ant help developers to compile, fetch dependencies, release their packaged applications, and so on.

For NetDevOps, programming languages such as Java are not commonly used. Hence, no compiled code is produced, and there will be no need for tools such as Maven and Ant. Therefore, these tools are not covered further in the book.

Test

As NetDevOps engineers continue to create software code such as Ansible playbooks, there is a need to continuously test the quality of that code as part of the end-to-end solution test process. This testing should not slow the overall delivery of new code; hence, the use of test automation is also critical at this stage. The goal of the testing should be to provide maximum possible coverage for network components and a complete solution that can validate the technical and business goals.

To validate the expected results of that code and to confirm the behavior on the network, test environment(s) must be used for quality assurance (QA). As a best practice, it is recommended to have multiple environments. The following list provides example of three environments that may be used:

- **Testing environment:** Only specific tests related to new features may be done in this setup. Hence, this environment may only have a subset of production devices—and only have virtualized or emulated devices. Unit testing can be performed in such an environment.

- **Staging environment:** Full integration testing can be done in this setup. It may contain virtualized-only, physical-only, or a combination of virtualized and physical devices. The goal should be to perform full integration testing in this environment, so it may be created on a smaller scale, or it could be a fully virtualized staging environment.

- **Pre-production environment:** This is an identical replica of the production networking environment. This environment should mimic the production environment, including multivendor components. It should use the exact same devices and topology as the production environment. In an ideal scenario, this environment should allow for full coverage of tests and for validation of all traffic flows and integrations with applications and multivendor products used in the production network. Sometimes the staging and pre-production environments are the same.

The capital expenditure and operational expense of procuring and managing resources such as routers, switches, virtualized and physical servers, and appliances can be an inhibitor. Hence, virtualization technologies are commonly used in the testing, staging, and pre-production environments. However, there may be restrictions on the features and data flows supported on virtual network devices. What's more, not all the vendors offer virtual network devices for the appliances or physical network devices they offer.

Various open-source and commercial products provide the capability to emulate the networking environments by using virtualization technologies. Emulated Virtual Environment (EVE-NG) and Cisco Modeling Labs are two such software products. EVE-NG provides multivendor network emulation capabilities. You can find more details about EVE-NG in Chapter 5, "How to Implement Virtual Networks with EVE-NG."

Setting up the test environment itself can be a time-consuming exercise; hence, automation is used for deployment and provisioning—that is, for instantiating (if any), setting up, and configuring the test environments. Tools and scripting languages such as Ansible, Terraform, and Python, along with other options, are commonly used for this purpose. Various examples of using such tools for on-premises and cloud infrastructure automation are provided in this book.

Release

This is a critical stage where the code is released for production. Once the code has passed through the earlier testing stages, the operations team can have high confidence in its readiness and quality.

NetDevOps engineers, like software engineers, are expected to make small changes frequently, often referred to as iterations, producing new network configurations in the form of code. Thus, automation is used to move through all the prior and subsequent stages. The tools that provide such automation capabilities through the various stages are sometimes referred to as "release management tools." These tools initiate a series of automated steps to help streamline the process for the building, testing, and release of the actual compiled code as a product. This series of steps is also referred to as a "pipeline."

Jenkins, Jira, and CircleCI are some examples of the tools used for the Release stage. An organization's choice of tool depends on many factors, such as expertise in and level of knowledge about a tool, whether a support mechanism for the tool already exists within the organization, the need for an on-premises or cloud-based delivery model, existing commercial agreements covering product procurement or licensing costs, and support costs.

Jenkins is one of the most popular tools used in the software development lifecycle and in NetDevOps for release management. More details related to installing and configuring Jenkins can be found in Chapter 3, "How to Implement CI/CD Pipelines with Jenkins."

Let's look at the following use case to understand the release management lifecycle and pipeline concepts.

Use Case: Release Management for NetDevOps   In this simple use case, Jenkins is used to create a NetDevOps pipeline for a data center environment. The Jenkins pipeline is configured to trigger steps for automated building and testing of code. It is assumed that Cisco Nexus switches are used within the data center to provide connectivity to bare-metal, virtualized servers and to the corporate intranet. And Jenkins is integrated with a centralized GitHub repository to automatically trigger this pipeline. Also, Ansible is used for the automation of deployment and configuration management of this environment.

It is assumed that the data center is already fully operational. Connectivity of the new bare-metal and virtualized servers to Cisco Nexus switches must be configured in the data center. Thus, new VLANs and physical interfaces on those switches must be configured to allow connectivity to those servers. Ansible code will be written to achieve this configuration. Ansible code for automating these tasks is saved in files called "playbooks" (in Ansible terminology). This code (that is, the playbook files) defines the desired state using YAML syntax, and the playbooks are saved with an extension of .yml (YAML).

Refer to Figure 1-3 for the NetDevOps pipeline steps. This pipeline executes a series of automated steps on a testing environment to validate the Ansible code. Such validation prior to making those configuration changes in staging, pre-production, and/or production environments reduces risks for any misconfiguration and potential network downtime. In Jenkins, the steps are grouped together in the form of stages. The logical grouping of one or more steps in a stage is used to reflect the different phases in a pipeline. Detailed procedures for the configuration of Jenkins and git are covered in multiple chapters—namely, Chapter 3, "How to Implement CI/CD Pipelines with Jenkins," Chapter 4, "How to Implement NetDevOps Pipelines with Jenkins," and Chapter 6, "How to Build Your Own NetDevOps Architecture." The following paragraphs provide a high-level overview of the steps and stages in the pipeline.

A new Ansible playbook named "vlan.yml" is authored by a NetDevOps engineer. It's a simple playbook that creates a new VLAN and adds interfaces on multiple switches. The NetDevOps engineer pushes the playbook to the centralized git repository on GitHub. In git terminology, this is done by performing a **git commit** and then a **git push** to the existing centralized GitHub repository. Jenkins is configured to automatically trigger the following series of steps in a pipeline upon the merging of code in the git centralized repository:

1. The Jenkins pipeline stage automates the launch of a Docker container from the pre-existing Docker image in the test environment.

   It is assumed that the Docker image, along with the required packages, has already been created with git and Ansible and made available in the test environment.

   Furthermore, an automated step in the same pipeline stage copies the code, in the form of playbooks, from the centralized git repository on GitHub within the Docker container. In git terminology, this step of copying a repository to local machine is performed using **git clone**.

2. The next pipeline stage performs lab validation tests. It includes an automated step that performs a syntax check of the Ansible playbook. This is performed by automatically executing the following Ansible command, as per the pipeline, within the Docker container:

```
$ ansible-playbook vlan.yml --syntax-check
```

Next step in this pipeline stage performs a dry run of the Ansible playbook on the test environment by automatically executing the following command within the Docker container:

```
$ ansible-playbook vlan.yml --check
```

3. It's always a good practice to clean up at the end of the pipeline and remove resources that have been created for testing purposes; otherwise, stale or unwanted resources stay in the environment and unnecessarily consume computing resources. Hence, this step in the next pipeline stage removes the Docker container in the test environment.

   This cleanup step can be configured to run unconditionally in Jenkins, regardless of the failure of one or more steps in the pipeline.

Figure 1-3 summarizes these steps in a pipeline.

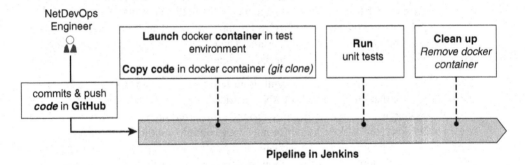

Figure 1-3 *Jenkins Pipeline for Building and Testing*

A successful completion of the pipeline means that the code is ready for solution integration testing in the pre-production environment.

Deploy

This stage deals with the deployment of the actual executable code into the production environment. In the case of NetDevOps, configuration management tools such as Ansible, Terraform, and an interpreted language like Python are commonly used to provision and deploy new capabilities or enhancements into the production networks. Assuming that one of these tools is used, the code developed by NetDevOps teams can be Ansible playbooks, Terraform scripts, or Python scripts. The use of automated software delivery methodologies for deployment is also referred to as "infrastructure as code" (IaC).

Note that some of these tools are customizable to extend their coverage. For example, a new Terraform provider can be developed or a new Ansible module can be developed by an organization to cater to its needs. Such activity can be considered to be part of a software development lifecycle and not necessarily part of the NetDevOps lifecycle.

Automated testing on a production network is an essential milestone for successful deployment. The goals and benefits of automating the deployment are very similar to the overall theme of NetDevOps, including providing speed and agility in adding capabilities to the network, improving the reliability of the network, and minimizing the risk of network issues, failures, or outages due to human errors and enhanced automated testing. Tools and capabilities such as the Robot framework, Cisco pyATS, and more are covered later in this chapter and can be used for automated testing during the Deploy phase.

Operate

Once the new code, new features, or enhancements to existing capabilities are deployed on the network, usually the operations team is solely responsible for the day-to-day operations of this network within a traditional environment. As part of the NetDevOps lifecycle, the development team gets to work closely with the operations team and could even be engaged in the day-to-day operations of the network. This enhanced collaboration between the development and operations teams helps to smooth the daily operations, reduce surprises for both teams, and achieve the goal of agility and reliability within the operating network. Effective collaboration between the two teams also leads to improved productivity within the organization and, in fact, can help to reduce the overall operating costs. NetDevOps, with its iterative model and smaller changes (rather than large changes), also positively impacts the Operate stage as the network behaves in a more predictable and reliable manner.

Monitor

Monitoring deals with gathering data and generating insights from the network. Modern capabilities of the networking products, such as streaming telemetry, allow enhanced, near real-time, rich data collection capabilities. The insights into networks provide data for measuring the usage and performance of the networks. Monitoring also enables you to get insights related to challenges faced by end users. This feedback is consumed by product owners and other team members working in the Plan phase. As a result, this helps in modifying the strategy and improving the capabilities of the future iterations of the product and NetDevOps pipeline.

Besides the monitoring of network elements, monitoring various stages of the NetDevOps pipeline is highly beneficial in improving the stages. Monitoring allows you to identify obstacles and bottlenecks within the stages of the pipeline. This information allows you to make improvements, to make the pipeline more efficient, and to enhance the efficiency of the organization. As part of the monitoring of NetDevOps stages, the team members should investigate various factors such as the following:

- Which stages require the most effort and time?
- What are the inhibitors within the stages that take a lot of time and effort?
- What are the reasons for inhibitors?

■ Is the Test stage taking too long to complete? Can these tests be optimized further by using automation tools?

Monitoring helps to provide answers to such questions and optimize networks by optimizing the NetDevOps pipeline. Figure 1-2 from earlier in the chapter showed that the NetDevOps lifecycle is a continuous loop, and the feedback from monitoring becomes part of the next iteration of the NetDevOps lifecycle.

The various stages of the NetDevOps lifecycle were covered previously. Each stage links with another and helps to provide the benefits associated with NetDevOps.

Security is one of the fundamental requirements that must be considered and integrated into each stage of the NetDevOps lifecycle. Security tools and processes should be applied to each of the stages to ensure that security considerations are not overlooked for the sake of speed and agility. Each of the NetDevOps stages and the actual network components included as part of these stages and pipeline need to be hardened. The security considerations include how and where the credentials of devices are configured and stored in the automation code (such as Ansible playbooks). Also, security tasks could be automated as part of the NetDevOps stages. In summary, security guardrails are part of and are further reinforced in the NetDevOps lifecycle.

Continuity is an integral part of NetDevOps, so let's look at a few additional terms—namely, continuous integration, continuous delivery, and continuous deployment—associated with NetDevOps.

Continuous Integration/Continuous Delivery/Deployment (CI/CD)

Continuous integration, *continuous delivery*, and *continuous deployment* are terms used frequently in DevOps, and consequently in NetDevOps. Let's explore these terms further.

Continuous Integration

The capability to develop code frequently by making small changes, generating the compiled code, and validating and testing those changes is referred to as *continuous integration (CI)*. Version control systems (such as GitHub) are utilized to track code changes and their versions used within the CI process, which enables organizations to develop code faster and reliably.

As explained previously, release management tools initiate a series of automated steps (referred to as a pipeline) to help streamline the process of building, subsequently testing, and releasing the actual product. Through the use of an automated pipeline, the time for releasing multiple iterations of software code (new or incremental) is reduced or made insignificant. In addition to frequent releases, the code quality is improved by way of testing the incremental changes.

Continuous Delivery

After the CI process, the compiled code is deployed in a test environment, goes through integrated solution testing, and then is released for deployment into production. This capability to continuously automate the delivery of the packaged code to a testing, staging, or production environment is referred to as *continuous delivery (CD)*.

The continuous integration and continuous delivery processes go together and are referred to as CI/CD. Because compiled code is produced frequently through the iterative process within CI, the CD process must continuously validate and release the code.

Continuous Deployment

After successfully completing the CI and CD processes, deployment of this high-quality code into the production environment is the last piece of the puzzle. This capability is referred to as *continuous deployment.* Sometimes continuous delivery and continuous deployment are used interchangeably because deployment to production can be automated or, alternatively, the NetDevOps team can control this manually. If the deployment to production is done automatically after CI, the acronym CD can be considered "continuous deployment." If there is a manual step involved to trigger the deployment to production, the acronym CD is assumed to be "continuous delivery."

Refer to Figure 1-4 and Figure 1-5 to see the differences between continuous integration, continuous delivery, and continuous deployment through manual or automated execution. Figure 1-4 shows an approach where the deployment of code, after release, is done via a manual step. Hence, all three stages (integration, delivery, and deployment) are unique from one another.

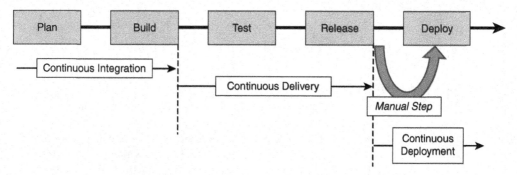

Figure 1-4 *Continuous Integration, Delivery, and Deployment*

Figure 1-5 refers to the approach where deployment to production is performed via an automated step. Since continuous deployment is an automated step after the release of code, continuous delivery is not considered a separate process. In this scenario, continuous delivery and continuous deployment are used interchangeably.

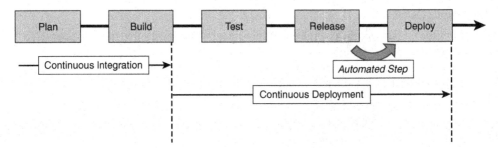

Figure 1-5 *Continuous Integration and Deployment*

The continuous integration/continuous delivery/deployment (CI/CD) process is considered fundamental to the NetDevOps (or DevOps) framework, providing the benefits such as the following:

- Enhanced collaboration between the development and operations teams

- Reliable and faster delivery via automation across all phases, such as build, unit testing, solution integration testing, and so on

- Improved time to market by using iterative development and automated and continuous deployments

- High-quality products and reliable networks using a feedback mechanism to produce frequent software releases, resulting in happier consumers and end users

Tools/Components

Let's look at some additional details of the tools that play a pivotal role in NetDevOps and in achieving the benefits associated with it.

Configuration Management

The ability to configure network products, through tools, by utilizing the programmable interfaces exposed by those products is a pivotal function in achieving high efficiency for reliable networks. Ansible and Terraform are popular configuration management tools for networking products, cloud, and applications. Each has its own unique strengths, and often multiple tools are used to deploy and manage the infrastructure and the applications running on that infrastructure. Therefore, the organization's use cases lead to its choice of tools.

As discussed earlier, existing knowledge, support, and commercial agreements also play a role in decision making when choosing a tool. Keep in mind that quite often both Ansible and Terraform are used together since they complement each other. The use of Terraform for automating the configuration of the networking infrastructure along with application installation using Ansible is one such scenario where both tools are used.

The ability to manage the infrastructure using code instead of using manual and interactive management techniques is known as infrastructure as code (IaC). As discussed earlier, in the context of networks and NetDevOps, the term *code* means that the configuration and day-to-day management of networking devices are performed by writing reusable code instead of performing those tasks manually by using the CLI.

Further, IaC utilizes the software development practices and CI/CD pipeline to build, test, and deploy. In other words, IaC aligns with the NetDevOps practices, although it's not mandatory to use the CI/CD pipeline.

Instead of configuring each network product separately, you can use a central host or a cloud-based service hosting the configuration management tool to push the configurations to one, two, tens, hundreds, or thousands of network devices.

Let's look at Ansible and Terraform in depth.

Ansible

Ansible is an open-source automation tool commonly used for configuration management of the network and cloud infrastructure as well as for deployment and management of applications. It is a tool that uses a centralized control machine—also called control node—to perform all the tasks centrally. Ansible is idempotent, agentless, and uses YAML syntax format for its scripts.

Here are some additional details about these concepts and Ansible's functionality:

- *Idempotency* means that, upon execution of a task, if the target device is already in the desired state, then no change is made. It is quite a powerful concept since the configuration changes are pushed only if the target device is not in the desired state. As an example, if a VLAN is to be configured in a network switch then, for idempotency, the Ansible control node pulls the configuration from switch, validates that the VLAN is not present, and only then configures the VLAN on the switch. During the control node's validation step, if it's found that the VLAN is already present, it is not reconfigured in the switch.

- *Agentless* means that the target device does not need any agent for the execution of automation tasks.

- Installation of Ansible is supported on many operating systems, including Red Hat, Debian, CentOS, and macOS. As mentioned previously, this machine is called a control node. The control node must have other dependencies, such as Python, installed prior to the installation of Ansible.

- The control node communicates with and performs automation activities on the target device using the library plugins. These library plugins are called "modules" in Ansible, and each one performs automation tasks, as per the module specifications developed and as per the capabilities supported by the target device.

- There are thousands of Ansible modules that are broken down into many categories, such as networking and cloud. The modules are developed such that the communication between control node and target device is facilitated by APIs, SSH, or other mechanisms supported by the devices.

■ Automation tasks can be executed by running ad-hoc commands. This mechanism is useful for validating and testing purposes but, as expected, is not scalable. Alternatively, a series of tasks written in a form of script can be used.

■ The automation scripts that perform a series of tasks are written in YAML format and saved in files with the .yml file extension. This is called a playbook.

■ A playbook consists of many plays, and each play has one or multiple tasks. The tasks execute the actual instructions on the target devices by utilizing the modules. The creation of a VLAN on a switch and the installation of a web server package on a server are examples of tasks. Each of these tasks will utilize modules for execution. For VLAN creation, a module named **nxos_vlans** within the **Cisco.nxos** collection can be used.

■ The list of the target devices on which the tasks are executed is defined in the inventory file. In Ansible terminology, the target devices are called "hosts." Hosts are referred to in the playbook's plays and tasks. Also, one or more groups of target devices can be defined within the inventory (hosts) file. The definition of "group" depends on the use case. For example, two groups of leaf and spine switches can be created if unique configurations need to be applied to these groups.

■ Variables in key-value pair format, which are required for the execution of tasks, can also be defined in the playbook or inventory file. However, for scalability and reuse purposes, these can be defined in separate files. The name and number of a VLAN are examples of where variables can be used.

■ The concept of playbook within Ansible has been introduced previously. Note that one starts to hit limitations when the playbook becomes large. To provide reuse and scalability, Ansible provides other capabilities, such as roles. Variables, tasks, templates, and various other functions are packaged within the roles. Ansible roles help with providing a scalable option along with reuse and sharing.

■ Since Ansible version 2.9, the modules are distributed within **collections** and need to be installed separately. In previous versions of Ansible, the modules were embedded and installed along with Ansible itself—there was no need to install modules separately.

■ Installation of the Collection module can be done by using Ansible Galaxy, which works as a distribution and installation mechanism of collections. Ansible Galaxy is a hub that allows for the sharing of Ansible content in the form of collections that can include modules, roles, and so on.

Figure 1-6 provides a high-level overview of the Ansible architecture where a control node executes plays and tasks, utilizing the modules for execution, on the target hosts defined in the inventory file.

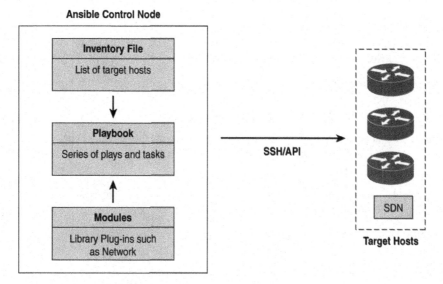

Figure 1-6   *Ansible Overview*

Use Case: Creation of VLANs   Now let's look at a sample Ansible playbook for creating VLANs on Cisco Nexus switches. As discussed earlier, an inventory file with a list of the target hosts must be created on the Ansible control node. In this case, the inventory file named *hosts* contains two switches. The credentials of those switches are also added as variables in this file. The inventory file with switches and variable configurations are shown in Example 1-1.

Example 1-1   *Ansible Inventory File*

```
$ more hosts
[all:vars]
ansible_connection = ansible.netcommon.network_cli
ansible_network_os = cisco.nxos.nxos
ansible_user=admin
ansible_password=Admin_1234!
[leaf_one]
sandbox-nxos-1.cisco.com
[leaf_two]
131.226.217.151
```

Here are some additional details about the hosts file:

- The group named **[all:vars]** lists the credentials and connection settings for the Ansible control node for the switches.

- The **ansible_connection** setting configures the control node to treat the connected device as a networking device and not as a server. Unlike servers, networking devices have limited functionality and allow limited connections over SSH.

- The **ansible_network_os** setting informs the control node about the network platform (operating system) of the target device. In this case, the configuration shows Cisco Nexus using the Cisco NXOS operating system.

- The **ansible_user** and **ansible_password** variables define the credentials used by Ansible module to authenticate with switches.

- Two leaf switches groups, named **[leaf_one]** and **[leaf_two],** with their respective hostname and IP addresses, are configured.

Example 1-2 shows the YAML playbook for creating VLANs.

Example 1-2   *Ansible Playbook—vlan.yml*

```
$ more vlan.yml


---
- name: create new VLAN
  hosts: leaf_one

  tasks:
    - name: provision VLAN
      cisco.nxos.nxos_vlans:
        config:
          - vlan_id: "{{item}}"
            state: active
      with_items:
        -  101
        -  102
```

As discussed, YAML is case- and indentation-sensitive. Even incorrect spacing in the file can cause errors in execution.

Take note of the following in this playbook:

- There is one play with the name of "create new VLAN." The **name** argument can be configured to any text that helps in identifying the actual play.

- As per the **hosts** setting, the execution of this play will be performed only on a single leaf named **leaf_one**.

- There is one task within the play that uses the **nxos_vlans** module (part of the Cisco NXOS collection). Again, the name can be configured with text to help identify the task.

- Two VLANs, numbered 101 and 102, are created by using the **with_items** functionality to loop through the creation of the two VLANs.

- As per the **nxos_vlans** module, the operational state of the VLAN is configured by using the parameter named **state**, which is set to be active.

A syntax check and dry run can be performed initially. Example 1-3 shows the successful execution of the **--syntax-check** and **--check** commands.

Example 1-3 *Ansible Playbook—Syntax Validation and Dry Run*

```
$ ansible-playbook vlan.yml -i hosts --syntax-check          .


playbook: vlan.yml


$  ansible-playbook vlan.yml -i hosts --check
PLAY [create new VLAN] ***********************************************************
*****************

TASK [Gathering Facts] **********************************************************
*****************
ok: [sandbox-nxos-1.cisco.com]


TASK [provision VLAN] ***********************************************************
*****************
ok: [sandbox-nxos-1.cisco.com] => (item=101)
ok: [sandbox-nxos-1.cisco.com] => (item=102)


PLAY RECAP **********************************************************************
*****************
sandbox-nxos-1.cisco.com   : ok=2    changed=0    unreachable=0    failed=0
skipped=0     rescued=0     ignored=0


$
$
```

Like the earlier execution of a dry run (using **check**), this is just a simulation. It shows that two VLANs, numbered 101 and 102, will be added to a switch named sandbox-nxos-1.cisco.com.

Terraform

Terraform is another open-source automation tool that is used for IaC capabilities in cloud and networking products. In Terraform, the configuration files use HashiCorp Configuration Language (HCL) syntax. This language is also declarative in nature (that is, the intended goal using HCL syntax is described in the Terraform configuration files) instead of the actual steps to reach the desired state being written out.

Here are some additional details about Terraform's functionality:

- Terraform was originally developed by HashiCorp. Both on-premises and cloud-hosted options are provided by HashiCorp as part of its commercial offerings. The latter is called Terraform Cloud (TFC). The open-source version of Terraform can be installed on-premises as a binary file on various operating systems such as Linux and macOS.

- Terraform is idempotent in nature and, for the most part, agentless. As explained earlier, idempotent means that if the target device is already in the desired state, then no change is made to it by the configuration management tool. In the case of Terraform Cloud, agents can be used for managing private infrastructure behind corporate firewalls.

- At a high level, Terraform works in three simple steps:

  1. Define the desired state of the infrastructure using the HCL syntax in the configuration file.

  2. Perform a dry run (that is, execute the **terraform plan** step). In this step, Terraform reads the current state of the infrastructure, performs a comparison operation, and then shows you the proposed network changes per the configuration file created in the first step.

  3. Apply the desired changes (that is, execute the **terraform apply** step). If you are happy with the proposed plan (as per the dry run), the changes or configurations are pushed to the infrastructure.

- Terraform builds and keeps track of the current state of the infrastructure that it provisions. This state is built dynamically and stored in a JSON-formatted file. In the case of on-premises deployments, the current state can be viewed using the command line, while in the case of Terraform Cloud, multiple versions of the state file are kept in the cloud. Thus, the latter provides more flexibility.

- Terraform Cloud provides many other features, such as the secure storing of credentials and passwords for target devices, role-based access control (RBAC), support for APIs, and more.

- The plugins in Terraform, which allow it to communicate and interact with the infrastructure (target devices), are called providers. There are hundreds of providers for cloud, networking, and other products, developed by vendors as well as the open-source community. Cisco Nexus (NXOS) and Cisco Application Centric

Infrastructure (ACI) are examples of Terraform providers. At the time of writing of this book, you can search for Terraform providers at https://registry.terraform.io/browse/providers.

■ The configuration file, where the desired state of the infrastructure is defined using declarative HCL syntax, must be saved with the .tf file extension. There can be multiple such files.

■ The required provider is also defined in the configuration file. During the initialization process, Terraform downloads and installs the required provider from the default public or private registry location. The initialization step only needs to be performed once.

■ The Terraform configuration file contains many blocks. A block that describes the actual desired state of the infrastructure is called a "resource." Each provider has its own set of resources that allow it to provision the infrastructure: **resource aci_tenant** and **resource aci_application_epg** are examples of resources that allow you to manage a tenant and EPG, respectively, as per the Cisco ACI provider. The resource block is configured as shown in the following example, where **some_local_name** is locally significant to Terraform. The **name** argument is the actual name configured on ACI:

```
resource "aci_tenant" "some_local_name" {
   name        = "tenant_name"
   description = "Tenant created by the Terraform ACI provider"
}
```

■ Another block in Terraform, called **data sources**, allows you to retrieve information from the infrastructure. This information, retrieved using **data source**, might have been provisioned by Terraform, by other methods (such as manually), or it could have been dynamically generated by the infrastructure. For example, a tenant may have already been created manually in ACI, or it may be added via another Terraform script by someone else. To add an EGP in this tenant, the tenant's ID is required. The ID and other attributes of the tenant (as per its **name** argument) can thus be extracted using a **data sources** block, as shown in the following example:

```
data "aci_tenant" "some_local_name" {
   name        = "tenant_name"
}
```

■ Terraform makes the deletion or decommissioning of infrastructure objects managed by Terraform quite easy. Terraform provides a **destroy** option that makes decommissioning resources very convenient, and there is no need to write separate code for it.

Refer to Figure 1-7 for a high-level overview of Terraform and the three steps of writing the desired infrastructure state as code, performing the dry run to make sure that the execution plan is in line with the expectations, and applying the configuration to the infrastructure to reach the desired state.

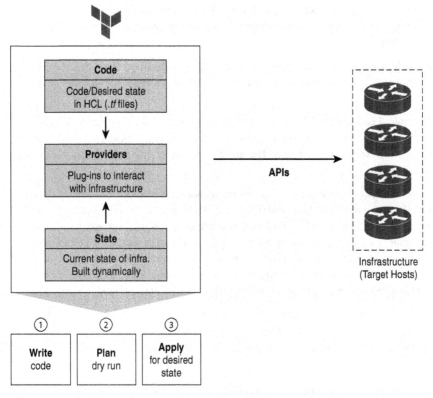

Figure 1-7   *Terraform Overview*

NetDevOps teams have the choice of using the Terraform as an open-source solution or using one of the commercial options provided by HashiCorp. At the time of writing this book, the choices for using Terraform include:

- **Terraform open source:** This is a great way to test out Terraform capabilities. It is locally installed on a workstation and does not allow a lot of extensibility or collaboration natively.

- **Terraform Cloud (TFC):** As the name indicates, this is the cloud-hosted offering provided by HashiCorp. There is a free version, but the commercial version of TFC provides additional features such as unlimited users and groups, policy management, and more. TFC also provides out-of-the-box integration with version control systems such as GitHub, GitLab, and Bitbucket. Features such as shared state maintenance in the cloud, password/secret management, RBAC, APIs, and workspaces make it a powerful option.

- **Terraform Cloud for Business:** This version extends TFC's capabilities by providing additional features such as the management of private infrastructure using Terraform Cloud agents, single sign-on (SSO), and more.

- **Terraform Enterprise:** This version provides organizations with the option to have an on-premises instance of Terraform that offers capabilities and features similar to TFC.

Use Case: ACI Tenant Creation   Let's look at a simple example for creating a tenant on Cisco ACI using the open-source version of Terraform on a NetDevOps engineer's workstation (that is, development environment). It is assumed that Terraform is installed in this development environment, and because the open-source version of Terraform is used, the execution steps are done via the CLI.

The Terraform version installed on the local workstation (macOS, in this example) can be confirmed by issuing the **terraform -v** command, as shown in Example 1-4.

Example 1-4   *Verifying the Terraform Version*

```
$ terraform -v
Terraform v1.2.8
on darwin_arm64

$
```

The next step is to prepare a config file that captures information related to the required provider, and this file also has the resource **aci_tenant** to add the tenant on Cisco ACI. This file must be saved with an extension of .tf (in this case, the file is named aci.tf and was created by the developer and saved in a folder on the local workstation). The contents of this file are shown, in Example 1-5, via the output of the **more aci.tf** command, where variables are also used for the URL and the username and password credentials of APIC.

Example 1-5   *Terraform Configuration File for ACI*

```
$ more aci.tf
terraform {
  required_providers {
    aci = {
      source = "ciscodevnet/aci"
    }
  }
}

provider "aci" {
  username = var.username
  password = var.password
```

```
  url      = var.apic_url
  insecure = true
}

variable "username" {
  type        = string
  description = "credentials for ACI"
  default     = "administrator"
}

variable "password" {
  type        = string
  description = "credentials for ACI "
  default     = "hidden!"
}

variable "apic_url" {
  type        = string
  default     = "https://sandboxapicdc.cisco.com"
}

resource "aci_tenant" "netdevops_tenant_1" {
  name        = "netdevops_tenant_1"
  description = "This tenant is created by the Terraform ACI provider"
}

$
```

Next, Terraform is initialized using the **terraform init** command, and this results in the installation of the ACI provider, as shown in Example 1-6.

Example 1-6   *Initializing Terraform*

```
$ terraform init

Initializing the backend...

Initializing provider plugins...
- Finding latest version of ciscodevnet/aci...
- Installing ciscodevnet/aci v2.5.2...
- Installed ciscodevnet/aci v2.5.2 (signed by a HashiCorp partner, key ID
  433649E2C56309DE)
```

```
Partner and community providers are signed by their developers.
If you'd like to know more about provider signing, you can read about it here:
https://www.terraform.io/docs/cli/plugins/signing.html


Terraform has created a lock file .terraform.lock.hcl to record the provider selec-
    tions it made above. Include this file in your version control repository so that
    Terraform can guarantee to make the same selections by default when you run "ter-
    raform init" in the future.
Terraform has been successfully initialized!


$
```

Next, the dry run is executed by using the **terraform plan** command. Example 1-7 shows that a tenant named **netdevops_tenant_1** will be created.

Example 1-7   *Terraform Dry Run*

```
$ terraform plan


Terraform used the selected providers to generate the following execution plan.
Resource actions are indicated with the following symbols:
  + create


Terraform will perform the following actions:

  # aci_tenant.netdevops_tenant_1 will be created
  + resource "aci_tenant" "netdevops_tenant_1" {
      + annotation                  = "orchestrator:terraform"
      + description                 = "This tenant is created by the Terraform ACI
provider"
      + id                          = (known after apply)
      + name                        = "netdevops_tenant_1"
      + name_alias                  = (known after apply)
      + relation_fv_rs_tenant_mon_pol = (known after apply)
    }

Plan: 1 to add, 0 to change, 0 to destroy.


$
```

The result of the **terraform plan** is as expected. Hence, it can be applied by using the **terraform apply** command. As per the execution of this command, a dry run is performed initially. Once the NetDevOps engineer is satisfied with this plan and enters **yes**, it is executed as shown in Example 1-8.

Example 1-8   *Applying Terraform Configurations to the ACI Infrastructure*

```
$ terraform apply

Terraform used the selected providers to generate the following execution plan.
Resource actions are indicated with the following symbols:
  + create

Terraform will perform the following actions:

  # aci_tenant.netdevops_tenant_1 will be created
  + resource "aci_tenant" "netdevops_tenant_1" {
      + annotation                   = "orchestrator:terraform"
      + description                  = "This tenant is created by the Terraform ACI
provider"
      + id                           = (known after apply)
      + name                         = "netdevops_tenant_1"
      + name_alias                   = (known after apply)
      + relation_fv_rs_tenant_mon_pol = (known after apply)
    }

Plan: 1 to add, 0 to change, 0 to destroy.

Do you want to perform these actions?
  Terraform will perform the actions described above.
  Only 'yes' will be accepted to approve.

  Enter a value: yes

aci_tenant.netdevops_tenant_1: Creating...
aci_tenant.netdevops_tenant_1: Creation complete after 3s [id=uni/tn-netdevops_ten-
  ant_1]

Apply complete! Resources: 1 added, 0 changed, 0 destroyed.

$
```

This is a simple use case that shows the capabilities of Terraform along with its configuration file to add a resource in Cisco ACI. This use case demonstrates how the Plan step shows what resources will be created, changed, or destroyed prior to actual execution.

Version Control System

As discussed in the "Code" section of this chapter, git is a distributed version control system (VCS) that enables versioning of the code, provides traceability capabilities for tracking changes made over time, keeps history and backups, allows collaboration among developers, provides authorization capabilities, and more.

Let's look further into the terminology associated with git to understand its distributed architecture, along with some examples to understand its capabilities and features.

Note   Users have the option of using the CLI or GUI for git operations by installing the appropriate git software package on their workstations—remember, that's the developer environment! In this example, the git package is installed on a terminal (bash).

- **Repository**: A folder that includes all the files and directories.

- **Remote repository**: In a decentralized VCS, there is one main repository that is used by all developers to share their work. In simpler terms, a remote repository can be considered a centralized repository that hosts the files and folders for exchange among all developers. The remote repository is usually provided on a cloud-hosting service such as GitHub, GitLab, or Bitbucket. GitHub is a web-based hosting service and is used for the examples in this chapter.

- **Local repository**: A repository on a developer's local workstation (that is, development environment) is a local repository.

Refer to Figure 1-8 to understand the high-level concept of repositories. We will look at a couple use cases to understand the local repository and remote repository operations further.

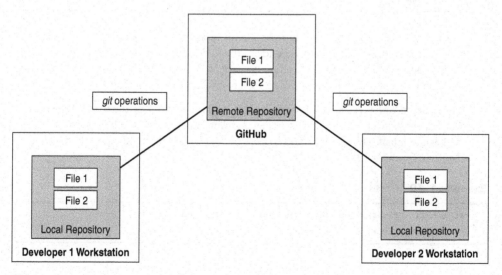

Figure 1-8   *Git Operations and Repositories*

Use Case: Local Repository

To understand the git operations for a local repository, let's consider a use case where a developer starts to work on a new network automation project.

Let's assume a clean-slate environment, where the organization is starting fresh on its NetDevOps journey. All the NetDevOps engineers have access to their working environment, which has git and other applications already installed.

A NetDevOps engineer (referred to as NetDevOps Engineer 1) authors a new Ansible playbook named vlan.yml for automation of the data center environment and now wants to collaborate further with the rest of the developers on that code. In addition, an inventory file named "hosts" is created that captures information about switches. The vlan.yml and hosts files are housed in a local directory named "netdevops" on the first developer's workstation. In the current state, git is not aware of and is not tracking this file.

As shown in Example 1-9, to initialize a new repository, the **git init** command is issued on the terminal within the "netdevops" directory. The response on the terminal confirms that the repository is initialized and a hidden .git folder is created. The hidden .git folder contains information related to files being tracked, their history, and so on. The users are not required to be aware of the details about the files within this hidden folder. The git CLI commands (aka git operations) provide the capability to retrieve information from the .git folder, such as commit history and such.

Example 1-9 *Initializing the Local Directory into a Git Repository*

```
$ git init
Initialized empty Git repository in /netdevops/.git/
```

This working space (or the working folder) in git terminology is called a "working directory." The working directory corresponds to the folder (complete directory/path) on the NetDevOps engineer's local workstation (as part of the local development environment). Also, git is not aware of and is not tracking any of the files within that directory.

As discussed earlier, git keeps track of changes and the identity of the user who makes the changes. For this reason, the username and email address need to be configured on the bash terminal. This is done by executing the commands for NetDevOps Engineer 1 shown in Example 1-10.

Example 1-10 *Git Configs*

```
$ git config --global user.email netdevops-1@netdevopsbook.com
$ git config --global user.name "netdevops-1"
```

The next step is to add the files in the staging area. As the name suggests, the staging area lets you review the files and the changes you are planning to execute (that is, you get ready before actually executing the files/changes to the local repository). Note that the staging area is also called an "index." To add the files in the staging area, **git add** commands are executed, as shown in Example 1-11. These commands add vlan.yml and hosts files to the staging area, and now git starts to track these files.

Example 1-11 *Adding Files to the Staging Area*

```
$ git add vlan.yml
$ git add hosts
```

The **git status** command provides the status of the files in the staging area, if any, and also provides the list of untracked files in the working directory. As shown in Example 1-12, this command validates the planned changes (that is, that the new files vlan.yml and hosts are in the staging area).

Example 1-12 *Verifying the State of the Git Working Directory and Staging Area*

```
$ git status
On branch main
No commits yet
Changes to be committed:
  (use "git rm --cached <file>..." to unstage)
        new file:   hosts
        new file:   vlan.yml

$
```

To add the vlan.yml and hosts files to the local repository (from the staging area), execute the **git commit** command, as shown in Example 1-13. A descriptive message should be part of the **commit** command. As shown in Example 1-13, the **-m** flag is used to add the message "ansible playbook to create VLAN."

Example 1-13 *A git commit to the Local Repository*

```
$ git commit -m "ansible playbook to create VLAN"
[main (root-commit) 67f8397] ansible playbook to create VLAN
 2 files changed, 28 insertions(+)
 create mode 100644 hosts
 create mode 100644 vlan.yml

$
```

When the commit is executed, git performs various steps for keeping the version history; for example, it takes a snapshot of the entire working directory, saves the information about the author who performed this commit, and generates an ID for tracking, and so on.

This information is highly useful if in the future the developer wants to revert to a specific version (past commit).

Since each NetDevOps engineer interacts with the files (network configurations as code) on their local workstation and in the local repository initially, git allows for fast execution of these steps.

This example shows a list of simple operations performed on the local repository. Refer to Figure 1-9 to see a graphical representation of the three steps:

Step 1.   NetDevOps Engineer 1 (username: netdevops-1) starts to work on the file in the "working directory."

Step 2.   Files are moved to the staging area within the local workspace via **git add** operations.

Step 3.   The files are placed in the local repository once the **git commit** is performed.

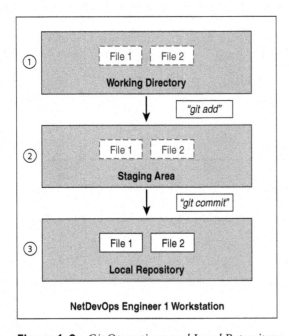

Figure 1-9   *Git Operations and Local Repository*

Use Case: Remote Repositories with Git Operations (Pull and Clone)   Let's continue the previous use case to see how git operations with the remote repository can be used by NetDevOps engineers for collaboration on the authored code (Ansible files for network configurations). Once the NetDevOps engineers are ready to share and collaborate on their work (that is, new code or changes to existing code), those files from the local repository are pushed to the remote repository.

In this use case, we will see how other NetDevOps engineers can access, review, and make changes to one of the files (that is, the Ansible playbook named vlan.yml, created earlier) as well as how the updated content can then be consumed by other collaborators via the remote repository.

> **Note**   Git is a flexible protocol. It provides multiple methods and a set of commands to achieve the same result. The following commands and steps represent one potential way of achieving the desired result. In this example, it is assumed that GitHub accounts have been created and are operational. Also, in the GitHub repository settings, the default branch name of "main" is configured. Further for authentication, a personal access token on Github.com is created under **Settings > Developer Settings > Personal access tokens.**

To create a remote repository, NetDevOps Engineer 1 (username netdevops-1), who developed the Ansible playbook file vlan.yml and the hosts file in the previous use case, accesses GitHub via a web browser (https://github.com). NetDevOps Engineer 1 (netdevops-1) then "creates a new repository" on GitHub through its web portal and initializes it by adding a README file with a description of the project.

Upon creation of the repository, its location is automatically generated by GitHub. The location is required for developers to view, fetch, or update the code to this remote repository. HTTPS and SSH URLs are two location options for accessing the content of this repository.

The following is an example for HTTPS URL syntax for the remote repository:

https://github.com/{userid}/{remote-repository-name}.git

In this example, **{userid}** is the username created during the initial account creation on GitHub (for example, netdevops-1), and **{remote-repository-name}** is the name of the newly created repository in the initial step (for example, dc-automation).

> **Note**   This is valid syntax used by GitHub at the time of writing this book.

To add the vlan.yml and hosts files to this remote repository, the URL of the remote repository must be configured on the bash terminal of the local developer environment (or local workstation). This configuration of the remote repository (URL) is performed by executing the **git remote add origin {remote-repository-url}** command, as shown in Example 1-14.

Example 1-14   *Adding a Git Remote Repository*

```
$ ls
hosts         vlan.yml
$
$ git remote add origin https://github.com/netdevops-1/dc-automation.git
$
```

This **git remote** command associates a remote URL with a name of origin. The default remote repository is usually called origin and is commonly used. The **git remote -v** command can be used to verify that the remote repository has been properly configured, as shown in Example 1-15.

Example 1-15   *Verifying a Git Remote Repository*

```
$ git remote -v
origin          https://github.com/netdevops-1/dc-automation.git (fetch)
origin          https://github.com/netdevops-1/dc-automation.git (push)
```

> **Note**   For HTTPS authentication to a remote repository on GitHub.com, a personal access token (PAT) must be used for the username authentication in the following step. To create a PAT, go to https://github.com and click your profile photo in the upper-right corner of the web page. Scroll to **Settings > Developer Settings > Personal access tokens** to generate a token that allows repo admin rights to push the code from the local repository to the remote repository. **git push** with the **force** option is executed, as shown in Example 1-16. The **force** option overwrites the history, which is a safe operation because the repository is newly created on GitHub. This command updates/publishes all the code to the remote repository (named "origin") from the local default branch of "main". In the password, the PAT will be used.

Example 1-16   *A git push to the Remote Repository*

```
$ git push origin main -force
Username for 'https://github.com': netdevops-1
Password for 'https://netdevops-1@github.com':
Enumerating objects: 4, done.
Counting objects: 100% (4/4), done.
Delta compression using up to 8 threads
Compressing objects: 100% (4/4), done.
Writing objects: 100% (4/4), 621 bytes | 621.00 KiB/s, done.
Total 4 (delta 0), reused 0 (delta 0), pack-reused 0
To https://github.com/netdevops-1/dc-automation.git
 + 0de7b6d...67f8397 main -> min (forced update)

$
```

At this stage, it can be confirmed on the GitHub web page that the main branch has the correct code files (vlan.yml and hosts). More details about the concept of git branching will be provided later in this chapter.

The other collaborators can now access and review this code. This developer can also add other developers as "collaborators" under the repository settings on GitHub. Let's continue the previous scenario to see how a peer developer (NetDevOps Engineer 2, with a user

ID of netdevops-2) can get this code and review it. It is assumed that the relevant GitHub accounts and the workstations for all NetDevOps engineers are already fully functional and operational with git.

NetDevOps Engineer 2, on the local workstation, creates a new directory and then navigates to that newly created directory on the bash terminal. Once NetDevOps Engineer 2 has navigated to that directory on the bash terminal, then, just like NetDevOps Engineer 1 (in the prior use case), the directory should be initialized for git and the username/email should be configured for git to track the user, as shown in Example 1-17.

Example 1-17   *Initializing the Git Repository and Git Configurations*

```
$ git init
Initialized empty Git repository in /netdevops/.git/

$ git config --global user.email netdevops-2@netdevopsbook.com
$ git config --global user.name "netdevops-2"
```

The Git configuration settings for NetDevOps Engineer 2 (netdevops-2) can be viewed by issuing the **git config --global -l** command, as shown in Example 1-18.

Example 1-18   *Viewing the Git Configuration*

```
$ git config --global -l
user.email=netdevops-2@netdevopsbook.com
user.name=netdevops-2
```

On the local bash terminal, NetDevOps Engineer 2 can copy the remote repository from GitHub by using the **git clone {remote-repository-url}** command, as shown in Example 1-19. This command copies the entire repository, and it shows up as a folder on the local machine of the developer, so they need to navigate to that directory using the **cd** command.

Example 1-19   *Cloning the Remote Git Repository*

```
$ git clone https://github.com/netdevops-1/dc-automation.git
Cloning into 'dc-automation'...
remote: Enumerating objects: 6, done.
remote: Counting objects: 100% (6/6), done.
remote: Compressing objects: 100% (2/2), done.
remote: Total 6 (delta 0), reused 3 (delta 0), pack-reused 0
Receiving objects: 100% (6/6), done.

$ ls
dc-automation

$ cd dc-automation
$
```

Now the code within the main branch is accessible to the NetDevOps engineer, as shown in Example 1-20, by using the **ls** command.

Example 1-20 *Listing the Files after git clone*

```
$ ls
hosts    vlan.yml
$
```

Let's assume NetDevOps Engineer 2 decides to update the Ansible playbook file so that it runs on all the switches instead of just one host. As shown from the output in Example 1-21 of the **more vlan.yml** command, the hosts configuration in the playbook has been changed to **all**. In Ansible, a group named **all** exists by default and contains every host (that is, all target devices) and does not need to be explicitly configured in an inventory file.

Example 1-21 *Contents of the Modified vlan.yml File in the Working Directory*

```
$ more vlan.yml

--
  - name: create a new VLAN
    hosts: all

    tasks:
      - name: provision VLAN
        cisco.nxos.nxos_vlans:
          config:
            - vlan_id: "{{item}}"
              state: active
        with_items:
          -  101
          -  102
```

Since git is tracking the vlan.yml file, once the file is modified, it is reflected by **git status** as shown in Example 1-22.

Example 1-22 *Checking the Status of the Git Staging Area and Working Directory*

```
$ git status
On branch main
Your branch is up to date with 'origin/main'.
Changes not staged for commit:
  (use "git add <file>..." to update what will be committed)
```

```
(use "git restore <file>..." to discard changes in working directory)
    modified:    vlan.yml

no changes added to commit (use "git add" and/or "git commit -a")
$
```

NetDevOps Engineer 2 can add the file to the staging directory and then to the local repository. The updated file is subsequently uploaded back into the GitHub repository using the appropriate credentials and personal access token generated earlier. This update/commit on GitHub will show the updated version of the file. This is done by using the commands shown in Example 1-23.

Example 1-23 *Adding the Modified vlan.yml File to the Git Staging Area and Pushing It to the Remote Repository*

```
$ git add vlan.yml

$ git commit -m "changed for all hosts in playbook"
[main 5be87b8] changed for all hosts in playbook
 1 file changed, 1 insertion(+), 1 deletion(-)

$ git push
Username for 'https://github.com': netdevops-2
Password for 'https://netdevops-2@github.com':
Enumerating objects: 5, done.
Counting objects: 100% (5/5), done.
Delta compression using up to 8 threads
Compressing objects: 100% (3/3), done.
Writing objects: 100% (3/3), 351 bytes | 351.00 KiB/s, done.
Total 3 (delta 1), reused 1 (delta 0), pack-reused 0
remote: Resolving deltas: 100% (1/1), completed with 1 local object.
To https://github.com/netdevops-1/dc-automation.git
   5be87b8..dbde804  main -> main

$
```

NetDevOps Engineer 1 (netdevops-1) can now display the commits on the remote repository using **git log origin/main**. The partial snippet of commands in Example 1-24 (**more vlan.yml**) shows that the current playbook in NetDevOps Engineer 1's local repository is only pointing to one switch (**leaf_one**). NetDevOps Engineer 1 can then download the updated Ansible playbook file from the remote repository by using the **git pull** command shown in Example 1-24.

Example 1-24 *Viewing the Git History on the Remote Repo and the Contents of the Local vlan.yml File and Pulling Down the Updated Version*

```
$ git log origin/main
commit 5be87b823862bdafaf9fb5e9261709b547a3f32b
Author: netdevops-2 <netdevops-2@netdevopsbook.com>
Date:    Thu Sep 1 16:57:35 2022 +0400
    changed for all hosts in playbook

commit 67f8397c61706d81c16830444b66155dfb771671 (HEAD -> main)
Author: netdevops-1 <netdevops-1@netdevopsbook.com>
Date:    Thu Sep 1 15:40:38 2022 +0400
    ansible playbook to create VLAN

$ more vlan.yml
---
  - name: create a new VLAN
    hosts: leaf_one
#OUTPUT OMITTED#

$
$ git pull origin main
From https://github.com/netdevops-1/dc-automation
 * branch              main        -> FETCH_HEAD
Updating 67f8397..c368b7f
Fast-forward
 vlan.yml | 2 +-
 1 file changed, 1 insertion(+), 1 deletion(-)

$
```

At this stage, NetDevOps Engineer 1 (netdevops-1) can display the commits using **git log**. The partial snippet of the updated vlan.yml file in Example 1-25 shows the **hosts** entry is now pointing to **all** switches.

Example 1-25 *The Git History of the Local Repo and Updated vlan.yml File on NetDevOps Engineer 1's Workstation*

```
$ git log
commit 5be87b823862bdafaf9fb5e9261709b547a3f32b
Author: netdevops-2 <netdevops-2@netdevopsbook.com>
Date:    Thu Sep 1 16:57:35 2022 +0400

    changed for all hosts in playbook
```

```
commit 67f8397c61706d81c16830444b66155dfb771671
Author: netdevops-1 netdevops-1@netdevopsbook.com
Date:    Thu Sep 1 15:40:38 2022 +0400

    ansible playbook to create VLAN

$
$ more vlan.yml
---
  - name: create a new VLAN
    hosts: all
#OUTPUT OMITTED#

$
```

This use case shows how the following git operations are used for collaboration among multiple NetDevOps engineers via the centralized remote repository. Refer to Figure 1-10 to see a graphical representation of these operations:

Step 1. Files are added to the local repository by NetDevOps Engineer 1 (netdevops-1) in a git branch.

Step 2. The git operation **git push** is used to copy the files from the local repository to the remote repository on GitHub. Now other collaborators with appropriate access rights can fetch, view, and update the content of the remote repository.

Step 3. The git operation **git clone** is used to copy all the branches of that remote repository from GitHub by NetDevOps Engineer 2 (netdevops-2).

Step 4. Files are now accessible in the local repository of NetDevOps Engineer 2 (netdevops-2), and any future modifications performed on these files are tracked by git. In this use case, the content of one of the files is modified.

Step 5. The git operation **git push** is used by NetDevOps Engineer 2 (netdevops-2) to copy the updated files from the local repository to the remote repository on GitHub.

Step 6. The git operation **git pull** is used by NetDevOps Engineer 1 (netdevops-1) to download the updated content from the remote repository on GitHub and to the local repository.

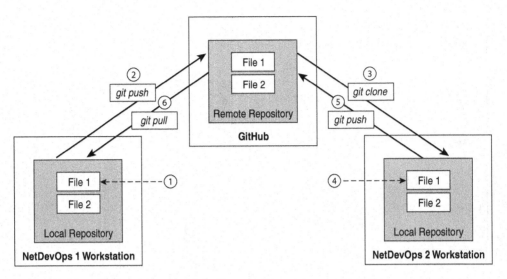

Figure 1-10   *Git Operations and the Remote Repository*

Git Branches

The git branches feature delivers ease of use by allowing NetDevOps engineers to develop, modify, or change code independent of each other, thus providing them the ability to operate in an error-free environment without impacting each other's work. Fixing bugs and adding new capabilities to existing code are some of the common use cases of git branches. When the git branches feature is used, the code in the main branch is protected. Think of git branches as the branches that offshoot from the trunk of a tree. The main branch is the trunk, and a "new" branch is created from this "main" branch by developers. There can be any number of branches. The development work (such as developing new features or modifying existing features) within each branch is independent of the main and other branches. Thus, the branches do not affect each other.

Once the development work within a branch is complete, the code can be integrated or combined back into the main branch. This integration is called "merging" in git terminology. Reviewing and agreeing on the code additions or changes (for feature development or enhancements) is done as part of the merge process.

In summary, branches and the merging process allow multiple developers to work in parallel and independent of each other.

Figure 1-11 is a graphical representation that shows the following:

- The main branch for Ansible code to create VLANs. The **main** branch has multiple commits and contains the vlan.yml and hosts files.

- A branch named **SVI** is created from **main**. In this branch, the Ansible role is created for configuring switched virtual interfaces (SVIs) with IP addresses for VLANs. SVIs will allow inter-VLAN routing on the Nexus switches in a data center environment. Once the Ansible role for SVI configuration is validated and reviewed, the branch is merged back into the main branch.

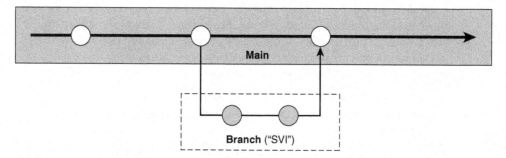

Figure 1-11   *Git Branching and Merging*

This is a very simple example of branching and merging in git. During the development of Ansible artifacts for the SVI configuration feature, there is no impact to the code on the main branch. Like in this example, there can be many additional branches for development of other features using Ansible.

CI/CD

Details about CI/CD were covered earlier in this chapter. More details about installing and using Jenkins are provided in Chapter 3.

Testing

Test automation is a critical part of NetDevOps. Various tools and techniques are available for automated testing, including the following:

- Use of an open-source automation framework such as Robot for test automation. The Robot framework uses human-readable keyword-based testing and provides an easy syntax for writing test cases. The framework is open and extensible. It provides a combination of pre-packaged (built-in) libraries and an option to install developed libraries separately. These libraries provide extensive coverage for device testing, and additional libraries can also be developed, as required. Examples of built-in libraries include the ability to generate and compare strings and execute tasks on operating systems. Web testing using Selenium and executing commands over SSH are examples of a few libraries that can be installed. The Robot framework can also be integrated with external systems, meaning it can be integrated into the NetDevOps environment and software development lifecycle. It also generates reports for test cases, providing easier consumption and distribution of the test results. Refer to https://robotframework.org/ for more information on the Robot framework.

■ Use of test automation suites such as Cisco pyATS, a Python-based automation test suite, for NetDevOps. Cisco pyATS has extensive coverage of networking devices (namely, routers, switches, and firewalls). It was originally developed by Cisco engineering teams for internal use but now has been shared with the external community for wider consumption via Cisco DevNet. Cisco has been extending its coverage and capabilities by adding additional SDK and libraries such as the Genie framework, which provides the flexibility of using the Python programming language and libraries to interact with networking devices. Refer to https://developer.cisco.com/docs/pyats/ and https://developer.cisco.com/docs/genie-docs/ for more on pyATS.

■ Use of Python to automate test cases of networking devices. Existing Python libraries such as Netmiko, NCClient, and Requests, for example, are used for test automation of networking devices.

■ Finally, a combination of any of the listed tools, as well as other tools, may be used.

As discussed earlier in this chapter, emulation of networking environments is important for validation and testing. Details about Emulated Virtual Environment (EVE-NG) are provided in Chapter 5.

Summary

In this chapter, you learned about NetDevOps and how it helps organizations add value to their overall business. Other benefits include improved speed of delivery, overall reliability and quality of networks, and enhanced collaboration among business, development, and operations departments. In this chapter, you learned about the following topics:

■ Modern networking products that provide APIs for model-driven programmability and telemetry

■ The stages of NetDevOps (that is, Plan, Code, Build, Test, Release, Deploy, Operate, and Monitor)

■ Various tools associated with these stages and how they help us realize the benefits of NetDevOps

■ Concepts and activities involved in continuous integration/continuous delivery/deployment (CI/CD)

■ Source control using git as well as how git operations help developers maintain version history and collaborate using remote repositories via GitHub

■ The importance of configuration management tools such as Ansible and Terraform

Details about various use cases of NetDevOps are provided in Chapter 2, "Getting Started with NetDevOps." In addition, implementation details about the CI/CD tool can be found in Chapter 3, and the implementation of pipelines using Jenkins is covered in Chapter 4.

Review Questions

You can find the answers to these questions in Appendix A, "Answers to Review Questions."

1. What are the benefits associated with NetDevOps?

    a. Increased speed in delivering new capabilities (that is, agility)

    b. Improved network reliability

    c. Enhanced collaboration among developers and operations teams

    d. Improved networks operations

    e. All of the above

2. What does the acronym CI/CD stand for?

    a. Continuous integration/continuous delivery/deployment

    b. Confidential information/continuous deployment

    c. Continuous integration/continuous design

    d. Continuous improvement/continuous delivery/deployment

3. Which of the followings statements is true about Ansible?

    a. It uses agents and a pull-based mechanism for configuring target devices.

    b. It requires the installation of additional software on the target device.

    c. It is an agentless and idempotent tool.

    d. The control node does not depend on additional packages such as Python.

4. Which of the following are valid git operations for the remote repository?

    a. git clone, git add, git commit, and git push

    b. git init, git branch, git checkout, and git monitor

    c. git pull, git push, git checkout, and git branch

    d. None of the above

5. What element in a Terraform configuration file declares the desired state of infrastructure?

    a. provider

    b. state file

    c. resources

    d. data sources

6. Which tool can be used for the automation and implementation of pipelines in NetDevOps?

    a. EVE-NG

    b. Maven

   c. Robot framework

   d. Jenkins

7. Test automation can be implemented using which tool?

   a. Cisco pyATS

   b. Jenkins

   c. GitHub

   d. Slack

8. Modern networking products offer which type of capability to retrieve as much data as possible and as quickly as possible?

   a. SNMP

   b. Streaming telemetry

   c. NETCONF

   d. YANG

9. Both Ansible and Terraform build and store the current state of the infrastructure that is provisioned by these tools.

   a. True

   b. False

10. For the Test stage of NetDevOps, the use of virtual network devices will offer all the capabilities of physical network devices.

   a. True

   b. False

## Chapter 2

Getting Started with NetDevOps

In this chapter, we describe the main use cases where NetDevOps excels. We go over what the use case is, how it is handled in a traditional networking fashion and finish with the NetDevOps approach and its benefits. We also describe common decisions in the adoption of NetDevOps such as tooling choices, skills required, and possible starting points. This chapter finishes with lessons learned from many NetDevOps adoption processes: common challenges and mitigations. In summary, you will learn the following about NetDevOps:

- What does it solve
- How does it solve it
- Possible starting points
- Decisions and investments
- Common pitfalls and recommendations

Use Cases

In Chapter 1, "Why Do We Need NetDevOps?", you learned what NetDevOps is, its benefits, and its components. In this section, you will learn what specific use cases you can benefit from by applying NetDevOps practices and tools.

More specifically, this section goes into detail on each individual use case NetDevOps can help you with. Although this is an extensive list, as you can see in Figure 2-1, it is possible that not all use cases are represented here.

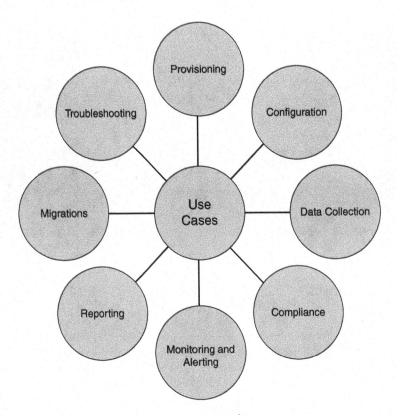

Figure 2-1 *NetDevOps Use Cases Mind Map*

The use case deep dives focus on the stages a typical continuous integration/continuous delivery/deployment (CI/CD) pipeline should have rather than on the automation scripts or infrastructure as code (IaC) that performs the actual actions. The reason for this choice is that we consider network automation a well-documented topic that is highly dependent on tool choices and desired automated actions, and we want you to learn the orchestration process behind each use case while keeping this chapter's stages and practices mostly tool and technology agnostic.

Note   This chapter's use cases assume you use all of NetDevOps' components; however, it is possible you are only using some (for example, only IaC), in which case you will see a subset of the benefits.

These use cases are focused on the usage perspective, meaning that you can and should have CI/CD pipelines to merge developed code into your source control. However, this is not our focus. The following pipelines are the pipelines you, someone from your team, or an automatic trigger would start when you need to perform an action in your network. Note the pipelines that are triggered when you modify your automation code.

Triggers are a topic we will dive into in Chapter 3, "How to Implement CI/CD Pipelines with Jenkins." However, for this chapter, it is important to understand that pipelines can be triggered in many different ways: manually by a user, automatically by a change in a code repository, automatically in response to an event (for example, a high % of CPU), and so on. Throughout this chapter, you will see mentions of possible triggers for each use case.

Provisioning

Provisioning, which is often confused with configuring, is the process of setting up the IT infrastructure. Infrastructure in this context can mean many things: virtual machines, containers, virtual network devices, services, and so on. However, when you want to create a virtual local area network (VLAN) and consult the documentation, you will often see "Configuring a VLAN." That's because configuring comes after provisioning; when you configure a VLAN, the switch was already provisioned.

In a physical environment, you provision a switch (cabling, racking, and stacking) and then configure it (VLANs, IP addresses, interfaces, and so on). In a virtual environment, you provision a virtual machine (number of CPUs, amount of RAM, or amount of storage) and then configure it (installing a software package, patching a security vulnerability, and so on) or you provision a virtual switch (virtual-to-physical port mappings) in a hypervisor environment and then configure port groups (VM-to-VLAN mappings).

In this book, provisioning refers to creating resources in networking environments. Mostly this happens in cloud environments—not necessarily only in public cloud environments, such as Amazon Web Services, Google Cloud Platform, and Microsoft Azure, which are the more famous options, but in any cloud environment, such as the less popular private clouds like Red Hat OpenStack and VMware environments.

These provisioning actions can take effect in different forms, such as command-line interfaces (CLIs), graphical user interfaces (GUIs), and application programming interfaces (APIs). In our NetDevOps context, and because automation is one of our core components, you will more often see an API as the default choice.

A traditional networking provisioning workflow is usually orchestrated as a series of manual steps executed by one or more individuals. This workflow is achieved either manually, by clicking through the GUI for simpler actions, or manually, by executing a series of automation scripts that make use of the product's API or CLI.

So, what does a typical provisioning NetDevOps pipeline look like and how does it differ from a traditional one? Figure 2-2 shows an example. This pipeline starts by retrieving the required code from a code repository, which is a version control system (VCS). In this repository, you will likely find the automation code to perform the provisioning action, which can be implemented by a variety of different tools (for example, Ansible, Terraform, Python, Unix shell, and so on), but also some specific variables required for this code to run. In concrete terms, this could be a generic Ansible playbook to replace the running-config on an IOS-XE switch and a variable file with the specific running-config to push.

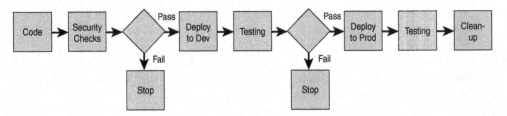

Figure 2-2 *Provisioning Pipeline*

For some automation workflows, there will be no variables file, either because it is a static workflow without any possible variation (for example, a script that saves the running-config to the startup-config in all your network switches) or because the pipeline prompts the user for the required variables at the time of execution. We call these "run-time variables" because they are provided at runtime.

The second stage, labeled "Security Checks," is a security verification stage. This is often ignored, not because people do not like security, but because it is, in many cases, hard to implement. In this stage, you verify that the combination of automation plus variables does not violate any security policy in a static way ("static" because you do not execute this automation to make this verification). Some tools can make this verification easier (for example, tfsec for Terraform). A common verification for cloud environments is to make sure the firewall rules are not open to the world.

Note   This is the pipeline for the execution of a provisioning workflow. Static code analysis tools are quite common in development workflow environments.

The third stage, "Deploy to Dev," is also a stage often missing from many production implementations. This is where you execute the automation code against a test/develop-ment/staging environment. This stage is meant to be executed against an environment that mirrors your production environment to give you confidence before you possibly make environment-breaking changes. Because of costs, historical reasons, or other factors, as we discuss later in this chapter, this stage is often skipped.

The pipeline's development deployment stage is followed by a more thorough testing than static analysis. In this stage, you can go as deep as you want with your testing. From the simple "are the resources created with my parameters?" test to actual functional testing of the created resources—anything is possible. This serves as a decision point of either to continue and provision the same resources in your production environment or to stop (in the case of discovered unexpected behaviors).

Assuming you did not abort, it is time for the production deployment stage. In this stage, you execute the same code as you did in the development environment but with a differ-ent target—production. This should have the exact same effect, and hopefully you now understand the value of the previous stage and the added assurance you get from having a testing environment.

Although you tested in the staging environment, the following stage involves testing in production. Here, oftentimes you do even a more thorough testing, and you include some end-to-end tests that you could not run in your testing environment. It is common that testing environments are smaller in size and complexity, and because of that some tests can only be run in production. Likewise, load tests (meaning putting a resource under simulated demand) are typically run in this stage.

The last stage is the clean-up stage, and it is optional. In this stage, you often clean up your testing environment (in the case that is virtual). However, if you have a static testing environment that mimics your production environment, you would not delete it in this stage.

Using Terraform to provision a tenant in Cisco Application Centric Infrastructure (ACI) is a concrete implementation of this use case. First, as shown in Example 2-1, you need to have Terraform code to implement a Cisco ACI tenant. With this code in a code repository, you can create a CI/CD pipeline with the previously mentioned stages.

Example 2-1 *Source Code for aci_tenant.yml*

```
resource "aci_tenant" "vmotion_tenant" {
    name        = "vMotion"
    description = "Tenant for vMotion"
}
```

In the first stage, you check out the code from the code repository. In the second stage, you can use a script to verify whether the tenant's name complies with your naming standards (for example, whether it uses CamelCase), or you can use tfsec to verify that the security configurations of the tenant are compliant with best practices.

In the third stage, you execute your Terraform code against a test/development/staging Application Policy Infrastructure Controller (APIC) using the Terraform syntax:

```
$ terraform apply aci_tenant.yml
```

In the fourth stage, you verify that the new tenant was successfully created and nothing broke. Your ACI fabric should still be working as expected. If that is the case, your fifth stage should apply your Terraform code to your production APIC. You can use environment variables to choose what environment to deploy to in each stage, or you can use other techniques, as you will see in Chapter 6, "How to Build Your Own NetDevOps Architecture."

In the sixth stage, you verify your production environment after provisioning your new tenant.

Normally, APICs are long-lasting appliances and are not spun up and spun down; instead, they run continuously. Because of that, you would not have the last optional stage to delete your test environment.

Note that error handling was not mentioned in this example of a typical CI/CD provisioning pipeline. If any of the stages fail, the pipeline would stop and human intervention would be required to set it right. There are different ways to handle errors; for example, you could retry the same action or you could roll back. In networking, retrying the same action is typically not advised without first checking the error logs. Because of that, rollbacks are the most common way of handling provisioning errors. Depending on the automation tool used, rollbacks for the most part only remove what was provisioned and therefore are easy to achieve. In Chapter 4, "How to Implement NetDevOps Pipelines with Jenkins," you will learn how to implement rollbacks in code.

Lastly, provisioning workflows are typically triggered manually by a user or by changes in the configuration variables in a code repository.

Configuration

Configuration, as mentioned, comes after resources are provisioned. This is the most common use case in NetDevOps. As the name implies, this use case consists of configuring resources, and both changes to an already existing configuration or new configurations fall within this use case's umbrella. Specific examples include configuring a VLAN on a router, configuring a virtual machine with a software package, and configuring a new virtual switch port group in a VMware environment.

In order to configure your target resources, besides the desired configurations, you will need a configuration tool. Many different tools with different features are available, including Ansible, Terraform, Chef, vendor-specific tools, and even programming languages such as Python. In our context of networking, the predominant tool is Ansible. However, choosing a tool is complex and a topic described later in this chapter.

A traditional configuration workflow can be described as a series of steps executed in sequence:

Step 1.   Connect to a resource.

Step 2.   Verify the current functionality.

Step 3.   Optionally retrieve the current configuration and functionality.

Step 4.   Optionally compare the current configuration to the desired configuration.

Step 5.   Configure the resource with the new configuration.

Step 6.   Verify the desired functionality.

Note   The workflow assumes the intended configurations were previously created.

These steps are usually manually executed by an operator from a workstation or executed by an operator in an automated fashion. For example, in a networking setup, an operator can either SSH to a device and issue a **show** command from their workstation (steps 1 and 2) or run a script from their workstation that does the same two steps in an automated fashion. The fully manual approach is more error-prone.

In a NetDevOps fashion, you take the previous automated approach a couple steps further. Figure 2-3 presents a complete NetDevOps configuration pipeline.

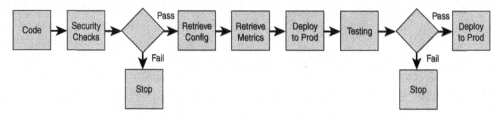

Figure 2-3 *Configuration Pipeline*

This pipeline is similar to a provisioning pipeline, but this section focuses on the differences.

One interesting difference is due to the fact that configuration workflows are often configuration changes made to previous configurations. Unlike in the provisioning use case, where you create net new assets, in this scenario you need to take into consideration what was configured before. In the third stage of the pipeline, you do that by retrieving the current resource's configuration. In this same stage, you can also retrieve information about the current functionality. However, many organizations prefer to separate these stages into two different ones, as shown in Figure 2-3 as the "Retrieve Metrics" stage; this allows them to manage the scripts to gather information independently of each other and achieve a higher level of decoupling.

Imagine you want to configure a new Open Shortest Path First (OSPF) neighbor in a Nexus switch. In the third stage, "Retrieve Config," you retrieve the running-config section of OSPF and the configuration of the interface where the new neighbor exists. In the fourth stage, you retrieve the **show ip ospf neighbors** and the **show ip route** commands' output.

The information gathered at this stage can be used to derive what configuration changes are needed. For example, if you want to replace a Simple Network Management Protocol (SNMP) key, it is different from configuring a new SNMP key on top of another existing one. This would result in having two SNMP keys instead of a single changed one. This type of logic needs to be implemented by you and is highly dependent on the configuration tool used.

In the fifth stage, "Deploy to Dev," you configure the resource in the test/development/ staging environment with the new configuration.

The next stage verifies that these configurations were applied correctly. You can, again, have a single stage that verifies both configuration and functionality, or you can use two separate stages. Figure 2-3 shows a single stage, "Testing," but it's recommended to use two.

Continuing with the previous example of configuring a new OSPF neighbor in a Nexus switch, in this stage, you would again retrieve the Nexus's running-config section of OSPF and the configuration of the changed interface and make sure it has the newly configured parameters. On top of that, you would retrieve the same **show** commands and verify the command output shows the new neighbor along with new routes. In this stage, like in the provisioning use case, you can take your testing further and also test functionality (for example, a connectivity test to an endpoint behind the new OSPF neighbor). The depth of the testing should depend on the criticality of the change and your willingness to accept risk.

So far, all the previous stages were executed against a development environment. This is a major difference from the traditional workflow, where there's a single environment—production. If everything functions as expected at the end of the verifications, you repeat the same stages but with a production resource as the target, represented by the "Deploy to Prod" stage.

Configuration workflows, just like the provisioning workflows, are typically triggered manually or by variable changes in a source control repository.

Data Collection

The simplest use case is data collection, where the goal is to gather data from resources. Although the target resources can differ (virtual machines, physical network equipment, controllers, and so on), the pipeline architecture is the same. Data collection is more often triggered on a schedule, like a cron job, than performed manually by an operator. However, these two are the usual triggers.

Tip Cron jobs are tasks that run periodically at fixed times. The name originates from the command-line utility cron of Unix-like operating systems. Cron is a job scheduler, and a job in this context can be a script or command.

In a traditional scenario, operators can use different ways to retrieve data. In networking, a common technique is to connect to devices using SSH and retrieve **show** command outputs. Other data-gathering techniques include SNMP polling and using a device's APIs.

It is important to note that all of these techniques are being increasingly automated. Instead of operators manually connecting to every device and gathering the command outputs, they now run scripts from their workstations that do this for them. However, NetDevOps takes this further by adding consistency, history tracking, and easy integrations to the process. Figure 2-4 presents a data collection pipeline.

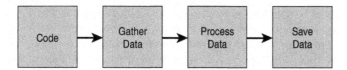

Figure 2-4 *Data Collection Pipeline*

It starts with the usual stage of retrieving your source code from a code repository; in this case, the most commonly used code is automation scripts, namely using Python. Python's network modules, vibrant developer community, and its easy-to-learn features, such as human-friendly syntax, make it the most used tool for this purpose. Nonetheless, Ansible and other tools can also effectively retrieve data.

In the second stage, "Gather Data," the scripts run and the results are stored locally. This step can be time-consuming if there are several target resources or if the scripts retrieve a large amount of data from each resource. In the first case, you can speed up the process by having multiple data-gathering stages running in parallel. You will learn more about this technique in Chapter 4.

The third stage, "Process Data," is optional but highly recommended. Data gathered from devices comes in its raw form, meaning it comes in whatever format the device outputs it in. Most of the time, this format is not the one you need. In this stage, you can use a programming language to parse the collected data into useful insights.

For example, if you issue a **show cdp neighbors** command, you get something similar to Example 2-2. This output is very verbose, and you might only need the name and the remote and local interfaces of the device's neighbor to store in a database. This is where a script could parse the output and save it in a simplified format.

Example 2-2 *Output for show cdp neighbors on a Cisco Switch*

```
Switch#show cdp neighbors
Capability Codes: R - Router, T - Trans Bridge, B - Source Route Bridge
                  S - Switch, H - Host, I - IGMP, r - Repeater, P - Phone,
                  D - Remote, C - CVTA, M - Two-port Mac Relay


Device ID          Local Intrfce     Holdtme    Capability  Platform  Port ID
Switch3.cisco.com
                   Gig 1/0/19        136                    R S I  WS-C3850- Gig 1/0/23
Switch2.cisco.com
                   Gig 1/0/17        126                    R S I  WS-C3850- Gig 1/0/24
Switch1.cisco.com
                   Gig 1/0/2         191                    R S I  WS-C3650- Gig 1/0/24

Total cdp entries displayed : 3
```

The last stage, "Save Data," is also optional. There are times when you are just collecting data for real-time verifications and you do not want to store what is collected; this is the equivalent of connecting to a network device by issuing a **show** command to verify something and immediately terminating that connection. However, if you do want to store what was gathered, you use this last stage. This stage is especially useful when you want to send the gathered data to multiple systems (for example, a monitoring system and a long-term archive). One goal for this last stage might be to anticipate network issues through the use of predictive machine learning (ML) models.

Compliance

There are many compliance frameworks and requirements. Most companies have to comply with regulatory requirements, such as HIPAA, PCI-DSS, SOX, DORA, and GDPR, on top of their own compliance policies.

In order to be compliant, companies have to prove their compliance. It is not enough to say they are applying the measures; in most cases, they have to prove the measures are actually in place. Historically, this was done through a series of manual steps executed by operators. Fast-forward to today, the process is a mix of manual and automated steps, mostly via manually operated automation tools. For example, if you must prove your organization is using SSH version 2 for all its network devices access instead of the older (and less secure) version 1, you must connect to every device in the network and retrieve and verify its configuration to show that.

> **Note**   You can see that compliance verification is very much like data collection, with extra steps for verifying whether the collected data complies with a set of predefined rules.

As previously mentioned for the data collection use case, connecting to devices today is commonly achieved by an operator running a script on their machine rather than actually connecting and issuing a **show** command. However, for compliance, you want something more reliable for recordkeeping than a human operator. A NetDevOps pipeline, as shown in Figure 2-5, adds these benefits.

Figure 2-5   *Compliance Verification Pipeline*

The second stage, "Gather Data," and third stage, "Verify Compliance," can be implemented in a single stage if your automation script does both of those tasks together. Beyond just gathering data, you also need to parse it into a format you can use for the verifications. This should all be achieved by your automation scripts.

The fourth stage, "Apply Remediations," is optional. However, it is a nice way of maintaining your environment's compliance. It is hard to achieve in a general-purpose way; nonetheless, for common attributes that tend to fall out of compliance, you can develop a script to fix them. For example, in networking, you can forget to enable BPDU Guard on newly configured access ports. After the automation identifies these ports as noncompliant, your remediation script adds this configuration to the affected ports. Another example is forgetting to enable password encryption. This can be achieved by triggering a configuration pipeline.

Lastly, the "Generate Reports" stage aggregates all information into a report format. Compliance officers typically want a document with a set structure. This can be a single report or multiple reports. There are many ways to generate these reports, but the most common is to use a programing language to produce markdown documents that can also be tracked under version control systems. If you do not need to generate a specific report, the logs generated by the pipeline run itself can be enough to document compliance, and you could then delete this last stage.

Case Study: PCI-DSS Networking Compliance in a Bank

Banks, because they are part of the payment industry, have to comply with the Payment Card Industry Data Security Standard (PCI-DSS), which is a set of security standards designed to ensure that all companies that accept, process, store, or transmit credit card information maintain a secure environment.

AnyBank, a large bank with a global presence in multiple countries across multiple continents, has a very large install base with different types of equipment from various vendors.

Because PCI-DSS standards are generic, AnyBank developed an internal document that details what kind of security controls are mandatory in all of its networking equipment. However, the bank faced a complicated challenge: each networking vendor implements its own command syntax, and unfortunately for AnyBank, it has multiple different vendors' equipment in its production network. In order for compliance not to be left to the discretion of network operators, AnyBank developed its internal security controls document further, to the point that the document had a specific command for each platform expected for PCI-DSS controls.

To put this document to use, twice a year AnyBank hosted a compliance manual verification exercise, where each of its local branches verified its equipment configuration compliance against the document. This was an expensive and tedious exercise for everyone involved. Connecting to multiple devices and checking configuration databases against a set of practices is not fun. Additionally, after this exercise, the same engineers involved in the verifications needed to document their findings so that a central entity could generate a consolidated report.

AnyBank realized this process could be improved. It started by creating automation scripts, using Python, that pull the configuration from the devices in the network and match it against a set of compliance templates built from the initial document. The result was a simple status report stating whether a device is compliant and, if not, why.

These automation scripts greatly improved AnyBank's ability to verify its compliance status; however, it still required operators to know how to run the scripts and had to point them to the right device types. Furthermore, AnyBank wanted this process to run continuously to achieve the best possible security posture.

Therefore, AnyBank evolved its solution to NetDevOps pipelines that use these previously created scripts to verify the bank's compliance status on a scheduled basis. AnyBank developed multiple pipelines, each targeting a different geography, that can run separately. It also created a pipeline that aggregates all available compliance findings into a consolidated report.

On top of all of this, AnyBank exposed these pipelines to its network operators through a graphical user interface (GUI). With this solution, anyone, with or without automation knowledge, is able to assess the compliance status of the network at any time.

AnyBank had such success adopting NetDevOps practices for its compliance efforts that it further adopted these practices for other use cases. Currently, the bank does most of its provisioning, configuring, and data gathering in the same fashion.

Compliance verifications are typically only done during certain specific time periods (for example, when you are trying to achieve a compliance certification or at a certain time to comply with regulations). The automation capabilities discussed in this section allow for constant compliance verification, rather than the usual point-in-time verifications. Because these pipelines are automated and can run without effort, you are able to achieve a constant monitoring of your compliance status by triggering them on a scheduled basis. A benefit of this behavior is the ability to take faster remediation actions whenever non-compliant characteristics are detected. For point-in-time verifications, you can still trigger them in a manual fashion.

Monitoring and Alerting

Monitoring is observing something over time. In our context, it can be observing metrics, logs, or simply the configuration of our resources. This is not a new field; there are plenty of well-established monitoring techniques and tools out there.

Alerting is warning something or someone of a certain condition. In networking, this is typically associated with a numerical threshold or a specific error message. Monitoring and alerting are two sides of the same coin: without monitoring resources, you cannot accurately trigger alerts. Although you can monitor resources without creating alerts, you lose value. Imagine you are monitoring the CPU percentage of your network devices, and the monitoring solution identifies a specific router at 100% CPU usage. If you don't have any alert on this condition, monitoring it does not add much value other than being able to know, at a later time, that the condition happened. On the other hand, if you do have an alert set, you can notify someone to act on this condition and mitigate the issue (likewise, you can notify something that triggers an automatic action, such as running a script).

As mentioned, monitoring and alerting are an established field. Because of that, you will most likely use a commercial off-the-shelf (COTS) tool. They are easy to install, configure, and use. These tools can be split into two categories: full end-to-end tools that manage the consumption, processing, and visualization of data, such as Cisco DNA Center Assurance and Datadog Network Monitoring, and tools that only manage processing and visualization of data, leaving you the responsibility of taking care of data ingestion, such as Splunk and the ELK (Elasticsearch, Logstash, Kibana) stack.

In the first use case, NetDevOps does not really have a role to play. However, in the second use case, where you own the data ingestion, a pipeline such as the one previously shown for data collection is useful. In the last stage you send the data, in the correct format, to the monitoring tools rather than a historical database. Another architecture sends the data to the database and configures the monitoring tool to monitor the data in the database, although this is less common. Alerting in these use cases is done in the monitoring tool itself, which is a widely supported functionally of these tools.

Besides the previously mentioned scenarios, there are two more cases: one where you decide to build your own monitoring and alerting solution, and one where you do not build a solution but use NetDevOps pipelines to achieve a simple alerting flow.

In the case where you decide to build your own tool, think again—this is not an easy task. In the case where you just want a simple alerting mechanism but don't want to invest in any tool at all, you can use a pipeline like the one in Figure 2-6.

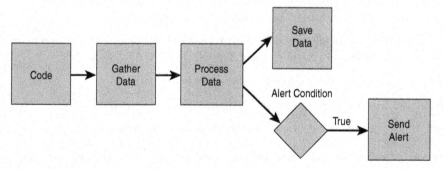

Figure 2-6 *Monitoring and Alerting Pipeline*

You can see the resemblance to the data collection pipeline, because monitoring is data collection over time. Therefore, you would trigger this pipeline on a scheduled basis.

> **Tip**   Independent of using a monitoring tool or triggering a pipeline on a schedule, think about the resource constraint this adds to your monitored resources. For metric data, you typically want a lower time interval than for log or configuration data.

At the end of the pipeline, you can see that when you send the processed data to storage, you also verify whether it passes a certain threshold or other configured alarm condition; if it does, you trigger an alarm. This does not need to be done in parallel, but doing it in parallel can trigger the alarm quicker.

Because the word "alarm" is used, you may think this needs to be a notification of some sort. However, this is not true. An alarm in this sense is just an action; it can be a notification such as an email or SMS, but it can also be an action such as calling an API or triggering another pipeline (for example, a remediation pipeline).

In a networking scenario, imagine you are monitoring the log file of a Layer 2 switch and you have configured an alert for the following error message format:

```
2022 Jul 14 16:04:23.881 N9K %L2FM-4-L2FM_MAC_MOVE2: Mac 0000.117d.
e03f in vlan 71 has moved between Po5 to Eth1/3
```

When your monitoring pipeline detects a MAC address moving between two different ports, which is sometimes a sign that an L2 loop is present on the network, it triggers a remediation pipeline that shuts down one of the two ports involved. On top of this, you could also notify someone that this action was taken, meaning there is no limit to the number of actions an alarm triggers.

Reporting

Creating reports is an activity many do not enjoy. However, they are needed for all sorts of reasons. Common reports in networking include hardware platforms, software versions, configuration best practices, and security vulnerabilities.

Each report has its own requirements and format. Drilling down on software version reports or software install base status reports typically requires three steps:

Step 1.   Connect to a device and gather the software version.

Step 2.   Verify the current version against recommended vendor version.

Step 3.   Repeat Steps 1 and 2 for every device and then generate a report.

Like many of the previous tasks, most companies today have part of the process (at least Steps 1 and 2) automated, but they run these automated processes/scripts manually from their workstations. Nonetheless, for Step 2, the operator needs to obtain, beforehand, the recommended version for comparison. In an ideal scenario, the automation could fetch the recommended version at the time of verification. For this to be possible, this information needs to be available from the vendor on a website or in an API, which is typically the case.

It is worth noting the higher the number of different operators running the scripts (for example, operators in different geographies or branches), the higher the likelihood of human error.

Other report types, independent of their nature, share the same sequence of steps to generate:

Step 1.   Gather data.

Step 2.   Verify the data against rules.

Step 3.   Generate a report.

A NetDevOps reporting pipeline architecture is presented in Figure 2-7.

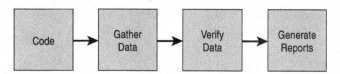

Figure 2-7   *Reporting Pipeline*

This is similar to a compliance pipeline, but in this case, we do not want to apply remediations, at least not at this stage, because the goal is just visibility.

As previously mentioned, some reports require data from outside of your environment to be generated. In the software versions example, the required data is the recommended vendor version, and in the case of security vulnerabilities you need a matrix of vulnerabilities per software version. This information gathering can and should be implemented as a separate stage. You can implement it in parallel with the data gathering stage from your environment, as shown in Figure 2-8, or before that stage, right after checking out your code from the code repository, as shown in Figure 2-9.

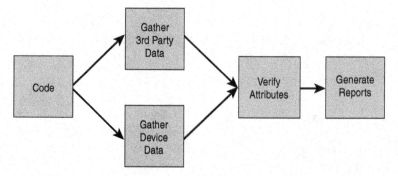

Figure 2-8   *Reporting Pipeline Integrated with a Third Party in Parallel*

Having it before instead of in parallel has the advantage of saving compute resources in the case that the needed information is not available. This means that your pipeline will fail without trying to gather information from your network because the verification data was not available.

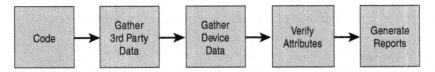

Figure 2-9   *Reporting Pipeline Integrated with a Third Party Sequentially*

Also, the previous examples show a capability offered by some proprietary network controllers such as Cisco DNA Center. A major advantage of this approach is reusability. You are able to create reports for anything you need using the same pipeline structure and automation scripts, with only minor modifications. You may have reporting needs beyond the typical ones; for example, you might have to report how many of your devices are running at or below 50% CPU usage or which of your devices are running out of physical memory. For these custom reporting needs, the proprietary controllers fall short.

Migrations

Network migration is a complex task that typically entails changing something to something different. Tasks can range from changing network configurations, provisioning new software, to replacing hardware. Nonetheless, it is important for you to understand that migration procedures are a combination of many smaller and simpler tasks.

Because of the criticality of some networks and the downtime some migrations cause, these are usually performed within maintenance windows. A maintenance window is a period of time, scheduled in advance, during which changes are made and service interruptions can happen. This concept is wider than networking or IT and is used in multiple other industries such as manufacturing and retail.

Note   Not all migrations require a maintenance window. Some changes are nondisruptive, or the target network in question is simply not critical enough to justify a maintenance window. Also, take into consideration that maintenance windows often occur nightly, which can increase costs.

In networking, migrations are typically associated with a method of procedure (MoP) document. Although it can have various names, this document details the migration steps one by one. A network device hardware replacement migration, for example, typically consists of the following steps:

Step 1.   Gather configuration data from the current device.

Step 2.   Prepare configuration for the new device.

Step 3.   Gather operational data from the current device.

Step 4.   Configure the new device.

Step 5.   Replace the current device with the newly configured device.

Step 6.   Gather operational data from the new device.

Step 7.   Verify operation data changes.

This is just an example; the actual steps may differ, depending on the migration use case. In a scenario where you do not have extra rack space, you have to switch the order of Steps 4 and 5. In a scenario where you are replacing the physical hardware but no configuration changes are required, Step 2 is not needed, as you can simply use the configuration gathered in Step 1. All of this is to show that each migration is different, so take this into account.

Independent of the migration scenario, most of the steps can be automated. However, the physical moving of equipment and cables cannot, or at least requires a different type of automation not covered by this book. Nonetheless, data collection, device configuration, and virtual device provisioning can be automated, as shown in previous sections. Many network migrations do not involve physical activities; therefore, those can be fully automated.

Today's state-of-art migrations, as with many of the previous use cases, rely on automating these steps individually and rely on an operator to execute those automation steps. NetDevOps ties all the automation steps together while enhancing the overall experience.

Figure 2-10 shows a simple two-tier network topology composed of a single distribution switch and two access switches. The migration consists of replacing the distribution switch with a newer one.

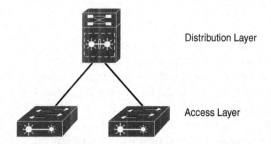

Distribution Layer

Access Layer

Figure 2-10   *Two-Tier Network Topology*

To replace this distribution switch, we rack and stack a new distribution switch and connect it to the available ports on our access switches. On top of that, we configure this new switch with out-of-band (OOB) management to enable remote management access. An example pipeline for the migration is shown in Figure 2-11.

Dev Pipeline

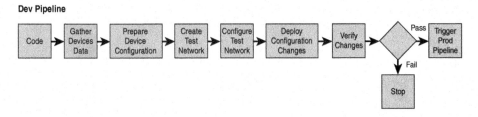

Prod Pipeline

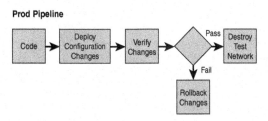

Figure 2-11   *Migration Pipeline*

This migration pipeline is divided into two pipelines: Dev and Prod. You can achieve the same functionality in a single pipeline, but the goal is to demonstrate the capability of a pipeline calling another pipeline.

You can see similarities between the migration pipeline and the configuration and data collection pipelines because this migration scenario is based on configuring a new device (configuration) using information from an already existing device (data collection).

> **Tip**   Although it's not represented in Figure 2-11, you can and should implement security verification stages before applying configurations to devices. This allows you to maintain a high security posture and prevents any noncompliant configuration from being applied.

In this scenario, you also see the return of the test/development/staging network. As mentioned, migrations tend to be critical, and using a test network to verify your changes before deploying them in production is a way to mitigate risk. In this particular example, you create a new test network to test the changes; this would be a virtual test network, as you will see in Chapter 5, "How to Implement Virtual Networks with EVE-NG." There are other possibilities to test your changes. For example, if you already have a test network, you could modify the pipeline to configure your test network the same way as your production environment, replacing the stage "Create Test Network," and then deploy and verify the changes there. In this case, the test network could be physical.

The provisioning use case briefly mentioned rollbacks. However, for migrations, rollbacks are a critical piece. As part of the MoP, network engineers prepare rollback configurations and actions in case the migration does not go as expected. This is fairly common. You see a rollback stage associated with a decision point in the pipeline in Figure 2-11; NetDevOps facilitates rollbacks in comparison to how they normally go. If you have been involved in migrations, you know that rolling back is almost always a high-pressure situation. If you are rolling back, things are already not going your way. On top of that, to roll back, you will need to make even more changes. When time is an important factor (for example, in very short service cut migrations), the pressure to roll back quickly is huge. This is a very error-prone activity. In the pipeline scenario, the rollback is prepared in advance without pressure. The rollback configurations can be tested beforehand, and you can be sure that the automation will not make any copy/paste errors.

Case Study: Migrations at an Energy Company

AnyProvider is an energy provider that powers millions of homes in AnyCountry. Like other energy providers, AnyProvider has a private network it uses to collect metrics and communicate across its many stations. On top of that, it also owns and manages several campuses across the country. For AnyProvider, networking is critical because an outage means loss of visibility of its infrastructure and potentially loss of business.

AnyProvider hired an external company, AnyCompany, to help migrate one of its campuses. This was a fairly large campus with four buildings, 12 floors per building, and around 4000 employees. This campus was powered by different types of networking equipment, among them around 800 switches, 2000 access points, and over 5000 other connected devices.

The migration consisted of replacing the current switch install base with a newer switch model while incurring the smallest possible downtime. To achieve this, AnyCompany needed to physically install the newer switches, configure them, and make the traffic switch while ensuring everything still worked as intended.

AnyProvider is a traditional company and hired AnyCompany to perform this migration in the traditional fashion, meaning network engineers onsite configuring the new switches with the required configurations and manually verifying that the same number of endpoints were active before and after the switch. The migration was divided into waves because of the size of the campus.

Once they started the migration, the planned method was going well, up until after the third wave of migrations. The network engineers onsite noticed that on one of the migrated floors some endpoints that were previously recorded to be working were no longer working. After a long night of troubleshooting, the engineers finally found the root cause. One of them had copy/pasted the wrong configurations in one of the switches on that floor. They fixed the error, and everything was working again. However, this mistake did not go unnoticed by management.

The management of AnyProvider was not happy with the extended service outage, and one of them suggested that they wanted AnyCompany to enhance their migration mechanisms to use automation and orchestration techniques so that this would not happen again.

AnyCompany involved extra engineers on the project to automate what could be automated. They started by creating Ansible playbooks to retrieve the current configurations from existing devices. Playbooks to create the configuration and then configure the new devices followed. By this time, manual errors were minimized because onsite engineers no longer copy/pasted configurations to and from Notepad. However, they were still facing long endpoint behavior-verification times. This was automated next; the engineers created Python scripts to retrieve "pre" and "post" information from the network devices so they could compare their status as well as created behavior verification scripts, such as Wi-Fi connection simulation and IP phone calls.

By the time all these automation scripts had been created and were being used, the onsite engineers were having a tough time running them in the correct sequence without losing the outputs created, which were critical for accountability.

The automation engineers took this migration a step even further with NetDevOps. They created migration pipelines that took care of the ordering of actions and maintained not only the outputs but also the accountability of who ran what pipeline and when.

These pipelines were not fully automated, and most of them had manual input stages asking for engineers' confirmation because some of the migration steps required changing cables, which was not automated.

In the end, this team of engineers was migrating six floors per night instead of the planned one floor—a sixfold increase in speed while minimizing errors and service downtime.

For migration pipelines, the only trigger is manual. You could use a different type (for example, a scheduled trigger), but migrations are typically such high-risk activities that they require human supervision, even when they are being executed by NetDevOps pipelines.

Troubleshooting

Some engineers love troubleshooting—the feeling of chasing and solving an unexpected behavior—but many others hate it. Troubleshooting is both a skill and an art, many times fueled by the rush of needing to fix something quickly because the issue is affecting a production service. Indeed, troubleshooting is often required in the worst moments. Do you remember the last time you had to troubleshoot something? Was it a calm situation in a development environment, or was it a production outage?

Troubleshooting often requires deep technical knowledge that not everyone in the company has. For example, if you are responsible for a production service that has a pager associated with it, do you let a newcomer, even if they are an expert on the technology, take part in troubleshooting the service. At least not initially, until the newcomer is fully onboarded and knowledgeable about the intricacies of the service. This shows that troubleshooting not only requires technical knowledge but often also subject matter expertise in the specific service itself.

Independent of all these challenges, a troubleshooting workflow is quite well-defined and includes the following steps:

Step 1.   Gather data from the affected resources.

Step 2.   Analyze the collected data and formulate hypotheses.

Step 3.   Experiment with the most likely hypothesis by configuring or reconfiguring resources.

Step 4.   Test for success.

Step 5.   Repeat Steps 3 and 4 until you're successful.

Not in every scenario can you apply Steps 3 and 4 multiple times and experiment with several hypotheses. In some scenarios, you need to analyze the data until you are certain of the problem and the solution. Nonetheless, after you are certain of these, you still apply Step 3. It is notoriously difficult to be 100% certain, and even if you are, you still need to apply the solution and verify the success.

In a networking-specific scenario, the aforementioned troubleshooting workflow is very similar:

Step 1.   Connect to the possible affected network devices.

Step 2.   Collect **show** command outputs.

Step 3.   Analyze the collected outputs and formulate hypotheses.

Step 3a.   (Optional but common) Repeat Steps 2 and 3 until you arrive at reasonable hypotheses.

Step 4.   Reconfigure/configure any identified missing feature in the network devices.

Step 5.   Test for success.

Step 6.   Repeat Steps 3 and 4 until you are successful.

Sounds pretty simple, right? Well, it is not. A network problem can manifest itself, and usually does, with pretty generic symptoms, such as loss of connectivity for some endpoints, increased latency, or users complaining their access is "slow." From such a generic description it's typically hard to pinpoint the specific network devices affected; therefore, your first step has a large number of target devices. On top of that, after connecting to your devices, assuming they are the correct ones, what **show** commands do you run? A common technique on Cisco devices is to start with the generic ones, such as **show logging**, as shown in Example 2-3, or **show running-config**. Other vendor devices have similar commands with different syntax.

Example 2-3 *Output for show logging on a Cisco Switch*

```
SWITCH1#show logging
Syslog logging: enabled (0 messages dropped, 3 messages rate-limited, 0 flushes, 0
  overruns, xml disabled, filtering disabled)


No Active Message Discriminator.
No Inactive Message Discriminator.



    Console logging: level debugging, 34 messages logged, xml disabled, filtering
  disabled
    Monitor logging: level debugging, 0 messages logged, xml disabled, filtering
  disabled
    Buffer logging:  level debugging, 34 messages logged, xml disabled, filtering
  disabled
    Exception Logging: size (8192 bytes)
    Count and timestamp logging messages: disabled
    Persistent logging: disabled


No active filter modules.

    Trap logging: level informational, 38 message lines logged
        Logging Source-Interface:        VRF Name:


Log Buffer (8192 bytes):


*Mar  2 00:00:01.137: %VIRTIO-3-INIT_FAIL: Failed to initialize device, PCI
  0/6/0/1002 , device is disabled, not supported
*Mar  2 00:00:01.381: %ATA-6-DEV_FOUND: device 0x1F0
*Mar  2 00:00:08.485: %ATA-6-DEV_FOUND: device 0x171
*Mar  2 00:00:08.704: %NVRAM-5-CONFIG_NVRAM_READ_OK: NVRAM configuration 'flash:/
  nvram' was read from disk.
*Feb  12 08:51:58.706: %PA-3-PA_INIT_FAILED: Performance Agent failed to initialize
  (Missing Data License)
*Feb  12 08:52:05.064: %LINK-3-UPDOWN: Interface GigabitEthernet0/0, changed state
  to down
*Feb  12 08:52:05.068: %LINK-3-UPDOWN: Interface GigabitEthernet0/1, changed state
  to up
```

Step 3 is highly correlated to Steps 1 and 2. You will formulate hypotheses based on your findings. And most of the time, you get stuck on Step 3a, bouncing between Steps 2 and 3 before you make any type of configuration change.

You make it to Step 4, however, and after you make your change, your users are still affected by their initial condition. Step 5 is a failure, but there is another thing you need to look out for: Did the change you make break something else? Maybe something else completely unrelated to the problem you were investigating? These are hard questions to answer in a traditional network setup, but you already have the solution: NetDevOps.

Troubleshooting is a collection of smaller use cases: data collection, configuration, provisioning, monitoring, and so on. What you have learned so far applies to this use case. Instead of manually connecting to devices and collecting **show** command outputs (Steps 1 and 2), you can run parameterized data collection pipelines that target the intended devices. Likewise, after formulating your hypothesis, you can codify those changes into a source control repository and run a configuration or a provisioning pipeline, depending on the troubleshooting scenario, and execute the changes with a higher degree of confidence. On top of that, the success criteria testing could be baked into the pipeline with an automatic rollback stage, as described previously.

When testing for your success criteria, be aware of the time it can take to propagate a change; likewise, when you are doing a manual change, you might issue a **show** command multiple times before it shows that the changed output using automation is the same. Another example is when you reboot a device: It takes time for the device to come up again and accept connections, and you often find yourself repeating the **ssh** command multiple times, or you have a ping running to the device and only reconnect when the ping is successful. In an orchestration scenario, take this into consideration. Add a wait time stage if you know the target device will not be immediately available. On top of that, you have a retry configurable option at the stage level in most CI/CD tools, which you can use in your verify success criteria stage.

All these changes combined, or even a subset of them, will not make you love troubleshooting if you hate it, but it can make troubleshooting easier, more reliable, and reduce mean time to repair (MTTR).

There are other applications of NetDevOps in troubleshooting. It can abstract the troubleshooting activity as a whole, disguised as a pipeline. This is not as simple to build as the previous example where you replaced the individual troubleshooting workflow steps with automated activities, but the reward is higher.

Figure 2-12 shows you a troubleshooting pipeline that is triggered automatically by a monitoring system when an alarm is triggered. The secret sauce of this pipeline lies in the step of automated machine reasoning. Automated reasoning is an area of computer science that is concerned with applying reasoning in the form of logic to computing systems. If given a set of assumptions and a goal, an automated reasoning system should be able to make logical inferences toward that goal automatically. In our context and put simply, it is a system that tries to understand what is happening in our network and infer potential solutions.

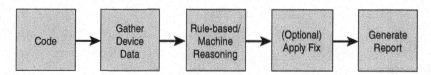

Figure 2-12 *Troubleshooting Pipeline*

How you build your own automated reasoning system is well beyond the scope of this book; however, you can partly accomplish this by using a rule-based system.

Imagine the following scenario: You manage a network that commonly suffers from L2 loops. You do not run the Spanning Tree Protocol because of fast convergence requirements, and sometimes your engineering team forgets that and creates looped topologies. In this scenario, you can benefit from having an automated rule-based engine that troubleshoots this issue for you. A subject matter expert (SME) would typically connect to the affected devices, identify interfaces with high utilization and possible packet drops, identify MAC address flaps either using the switch's log or the MAC address table, and then break the loop. However, if you are not a seasoned SME, you might lose time collecting other **show** command outputs and at the end create a hypothesis regarding problems other than the L2 loop.

With an "auto-troubleshooting" pipeline, you can abstract what is being collected and analyzed from the devices and output to the network operator only what it thinks the underlying issue is. Of course, it is also possible that this pipeline applies the fix directly, but most of the time in networking use cases, companies want human confirmation.

This works great for common issues such as BPDU Guard–blocked doors and mismatched protocol timers. However, for complex troubleshooting scenarios, you will need a very good rule-based system, which is not easy to create.

Note   Some vendors have automated reasoning tools embedded into their network controllers—Cisco DNA Center Machine Reasoning Engine (MRE) is one example. You can take advantage of these engines and embed their capabilities into your pipelines using APIs. They are typically much more complete than homemade systems.

Although the previous example was triggered automatically from a monitoring system alarm, you can create "auto-troubleshooting" pipelines for common issues of your network and let operators trigger these manually. This is a good first step, and it also reduces the subject matter knowledge required to troubleshoot common issues. If this does not solve the issue, it can be escalated to a higher-tier, smaller team.

Case Study: Insurance Troubleshooters

AnyInsurance is a global insurance company operating in four continents. It offers a variety of services, ranging from insurance to asset management. For AnyInsurance, maintaining minimal downtime is critical, not only because of its global time zone coverage but also because of the regulations it is subjugated to.

Although AnyInsurance has a big dependency on IT systems, it is not an IT company. This was reflected in its headcount, with only a few IT engineers maintaining their main two data centers located in Europe and the USA. This strategy was a disaster waiting to happen, and it did. In 2020, AnyInsurance had a data center–wide outage rendering it out of service for almost 24 hours. The data center was eventually recovered, and the root cause was identified to be a device misconfiguration on the border network—the network between the last devices and the Internet.

These kinds of outages happen, but what AnyInsurance identified to be a problem was the time it took to address the issue. Turns out the company's main engineer, the go-to guy for all things networking, was out the week before and the week of the outage. Because of that, changes were made to the network without his supervision, which would be normal in most companies; however, at AnyInsurance, this guru was one of the only SMEs. Without his knowledge, it took several hours to identify and fix the problem.

You could say that this is a staffing problem and has nothing to do with NetDevOps. However, AnyInsurance contacted a third-party consulting company for help, and the company's recommendation was to enhance the troubleshooting process and embed it with intelligence.

To accomplish this, the third-party firm worked jointly with the few AnyInsurance SMEs to identify what were common issues in the data centers and what technologies they were using, among other things. In short, they tried to pack some of the SMEs' knowledge into automated tooling, and they were successful.

They created automated pipelines that run on alarms as well as manually triggerable pipelines that more junior and less-knowledgeable engineers could point at specific devices. These pipelines outputted common **show** commands recommended by the SMEs as well as recommendations of possible issues that might be occurring based on those same outputs.

The pipelines did not replace the SMEs; however, they allowed AnyInsurance to keep its staffing model of having few SMEs and many operators while minimizing downtime by enhancing the troubleshooting capabilities of the common operator.

Combined

The two previous use cases, migrations and troubleshooting, are combined use cases. They aggregate the previous simpler use cases into more complex end goals.

In networking, complex goals are often what you will encounter. Nonetheless, these complex goals and tasks can be decomposed into smaller, more manageable subgoals and subtasks, and that is what you will learn about in this section.

An interesting combined use case is the use of one pipeline to gather data and store it in a database and the use of other pipelines in the same network for retrieving that data from the database instead of fetching it from the devices directly. A database in this context can be anything, even a local file. This type of interaction between pipelines will reduce resource consumption on end devices because you are not connecting to them for every action. Although all the use cases in this chapter so far have gathered data from the end devices, you can now see this is not necessary.

Another interesting combined use case is network optimization. While your data collection pipelines are collecting data from your network and storing it somewhere (for example, in a database), you can have a pipeline monitoring the stored data, looking for patterns or optimizations. For example, if you are collecting and storing information on the bandwidth utilization of your interfaces, it is possible that your monitoring pipeline will identify underutilized interfaces. In this case, it can trigger a configuration pipeline that alters some traffic-routing metrics to reroute traffic and better utilize your available infrastructure.

There are increasingly more uses for networking data. A practice that is becoming more common is to apply machine learning algorithms to identify patterns in networking data. Just like in the previous scenario, assume that you are collecting and storing your switches' data—this time percentage CPU utilization. You can build a machine learning model, which some consider to fall within the automation umbrella, and integrate it in a NetDevOps pipeline.

In simple terms, a machine learning model has two phases in its lifecycle: the first phase is where it needs to be trained, and the second phase is where you can use it to make predictions (called "inference"). In the first phase, you "feed" data to the model so it can learn the patterns of your data. In the second phase, you give it a new data point, and the model returns a prediction based on what it learned from past observations.

Continuing our previous example, you can train a model based on percentage CPU utilization per device family. CPU utilization is highly irregular—what is an acceptable value for a specific device doing a specific network function might not be an acceptable value for a different device in the same network. Because of this, it is very complicated to set manual thresholds. Machine learning can help you set adaptable thresholds depending on the specific device based on its historical CPU utilization.

Now what does all of this has to do with NetDevOps? You can have a pipeline that retrains a model when predictions become stale. Likewise, you can call the inference point of the model in one of your alerting pipelines and replace the static alarm thresholds.

Machine learning is starting to have many applications in the networking world—from hardware failure prediction to dynamic thresholds and predictive routing. It is important to understand that if you are using NetDevOps practices, adding machine learning into the mix is simple.

Do you have a use case not covered in this chapter? NetDevOps is only limited by what you can do with automation. So, if you can automate it, you can make it run on a CI/CD pipeline using source control and testing techniques to reap all the benefits you have learned in this chapter.

Decisions and Investments

Let's say that you love the use cases of NetDevOps because they resonate with your current challenges. So now you ask yourself, "How do I start, and do I buy something?"

In order to adopt NetDevOps, or any other technology, you will have to make several decisions and possibly some investments. This section covers the four main verticals you should consider:

- Starting point
- New skillsets
- New tools
- Organizational changes

These might seem like a lot of investments; however, considering the benefits, they are worth it. NetDevOps has some initial investments that decline over time, while its benefits grow over time, as shown in Figure 2-13.

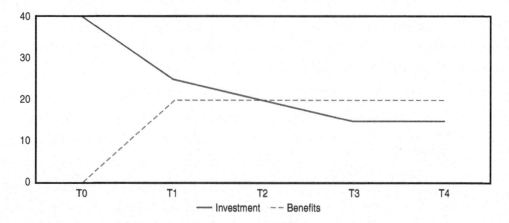

Figure 2-13 *NetDevOps Investments Versus Benefits Chart*

Because this is a fairly new field compared to others in networking, it is hard to find trustworthy resources about it. The four main verticals described in this chapter are derived from the authors' own experience in the field for the last five years working with NetDevOps. They are not industry standards.

Where to Start

When you start something new, you must begin somewhere. For example, when you are learning a new technology, you can start by reading a book or watching a video online. For some things, where you start does not matter because you'll ultimately reach the same destination; however, when it comes to adoption of NetDevOps practices, choosing the place to start is very important.

So where should you start? There is no silver bullet or a single place where all organizations should start; rather, each organization should undergo an analysis to decide what is best for its situation. This preliminary analysis should evaluate roughly where the organization is in terms of the following:

- Challenges/pain points
- Skills
- Technology stack

Why these three? There are other verticals you can consider, but evaluating these three typically results in a good starting point. Besides, the state of these three verticals is often well known to organizations, making this initial analysis cheap and fast. You do not need to produce a formal analysis with documentation, although you can do that if you wish. The result of this analysis should be an understanding of where you are in regard to these three topics.

After you have the understanding of where you are, either documented or not, you should add more weight to the first vertical, challenges/pain points. You should start your journey with use cases in mind. Do not try and embark on the NetDevOps journey because of trends or buzzwords. Solving the challenges you have identified that are affecting your organization is the priority.

Prioritize the identified challenges based on their importance for your business but at the same time measure the complexity of each challenge. The result should be an ordered list. This balance between complexity and benefit is sometimes hard to understand, so use your best judgment because this is not an exact science.

So far, you have not factored in the skills and the technology stack verticals from the analysis. This is where they come in. From the ordered list of challenges, add which technologies are involved from the technology stack and what skills would be required to solve them. Some of those skills you might already have, while others you might not. The same goes for the technologies.

Skills come in second in our three verticals. Although the next section focuses solely on skills and how they influence your NetDevOps journey, they also play a role in defining a starting point. Prioritize use cases that you already have the skillsets to implement. Technology comes next, because it is easier to pick up a new technology than a new skillset. However, this does not mean that adopting a new technology is easy, because it is not, and that is why we include it as our third factor.

For the technology stack, there will be many different nuances, and some use cases will not require all NetDevOps components to solve. For example, if your challenge is that people can make modifications to your network device configurations that go unnoticed, creating snowflake networks, and you need a way of maintaining a single source of truth, the only component you need is a version control system repository. Similarly, if your challenge is lack of speed and error-prone copy/paste configuration activities, you might just need to apply automation instead of also using CI/CD pipelines.

Understanding the minimum number of NetDevOps components you will need to adopt makes the journey to success shorter, which leads us to the highest contributing factor to the success rate of NetDevOps adoption: the ability to show successes at the early stages of adoption. Do not underestimate this. It not only motivates the teams involved, but it is a great way to show stakeholders their investments are paying off. Experiencing failures early or going for a long time without anything to show for it is the downfall of many adoption journeys.

However, you cannot really show success if you do not have success criteria. After you decide which use cases you will solve using which NetDevOps components, make sure you define what success looks like. Following up the previous example of snowflake networks and configurations changes that go unnoticed, the success criteria could be to have 80% of devices in the same functions with the same configuration, and to measure this you would audit the network. For the second example, in the slow and error-prone configuration changes environment, you could measure your current estimated time to implement a new configuration and the number of minutes of downtime caused by changes. Then you could define a success criterion of lowering this number by 20%.

Having specific success criteria allows you to show progress and improvement; however, it can also show that you are not actually solving your initial use case. This can be equally beneficial because it enables you to adjust your initial plan. In other words, failing quickly is less expensive.

To summarize, start with understanding where you are right now in terms of challenges, skills, and technology. Make identifying challenges the number-one priority because you want to ensure you are solving something relevant for your organization. Next, prioritize your challenges based on the skills you already have while minimizing the amount of NetDevOps components involved, prioritizing the ones you already have. Before you implement your NetDevOps strategy, make sure you have clearly defined success criteria and plan to show milestone successes early.

Skills

Skills are an influential factor in NetDevOps. In Chapter 1, you learned that many components of NetDevOps are not traditional networking components, and although some folks take them for granted, automation, programming, and orchestration are not an evolution of networking; rather, they are a horizontal domain of knowledge.

Most organizations have network engineers equipped with the traditional skillset of "hardcore" networking. This includes routing protocols, switching configurations, networking security such as access control lists (ACLs) or Control Plane Policing (CoPP), and all the rest. But in the same way that software developers do not know what the Border Gateway Protocol (BGP) is, traditional network engineers do not know what Jenkins or Groovy is.

The profile of a network engineer is evolving, and nowadays we're starting to see more and more a mix of networking, infrastructure as code (IaC), and orchestration knowledge. However, that might not be the case at your organization. If it is not, there are two schools of thought: upskilling/training and hiring.

You can choose to train your engineers in the skills you have identified to be missing from your "where to start" analysis, or you can hire folks who already have those skills. One option is not better than the other; each organization must make its own decision.

If you choose to train your engineers, you must take into consideration that, as previously mentioned, some of these NetDevOps skills are not a natural evolution of networking and can require considerable effort to learn. For example, software-defined networks (SDN) can be seen as an evolution of networking, and in some way they are the next networking topology. However, writing an automation playbook in a programming language is not an evolution of writing network configurations. Although the line is becoming blurry, and some terms like "network engineer v2" and "next-generation network engineer" have started to emerge, historically speaking, networking and automation have been two different domains.

Not all skills are generic skills such as automation or networking. A skill family that often is overlooked is tool skills. An engineer proficient at automation will not be an expert in all the automation tools; for example, the engineer might have worked extensively with Ansible but never with Terraform. This is particularly important if your chosen strategy is to hire, because most of the time you do not want to upskill a new hire on a new tool if you can hire someone with tool knowledge. In terms of training, this also factors in. Training someone in a tool is easier if that person already has knowledge of the tool domain. In other words, training someone in Golang is easier if they already know how to program in Python.

Another consideration is how you want to distribute your skills in each role; the upcoming section "Organizational Changes" covers how you can distribute your skills: all in one NetDevOps team or separate automation and networking teams. The number and distribution of engineers' skillsets differ based on each organization's needs.

Lastly, because you are reading this book, you probably want to become a NetDevOps engineer or transform your organization into one that uses NetDevOps engineering practices; however, not every network engineer will become a NetDevOps engineer. Expert-level networking skills are still required, and many folks may not have to take part in orchestration and automation tasks. This is a common misconception.

Tooling

Tools are an important part of NetDevOps. As you have learned, tools are enablers and not actual DevOps practices; however, some folks still commonly label tools as DevOps. Nonetheless, tools will still represent a big part of your investment. Not only because of their price but also because of tool-specific skills and knowledge. After you and your organization acquire these skills, changes result in added effort and cost.

Within the NetDevOps umbrella, you can separate the tools into the following different categories:

- Infrastructure as code
- Continuous integration/continuous delivery (or deployment)
- Source/version control
- Testing
- Monitoring

The following list provides examples of tools in each category. Note that this is not an exhaustive list; each category has a plethora of tools to offer.

- IaC
  - Ansible
  - Terraform
  - Pulumi
- CI/CD
  - Jenkins
  - GitHub Actions
  - AWS CodePipeline
- Testing
  - EVE-NG
  - GNS3
  - Cisco Modeling Labs CML
- Source Control
  - GitHub
  - GitLab
  - Bitbucket
- Monitoring
  - Datadog
  - ELK stack
  - Splunk

Note that the IaC, CI/CD, source control, and testing tools were covered in Chapter 1. Monitoring is a well-known tool vertical in networking that has evolved over time. From the older SNMP pull-based monitoring to the newer push-based telemetry models, common tools to achieve this functionality are proprietary network controls such as Cisco DNA Center, SolarWinds Network Performance Monitor, Splunk, and open source solutions you can tailor to your liking, such as ELK (Elasticsearch, Logstash, Kibana) stack. Monitoring in NetDevOps also encompasses the monitoring of CI/CD pipelines and automation tasks. This is an extended scope compared to only monitoring the network.

Here is a set of characteristics you can use to select the best fit for your organization in any of these tool categories:

- Cloud or on-premises

- Managed or unmanaged

- Open source, proprietary, or in-house

- Integration ecosystem

The first characteristic is where the solution will be hosted. All the tools have to exist somewhere, and some have a bigger footprint than others (for example, a CI/CD server with many agents versus an IaC tool that only needs a single server). For the location, you have two choices: the cloud or on-premises. Some folks will argue you have three options, with the third being a co-location facility (for example, a service provider data center). However, this option is encompassed in the on-premises category in this two-location system. The cloud refers to on-demand resources accessed over the Internet. It is a huge trend right now and typically benefits from a pay-as-you-go model. Of the many cloud vendors, the most well known are Amazon Web Services (AWS), Microsoft Azure, and Google Cloud Platform (GCP). The benefit from using the cloud is that you do not have to manage or secure the physical infrastructure. You can just access your resources as you need them. In contrast, the on-premises option will give you more flexibility when it comes to controlling the storage of your data, and you do not have to rely on Internet connectivity.

The second characteristic is manageability. In the cloud versus on-premises characteristic, you saw that with the cloud, physical management is the responsibility of the provider. Some tools offload more than that; they offload all the management to the provider, other than the actual configuration. For example, you can have access to a working Jenkins instance, and all you need is to create your workflows. You do not need to install Jenkins, configure networking for the instance, or anything like that. For on-premises setups, this is more uncommon, although some service providers manage the installation of tools for you. In general, you should only consider this a feature for cloud-hosted tools. Examples of managed tools are Amazon Managed Grafana, versus hosting your own Grafana in a virtual machine on the cloud; Amazon OpenSearch service, versus hosting your own Elasticsearch cluster in virtual machines; Terraform Cloud, versus hosting your own Terraform environment in containers or virtual machines; and CloudBees-hosted Jenkins, versus hosting your own Jenkins in AWS.

The third characteristic is of special importance because it greatly contributes to the price. All tool categories will have open source solutions; however, these solutions will not have support other than community support. For enterprise environments, this might be a problem. Nonetheless, many organizations offer enterprise-grade support for open source tools. Therefore, don't rule out open source tools just because they are open source. Ansible, for example, is a free and open source configuration tool, but Red Hat has enterprise support plans for it. An advantage of open source tools is the wealth of knowledge you will be able to find online versus the more exclusive proprietary tools. In contrast to open source tools, proprietary tools are solutions owned by the individual or company who published them. They are "closed" in the sense that changes must be made by the party that published the tool. However, this type of tool usually has several support offerings. This is the most widely adopted tool type in medium- and large-sized companies.

The other option is to build your own tools. Although this option is uncommon, it is not unheard of; some organizations decide to build their own in-house tools using programming languages such as Python and Java. This option requires highly specialized staff, and after the development phase, you will also need to provide support. The advantage is that the tool will have only the functionality you need and not numerous features you never use, as commonly happens with commercial off-the-shelf (COTS) tools. On top of that, if the tool needs modifications (for example, you find a buggy behavior), you are the vendor, so you can immediately apply a fix. If you are starting out in automation and orchestration, however, this option is not recommended for you.

The final characteristic is the tool ecosystem. This characteristic is sometimes undervalued, but having a tool integrate natively with the rest of your tooling can be a very big advantage (versus having to script a lot of functionality). For example, most source control tool vendors now offer CI/CD tools embedded together. This greatly simplifies integrations, and you can run your workflows directly from the source control repository. Examples of this are Gitlab CI/CD and GitHub Actions. You will also see very tight and native integrations when you are using all the tooling from the same cloud vendor, such as Azure DevOps ecosystem and Amazon Code* services.

Tip   Going back to the "Where to Start" section of this book, you should invest in tools that you need for your use cases. Do not adopt tooling based on new trends or use cases that are low on your list.

Ensure you are prioritizing skills over tools. A characteristic that did not make it on the list is the available skills in the market. Your prioritization should start with the tool skills you have available; however, you should consider how widely adopted within the industry a tool is because this will greatly improve your ability to hire folks who are proficient with the tool or to find training materials for your own folks.

Now that you know what characteristics to look for in a tool, you need to adapt this to your organization's needs and liking. Be aware of the tradeoffs; for example, continuing to use Ansible for provisioning while understanding Terraform might be a better solution for your use case if you already have Ansible skills and existing support from Red Hat. Again, there is no single "works every time" choice, but aligning your tool choice to your organization's strategy helps. For example, if your organization is implementing a cloud-first strategy, cloud-hosted tools are preferred. Likewise, if your organization is not an IT-focused organization and instead focuses on a different core business, offloading the management of the tools (sometimes called "undifferentiated heavy lifting") to focus your resources on differentiation activities is likely the right choice.

Finally, because so many tools are available right now, you need to be careful of tool sprawl, meaning having too many tools and even unused tools. It is okay to use special-ized tools that are very good at a specific task or action, but it is important not to let the tools take over your organization. Likewise, retire old tools if they are no longer being used. As you have learned, NetDevOps is a set of practices, not tools, but using the right tools for the job is one of those practices.

Organizational Changes

Network operators and network architects—that is, folks who design and configure net-works—are typically already on the same team or work closely aligned. In the develop-ment world, however, developers and operations were many times on completely separate teams. This is good because adopting NetDevOps has less of an impact on an organiza-tion's structure as DevOps did back in the day in software development.

However, being on the same team does not mean you do not need any organizational changes at all. For some more traditional teams, adopting these practices might require hiring new folks, as described previously in this chapter, which is an organizational change already.

You can tackle NetDevOps in one of two ways: join automation and networking together into one team or have automation and networking in separate teams but collaborating.

If you choose to separate automation and networking in different teams, which is not rec-ommended, your organization needs to find a way of bridging these two areas. For exam-ple, your networking folks create configuration templates per device type and platform, while your automation team creates the automation scripts and orchestration pipelines to deliver the configurations. If you chose this approach, remember that each of these teams has no idea about the others' domain expertise and challenges, so communication and collaboration are key. Working in isolation will greatly impair their ability to deliver fast and working solutions.

If you choose to relabel your networking team as a NetDevOps team, your folks will be doing end-to-end tasks. This is the recommended approach. With this method, everyone has an understanding of the use cases and challenges, which is beneficial in the successful adoption of these practices. This is the most ambitious approach, and you may face more resistance from folks who prefer the traditional approaches to networking.

Although this might seem like a simple rebranding exercise, it is not, and it is important to have support from the organization and key management stakeholders. This support is paramount to address resistance from less-inclined engineers as well as to address and justify a potential initial loss of productivity or higher costs due to ramp-up.

Another important organizational change is to adopt open communication and encourage failing fast. When new processes, tools, skills, and technologies are being adopted, mistakes will happen and questions will arise. It is important to foster a culture of collaboration and open communication, where engineers are encouraged to present their questions and doubts while experimenting and, in some cases, failing. This is a NetDevOps principle. Although this might not seem like an organizational change, many organizations do not openly embrace open communication and failing, and they are surprised by this aspect when adopting NetDevOps.

The junction of the networking and automation domains, which likely have been working separately until now, should be reflected in your organizational structure. However, independent of your decisions regarding skills, tooling, and where to start, you should understand that it can take time to successfully reshape your organization into this new paradigm.

Adoption Challenges

Adopting new practices can be challenging, and although you now know that NetDevOps is a mix of already well-known and battle-tested practices, it is still likely that you will face challenges in your journey.

This section describes common challenges and recommended mitigations associated with the adoption of NetDevOps in organizations of all sizes.

Note   This section covers the main challenges we have encountered in NetDevOps adoption from our experience in the field over the last five years. These challenges are not industry-wide.

Do not get discouraged if you face one of the following challenges. Adoption of new technologies often comes with initial challenges, but the benefits far outweigh the initial burden.

Remember the RIP routing protocol? Frame relay? Half-duplex Ethernet? When introduced, they were different, disruptive, and folks had to learn them. This initial hardship was, however, worth it. A lot of current networking technologies have evolved from these.

Traditional Mindset

The networking field is commonly associated with traditional or old technologies. Although this is not necessarily a true assumption, some networking practices are indeed rudimentary and old, such as physically connecting to devices via a cable and typing commands one by one on a command line. This is not to say this practice is wrong or that there was a better way of performing these tasks before—if a device was isolated on a network, there were not many options other than physically plugging in a laptop to it. Nowadays, there are more options, such as zero-touch provisioning (ZTP) for Day 0 configuration and the use of automation tools for Day 1 and Day 2.

One challenge you will encounter is dealing with organizations and folks who are attached to the old ways of performing tasks. Before, their way may have been the best way, as just described; however, now, there are likely better ways. Some folks will resist change and refuse to adopt new practices.

A common complaint is, "We've been doing it this way for X years." It is not easy to convince these folks of a better way of doing things; however, here's one way that typically works: instead of leading with the possible benefits of the solutions you are trying to adopt, perform a proof of concept (PoC) with other collaborating individuals and return to the skeptics with factual results, such as improved time to execute change requests or less downtime. It is harder to ignore results than a business pitch. Likewise, the competition factor of seeing others succeed with different techniques will often increase the likelihood of folks wanting to join in. In other words, they do not want to be left out.

Another important aspect, as mentioned previously, is senior stakeholder support. A clear request coming from senior leadership is harder to ignore than a colleague's request. For any organizational transformation, leadership support is vital, and NetDevOps is no different. Try to find this support early in your adoption journey, preferably right from the start.

Testing or Lack Thereof

Network testing has always been associated with acquiring additional expensive hardware and putting in extra work. Because of these reasons, and others, testing network changes is often kept to a minimum by most organizations, and many times happens in a production environment. When was the last time you copy/pasted commands into a production network device within a maintenance window without previous testing? What about the last time you tested a network configuration change in a test environment that mirrors your production environment? If you only remember the first scenario, you are not alone.

In the software development world, testing is part of the culture. Writing tests for your code and executing them is a standard practice across the industry. There are even software development processes such as test-driven development (TDD) where tests are written before the actual software implementation of a feature. DevOps embraces testing as a way that enables safe, continuous integration and aims to make sure nothing preexisting is broken with new modifications. Likewise, as you have learned in this book, NetDevOps also makes extensive use of testing for networking. Networks are critical, and network changes should be executed with confidence.

You will encounter two common arguments against the adoption of network testing. The first one is, "This was working fine until now without a test environment." The second common argument is, "A test environment is too expensive for the benefits it provides."

To answer to the first argument, you must show how new practices such as automated changes increase the number of changes and features that can be implemented in a shorter span of time, and you must show that testing greatly increases the chances of success without rollbacks. A single maintenance window per year, where all the change requests are executed, is no longer enough to support modern applications' changing requirements. With multiple changes being executed per month, or even per week in some cases, your organization can benefit from a test environment, which increases confidence in the success of these network changes.

For the second argument, yes, historically test environments were very expensive and required physical hardware. However, this is no longer the case. Although you still can acquire physical hardware and build a test environment, you are not required to because there are plenty of virtualized options.

In Chapter 5, you will learn how to install and configure EVE-NG to virtualize network topologies that can be used as a testbed. Although this is a commonly used tool for network testing, you will also learn about different options you can choose from.

Physical testbeds are still irreplaceable for some products and specific features (for example, when you are trying to load-test a specific hardware model). Nonetheless, network testing now has a lower barrier of entry, and many if not most types of functionality can be tested on virtualized network devices. If you manage a critical network, where you need the maximum amount of confidence in your changes, a physical setup that mirrors your production environment is likely still the preferred choice.

Success Criteria or Lack Thereof

In the "Decisions and Investments" section of this chapter, you learned the importance of having clearly defined success criteria. This is the biggest adoption challenge because it directly influences your ability to show successes. This challenge can manifest itself in one of two ways: lack of defined success criteria or unrealistic success criteria.

The first way is the most common. Folks embark on a NetDevOps journey without a measurable destination. They want to reap the benefits of automation and orchestration, so they set out on their way and make some initial investments; however, they end up quitting before they reach the point of seeing positive returns. Figure 2-13, earlier in this chapter, plots the relationship between investment and benefits. Other folks actually achieve successes, but without a goal or criteria to measure them against, so they end up being shut down by management, who do not understand what was actually achieved.

The second way this challenge manifests is when folks define success criteria that either are too ambitious or are cheatable. If you set success criteria that people can obtain by cheating, you may perceive you are getting benefits when in reality you are not. This contributes to resource waste and bad decisions.

An example of a cheatable criterion is one that measures success by achieving ten network changes a month. However, folks can break a single change into smaller changes, meaning one traditional network change can transform into the needed ten. Therefore, consider how "cheatable" your defined criteria are.

When you set success criteria too high, you might never achieve them. This is acceptable if you understand the context of these criteria or the way the criteria were set up. However, oftentimes senior stakeholders are not aware of either, and they simply look at these criteria as yes/no boxes. If you fail to meet the success criteria, your NetDevOps initiative might be shut down.

Defining success criteria might seem like wasted effort at first, and you might face resistance when you propose defining them. Therefore, explain the "why" behind this choice and how it will contribute later in the adoption journey when everyone understands the progress made.

New Skillset

You learned how NetDevOps requires not only networking skills but also automation and orchestration skills, which are not a natural evolution of networking. Although most folks who embark on the NetDevOps journey are completely aware of this fact, skills are usually still a big challenge in adoption.

You can face two types of challenges: folks not wanting to be upskilled and the organization not wanting to invest in the adoption of this new skillset, either through upskilling or hiring.

For the first challenge, there is not much you can do other than to adopt a hiring tactic instead of upskilling. You might find individuals who simply do not want to learn these new verticals and stick to traditional networking, and that is completely fine. You should not force them; instead, apply a different tactic.

For the second challenge, you can invest in explaining to the organization how these skills are different from the former networking landscape and what benefits they will bring. Many times, this challenge comes from the wrong understanding that NetDevOps is an evolution of networking and therefore the same skillsets apply.

Case Study: Skills Evolution at a Bank

YetAnotherBank is a large bank with a presence in multiple countries across multiple continents. Because of its global presence, YetAnotherBank has a very large install base of multiple types of equipment from various vendors.

Banks, because they are part of the payment industry, often have a very high aversion to risk. This also applies to networking changes, which are typically kept to a minimum. Often, these limitations have led banks to have outdated software releases running on their hardware or suboptimal configurations.

YetAnotherBank is a good example of a traditional organization. It only allowed network changes once every quarter, unless they were very critical or were fixes in the case of an outage. Moreover, any change required a chain of approvals with well-documented procedures and justifications.

This change process was put in place because, in the past, YetAnotherBank had production-level outages related to manual changes that were improperly applied.

Some stakeholders of YetAnotherBank wanted to adopt NetDevOps practices for network changes on their managed data center in order to decrease the risk associated with operator manual network changes and increase the number of changes from once a quarter to at least once a month. Naturally, they faced challenges. The most interesting challenge was the lack of support to evolve the networking team's skills.

Senior management for YetAnotherBank did not understand why evolving the network practices would require so much investment in retraining their current teams and/or hiring externally. Even when the team explained the benefits that NetDevOps adoption would bring, especially the reduction of risk for network configuration changes, the senior stakeholders were not supportive.

The data center team decided to procure automation and orchestration talent internally—inside the company but outside of the networking team—in order to produce a small-scope PoC to showcase the benefits instead of describing them.

Luckily, YetAnotherBank is a very large organization, so it had multiple software development teams, and it also had an internal program that allowed employees to devote a percentage of their time to activities outside their job responsibilities.

The team found four developers who agreed to help with the PoC. In one month they created an automated pipeline that delivered automated configuration changes to a specific device type; furthermore, the pipeline used network device virtualization to test the changes before applying them to the target device. The team was very happy with the results and started using this pipeline on their quarterly maintenance window.

More than using the pipeline, the team gathered metrics on the executions, such as average time to deploy a change, number of rollbacks, number of outages, and so on. With this data, they went back to the senior management team and showed them the data on these improvements.

The difference that these four developers made was very clear, and it was enough to convince the senior management team to fund a NetDevOps practice team within their geography.

Some months later, YetAnotherBank took its NetDevOps practice team further and made it a global team that enables local teams to improve their traditional networking processes.

Adding to this challenge is the lack of the needed skillsets in the market. NetDevOps is a mix of different domains and is still a relatively new trend. This, combined with a very competitive labor market, makes finding the right skillset typically very challenging. This also applies to the retention of talent when an upskilling tactic is adopted. Consider this when you find the right candidate or when you are trying to retain that special NetDevOps engineer.

Summary

In this chapter, you learned several use cases where NetDevOps improves the current state of the art of networking operations:

- Provisioning

- Configuration

- Data collection

- Compliance

- Monitoring and alerting

- Reporting

- Migrations

- Troubleshooting

- Combined

In Chapter 4, you will see code implementations of these use cases, together with real-life examples.

NetDevOps adoption is a journey. In this chapter, you learned how you can start that journey, by prioritizing starting points that usually work well, such as focusing on solving your use cases instead of following market trends as well as prioritizing skills over technologies. You also learned the different characteristics tools can have and how those characteristics can impact your tool choice.

This chapter finished with the common pitfalls and challenges organizations and teams suffer from during their NetDevOps adoption journey, along with recommendations on how to mitigate or circumvent them.

Now that you know the theory of NetDevOps, it is time to dive deeper into the specific components. In Chapter 3, you will dive deep into the orchestration component of NetDevOps and learn how Jenkins implements CI/CD logic.

Review Questions

You can find answers to these questions in Appendix A, "Answers to Review Questions."

1. What is the predominant configuration tool in networking use cases?

   a. Terraform

   b. Ansible

   c. Python

   d. Chef

2. What stage is common to all NetDevOps pipelines?

   a. Code

   b. Security verifications/linting

   c. Deploy to Dev

   d. Deploy to Prod

3. What is the most common data collection pipeline trigger?

   a. Manually executed by an operator

   b. Automatic by another pipeline

   c. Automatic by a change in the source control

   d. Automatic on a schedule

4. How many actions can you trigger using alarms?

   a. One

   b. Ten

   c. Fifty

   d. Unlimited

5. In NetDevOps pipelines, when an action can fail but is idempotent, which characteristic should you configure your stage with?

   a. Rollback

   b. Retry

   c. End

   d. Linting

6. What term is used in machine learning to describe the stage when a model is producing predictions?

   a. Inference stage

   b. Prediction stage

   c. Training stage

   d. Production stage

7. What is typically the biggest investment when adopting NetDevOps practices?

   a. Purchasing DevOps tools

   b. Acquiring new skills

   c. Purchasing networking equipment

   d. Hiring external consultancy

8. What should you prioritize first when starting your NetDevOps adoption journey?

   a. Existing skillsets

   b. The same technology stacks

   c. Solving current challenges

   d. Defining success criteria

9. Which of the following is not a type of NetDevOps tooling?

   a. CI/CD orchestration

   b. Infrastructure as code

   c. Monitoring

   d. Cloud

10. Do virtual network devices support all features needed for testing?

   a. Yes

   b. No

## Chapter 3

How to Implement CI/CD Pipelines with Jenkins

The execution of a series of automated steps through CI/CD pipelines is critical for the successful implementation of NetDevOps. The use of CI/CD pipelines results in improved speed, agility, and overall quality of the product. These benefits have been discussed in the first two chapters of this book. Further, the use of Jenkins as a tool for implementing CI/CD pipelines has already been discussed.

In this chapter, we will deep dive into Jenkins and learn about the implementation of pipelines using this product. This chapter will cover topics such as the following:

- Jenkins' architecture and capabilities

- Declarative and scripted syntax options for defining pipelines

- Jenkins installation

- What triggers are and how to configure them

- Options for integrating Jenkins with other components and tools such as version control systems (VCSs)

- Alternatives to Jenkins

By the end of this chapter, you should be able to install Jenkins and create pipelines.

Jenkins Architecture

Jenkins is an open-source tool used for continuous integration/continuous delivery (CI/CD). Jenkins is one of the most popular tools used for the implementation of CI/CD pipelines. It automates a series of tasks or steps that help in the process of building, testing, and releasing a product. In the context of NetDevOps, the product may include deployment, provisioning, and day-to-day management of a highly scalable network infrastructure. The process for automating these tasks is performed by configuration of a *pipeline* in Jenkins. The ability to integrate with other tools is one of the key capabilities for any CI/CD tool, and Jenkins provides this capability via plugins.

Let's review the key features of and functionality provided by Jenkins.

Jenkins supports hundreds of plugins that allow it to integrate with many other tools and systems, such as source control systems, cloud platforms, test frameworks, monitoring and analytics tools, and so on. These integrations allow Jenkins to fetch data from a system/tool and to invoke an action on another system/tool. Jenkins and similar CI/CD tools orchestrate steps across multiple systems via their integrations. Thus, Jenkins and other CI/CD tools are sometimes referred to as "orchestrators." Because Jenkins is an open-source platform, additional plugins can be developed as well, which allows the flexibility to extend Jenkins integrations to a platform that does not have plugins.

Jenkins can be installed on multiple operating systems, including Linux, macOS, and Windows. Jenkins itself and the plugins are developed using Java. The installation of Jenkins requires Java to be pre-installed on the host machine. The version of Java varies with Jenkins releases. However, Java version 11 or 17 is required since Jenkins version 2.357.

For initial trials and small deployments, a standalone Jenkins server can be installed on a single machine running a macOS, Windows, or Linux operation system. It can also be installed and run as a Docker container, virtual machine, Kubernetes cluster, bare-metal server, and so on. This single-node Jenkins server performs functions related to server administration, along with configuring and executing jobs.

The correct sizing of the Jenkins server depends on many factors, such as the number of jobs executed, the number of users accessing the user interface (UI), and so on. In addition, future requirements on how the organization or department plans to use Jenkins play a role in the sizing of the server. The documentation at https://www.jenkins.io/ provides guidance and recommendations about the hardware, CPU, memory, and other factors that should be considered for the Jenkins server.

Jenkins also supports a distributed deployment architecture that is implemented by way of the Jenkins controller and agents. In a distributed architecture, the centralized machine where all the administration steps are performed is referred to as the Jenkins controller. All the configuration, management, and orchestration operations are done on the controller, while the execution of tasks is performed by one or more agents. There is a primary/secondary relationship between controller and agents in this distributed cluster architecture. The controller instructs the agents (also referred to as build agents) as to the execution of the tasks. This distributed architecture is considered a best practice and is commonly used for production deployments.

The agents can run on a variety of platforms, such as a Docker container, virtual machine, Kubernetes cluster, bare-metal server, and so on. Just like the controller, the agent machine also requires Java to be installed.

This distributed model provides scalability since it allows for the execution of multiple activities in parallel. As expected, the agents and the controller require network connectivity. This connectivity, at the time of writing of this book, can be configured on a random or fixed TCP port (or ports) on the controller. If the controller is in a centralized data center while the agents are spread across the network, the configurations on any firewalls must allow communication on those random or fixed TCP ports between them. Figure 3-1 provides a high-level overview of the Jenkins architecture.

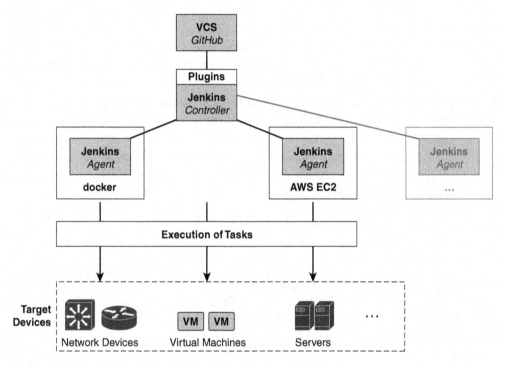

Figure 3-1   *Jenkins Distributed Architecture*

Jenkins provides a web interface that is used for administration and other tasks such as managing and monitoring Jenkins itself, installing plugins, integrating with other systems, creating a pipeline, and more. The Jenkins user interface (UI) is accessible via a web browser. In a distributed architecture, the controller provides the web interface for administrators to log on and perform all the configuration, administration, management, and monitoring activities.

The Jenkins web UI is used to configure a *job*, which is a specific task or series of tasks executed by Jenkins as per the job's configuration. In other words, a pipeline is created on the Jenkins UI. The job is also referred to as a "project," and these two terms can be used interchangeably to describe the same capability.

The Jenkins web UI provides options to create multiple types of jobs or projects. Freestyle, multibranch, and pipeline projects are some of the options available. Here are some additional details of these project types:

- A **freestyle project** is the most basic type of Jenkins job. It allows for the creation of tasks through the Jenkins UI, such as cloning git repository, executing any shell commands, and so on. Multiple freestyle jobs can be linked with each other to provide the same impact as a pipeline (that is, the execution of a series of steps). The ability to configure a freestyle job via the UI is both beneficial and restrictive. It's beneficial since the creation is done via workflows on the UI, so it is easier for not-so-complex jobs. However, it's restrictive since the UI must be used for the creation and requires going through many steps. Additionally, creating and managing any subsequent changes via the UI makes it less effective as well as slower.

- A **multibranch pipeline** scans the branches from the source code management (SCM) or version control system (VCS) and creates multiple pipeline projects accordingly.

- A **pipeline** project allows you to define a pipeline as code using a domain-specific language supported on Jenkins. This pipeline can be configured and saved natively on the Jenkins server itself, or it can be defined in a text file and stored on an SCM. If the latter mechanism is used, then Jenkins retrieves the pipeline defined on an SCM (git repository) and will automatically run the tasks defined in that file. Creating a Jenkins pipeline in a text file and storing that file on a git repository is a common scenario. The use case presented in the section "Use Case: GitHub Webhook and Jenkins," later in this chapter, provides more details for using a file to define a pipeline and storing it in git.

In summary, the options for creating a pipeline in Jenkins are as follows:

- Use the Jenkins UI to define the pipeline.
- Define the pipeline in a file named "Jenkinsfile" on the SCM.

Note   Jenkinsfile is a text-based file typically used to define a pipeline. More details about the syntax for defining a pipeline in this file are covered later in this chapter.

Once the job is defined in Jenkins, the execution of this job is called a "build." There are multiple options for initiating the execution of a job (that is, triggering a build). For example, a build can be triggered manually, periodically on a predefined schedule, based on events in GitHub or another VCS/SCM, and upon completion of another build. A commit or push of updated code in a GitHub repository is an example of an event that can be configured to trigger a build in Jenkins. The "Triggers" section in this chapter provides more details about the various options.

The Jenkins web UI allows you to view the execution of the build stages and all the steps. The results for each build of a job are also available, so historical data of the builds after execution is also available.

Jenkins Installation

The Jenkins architecture allows it to be used in multiple ways and installed on multiple operating systems. Let's look at some of the options for installing Jenkins.

First, Jenkins can run as a Docker container. The Jenkins open-source community officially distributes a Docker container image that can be used to run Jenkins. The container image is made available by the community on the Jenkins public repository on Docker Hub. It is identified as Jenkins/Jenkins repository on the hub. Installing Jenkins and all the prerequisite software packages on a self-managed Docker container is an alternate option.

Second, Jenkins can be installed and run in a Kubernetes cluster. Jenkins can also be installed natively on the Windows and macOS operating systems. Jenkins installers are made available for these operating systems.

Finally, Jenkins can be installed on a variety of Linux distributions such as Ubuntu, Red Hat, CentOS, and Fedora. This chapter provides a step-by-step procedure to install Jenkins on a Linux distribution.

At the time of writing of this book, Java version 11 or 17 is a prerequisite for the installation of Jenkins. Further, regardless of the operating system used for Jenkins, the correct sizing of the host machine is very important. As covered earlier in this chapter, hardware specifications of the host machine depend on the number of jobs being executed, the number of users accessing the UI, future usage of Jenkins, and more. It is recommended that you check the most up-to-date sizing requirements in the Jenkins documentation (https://www.jenkins.io/). At the time of writing this book, the recommended hardware specifications for a host machine are as follows:

- **RAM:** A minimum of 4GB of RAM should be used for the host virtual machine.

- **Hard drive (storage):** A minimum of 50GB of drive space should be made available to the host machine.

Network access to this host machine should be considered based on the usage of Jenkins. For example, if automation tasks in a pipeline will be executed on networking devices in a private data center, then the Jenkins server and associated agents can be installed as a Linux virtual machine in this private data center. If access to the Jenkins server is required from the Internet (for example, without VPN access to the corporate network), then the virtual machine that hosts the Jenkins server and agents can be installed on a public cloud infrastructure. Simultaneous public and private network access to Jenkins can be provided as well, which is explained further in the following section.

Infrastructure for the Jenkins Server

In this chapter, the Jenkins server is installed on an AWS public cloud infrastructure. The Jenkins server will run a pipeline that executes tasks on network switches in a private (corporate) data center. The public cloud infrastructure connects to this corporate network via a VPN. In addition, the Jenkins server is made accessible from the Internet and thus allows for integration with GitHub.

The underlying public cloud infrastructure details are shown in Figure 3-2. As shown in this figure, the cloud infrastructure has the following key components:

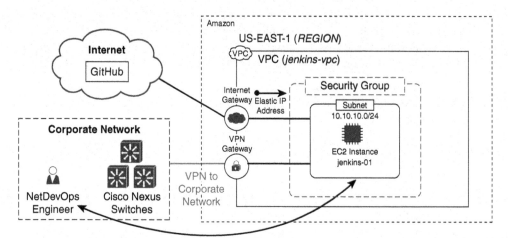

Figure 3-2   *Public Cloud Infrastructure for Jenkins Server*

A virtual private cloud (VPC) named "jenkins-vpc" is created and hosts the Jenkins instance. In AWS, the term "instance" is used to describe a virtual machine (VM) or virtual private cloud (VPC) that is a logically isolated infrastructure on a public cloud, like a traditional private network. Resources such as IP addresses and subnets, routing, the gateway for an Internet connection, VPN peering, security rules, and more are created as part of the VPC.

A subnet with an IP address range of 10.10.10.0/24 is created within this VPC. The Jenkins instance, after it is launched, gets the IP address from this subnet. Note that the subnet created within the VPC has a private IP address range.

To protect and control access to the Jenkins instance and other resources within VPC, a "security group" is defined in AWS. You can think of a security group as a traditional firewall that protects all incoming and outgoing traffic for one or more instances. The rules within the security group are configured to allow inbound traffic to the Jenkins instance from the corporate network. Similarly, outbound rules are created to allow outbound traffic from the Jenkins instance (that is, traffic that leaves the VPC). For access to and from the Jenkins instance, the following security rules are created:

- **Inbound rules for HTTP and SSH:** Multiple inbound rules are created to allow traffic on TCP ports 8080 and 80 and TCP port 22 for web access to the Jenkins UI and for SSH access to the Jenkins instance, respectively. The source IP address of the corporate network subnet is configured in these inbound rules. Hence, these rules allow traffic from the corporate network to the Jenkins instance.

- **Inbound rule for GitHub:** In this setup, the Software as a Service (SaaS) offering of GitHub is used as the VCS. The source IP address from the GitHub SaaS is also allowed and configured in an inbound rule on AWS. At the time of writing, GitHub meta API endpoint provides a list of IP addresses for various GitHub services (for example, webhook). This rule will only be required for use cases covering GitHub integration later in this chapter.

- **Outbound rule:** This rule allows traffic to any destination. This is required to allow the installation of Jenkins and updates for other Linux packages from the public Internet.

For Internet access, an "Internet gateway" (IGW) associated with this VPC is created in AWS. It allows Internet access to and from the Jenkins instance. Information about Elastic IP is provided in this section.

Further, for access to and from the corporate network, the AWS "VPN gateway" is used for site-to-site VPN connectivity, which uses IPSec for connections between the VPC and the corporate network. The corporate network needs its own device for the IPSec functionality. The AWS VPN gateway provides the option to use either static routing or a dynamic routing protocol (BGP) for routing traffic between the corporate network and the VPC.

The "route tables" within the VPC are configured so that traffic to the Internet is routed to the AWS Internet gateway, and traffic going to the corporate network is sent to the AWS VPN gateway.

The AWS EC2 service is used to instantiate an instance (virtual machine) within AWS us-east-1 region. The EC2 instance named "jenkins-01" is launched in AWS, with the following details:

- The instance is launched in "jenkins-vpc."

- The instance is launched in the 10.10.10.0/24 subnet within this VPC.

- An AWS machine image (AMI) of "Amazon Linux 2" is used.

- An instance type of "t2.micro" is used. At the time of writing this book, this instance type is a free tier within AWS for hundreds of hours for one year.

■ For SSH access to this instance, a "key pair" is used to generate public and private keys as security credentials. The AWS EC2 service automatically adds the public key when the instance is created. The private key must be downloaded by the administrator and used for SSH access to the instance.

■ The security group with the appropriate rules for access to the Jenkins instance is attached to this instance.

Since the Jenkins instance gets an IP address from the private IP address range (10.10.10.0/24), an Elastic IP address is used to provide one-to-one NAT on the Internet gateway. Elastic IP is a functionality provided by AWS that allows you to allocate and assign a public IP address to an instance. In this case, the public IP address of 44.208.200.59 (that is, "Elastic IP") is associated to the Jenkins instance after it is launched. This Elastic IP address serves multiple purposes. It is used for communication between GitHub and Jenkins as well as for installation of software packages and plugins on the Jenkins instance.

Once the Jenkins instance is launched, from AWS console we need to verify that this instance is fully operational without any alarms. We also need to verify that the Elastic IP address, the correct security group and rules, and so on are assigned to this instance, as shown in Figure 3-3.

Figure 3-3   *AWS Console for Jenkins EC2 Instance*

Installing the Jenkins Packages

After successfully launching the EC2 instance, we need to ssh to this instance to install the prerequisite software packages and then install the Jenkins software on this instance.

The steps for SSH access and the installation of Jenkins software are provided in this section.

A NetDevOps engineer (or administrator) initiates the SSH connection to the EC2 instance. The private key generated earlier in the AWS EC2 key-pair is required for authentication to access the EC2 instance via SSH. In Example 3-1, "privatekey.pem" is the name of the private key saved on the NetDevOps engineer's workstation. The default username of "ec2-user" on the AMI of Amazon Linux 2 must be used to access this instance

Example 3-1   *Authenticating to the EC2 Instance via SSH*

```
$ ssh -i privatekey.pem ec2-user@10.10.10.229


Last login: Tue Oct 11 11:06:41 2022
       __|  __|_  )
       _|  (     /    Amazon Linux 2 AMI
      ___|\___|___|


https://aws.amazon.com/amazon-linux-2/
[ec2-user@ip-10-10-10-229 ~]$
```

After SSH access, we need to verify that Internet access from the instance is working properly, as shown in Example 3-2. This means that the routing tables, Internet gateway, and Elastic IP address are all working properly.

Example 3-2   *Verifying Internet Access*

```
[ec2-user@ip-10-10-10-229 ~]$ ping www.google.com
PING www.google.com (142.251.16.147) 56(84) bytes of data.
64 bytes from bl-in-f147.1e100.net (142.251.16.147): icmp_seq=1 ttl=50 time=2.26 ms
64 bytes from bl-in-f147.1e100.net (142.251.16.147): icmp_seq=2 ttl=50 time=2.35 ms
64 bytes from bl-in-f147.1e100.net (142.251.16.147): icmp_seq=3 ttl=50 time=2.29 ms
^C
--- www.google.com ping statistics ---
3 packets transmitted, 3 received, 0% packet loss, time 2002ms
rtt min/avg/max/mdev = 2.263/2.303/2.351/0.036 ms


[ec2-user@ip-10-10-10-229 ~]$
```

The operating system version details can be checked by issuing the commands shown in Example 3-3. The output of these commands shows that Amazon Linux release 2 is running on this instance.

Example 3-3 *EC2 Instance OS*

```
[ec2-user@ip-10-10-10-229 ~]$ cat /etc/system-release

Amazon Linux release 2 (Karoo)
[ec2-user@ip-10-10-10-229 ~]$
[ec2-user@ip-10-10-10-229 ~]$ cat /etc/os-release
NAME="Amazon Linux"
VERSION="2"
ID="amzn"
ID_LIKE="centos rhel fedora"
VERSION_ID="2"
PRETTY_NAME="Amazon Linux 2"
ANSI_COLOR="0;33"
CPE_NAME="cpe:2.3:o:amazon:amazon_linux:2"
HOME_URL=https://amazonlinux.com/

[ec2-user@ip-10-10-10-229 ~]$
```

The software packages on this instance should be upgraded. This step is performed by using the **yum update** command as shown in Example 3-4. Yum is a package management tool for Red Hat–based Linux systems. It is used to install, update, and remove software packages on these Linux systems.

Example 3-4 *Updating Packages on the EC2 Instance*

```
$ yum update -y
Loaded plugins: extras_suggestions, langpacks, priorities, update-motd
amzn2-core                                                              | 3.7 kB
  00:00:00
Resolving Dependencies
#output omitted#
--> Finished Dependency Resolution

Dependencies Resolved

================================================================================
=========================
 Package              Arch        Version                 Repository
  Size
================================================================================
=========================
Installing:
 kernel               x86_64      5.10.144-127.601.amzn2        amzn2extra-
kernel-5.10            32 M
```

```
#output omitted#
Installed:
  kernel.x86_64 0:5.10.144-127.601.amzn2

Updated:
  initscripts.x86_64 0:9.49.47-1.amzn2.0.3        kernel-tools.x86_64 0:5.10.144-
127.601.amzn2
  kpatch-runtime.noarch 0:0.9.4-6.amzn2           libxml2.x86_64 0:2.9.1-6.amzn2.5.6
  libxml2-python.x86_64 0:2.9.1-6.amzn2.5.6       systemd.x86_64 0:219-78.amzn2.0.20
  systemd-libs.x86_64 0:219-78.amzn2.0.20         systemd-sysv.x86_64 0:219-78.
amzn2.0.20
  tzdata.noarch 0:2022d-1.amzn2.0.1               zlib.x86_64 0:1.2.7-19.amzn2.0.2

Complete!
```

To install Jenkins in the later steps, the location of the centralized repository that keeps all the Jenkins software packages must be added to this instance. This is done by issuing the **wget** command shown in Example 3-5 on the instance. It is a command-line utility that downloads files from the Web. As per the -O flag, the repository information is downloaded from https://pkg.jenkins.io/redhat-stable/jenkins.repo and stored as a file named jenkins.repo in the /etc/yum.repos.d/ directory of the instance.

Example 3-5 *Jenkins Repo on the EC2 Instance*

```
$ sudo wget -O /etc/yum.repos.d/jenkins.repo \
    https://pkg.jenkins.io/redhat-stable/jenkins.repo
--2022-10-14 10:26:18--  https://pkg.jenkins.io/redhat-stable/jenkins.repo
Resolving pkg.jenkins.io (pkg.jenkins.io)... 146.75.34.133, 2a04:4e42:79::645
Connecting to pkg.jenkins.io (pkg.jenkins.io)|146.75.34.133|:443... connected.
HTTP request sent, awaiting response... 200 OK
Length: 85
Saving to: '/etc/yum.repos.d/jenkins.repo'
100%[===========================================================>] 85
--.-K/s   in 0s
2022-10-14 10:26:18 (5.59 MB/s) - '/etc/yum.repos.d/jenkins.repo' saved [85/85]
```

For security and verification purposes, the Jenkins software packages are signed with keys. To verify Jenkins software packages, the associated key must be imported on the instance. This is performed by issuing the following command.

```
$ sudo rpm --import https://pkg.jenkins.io/redhat-stable/jenkins.io.key
$
```

At this stage, all the packages can be upgraded, and obsolete packages can be deleted by issuing the **yum** command found in Example 3-6.

Example 3-6   *Upgrading Packages on the EC2 Instance*

```
$ sudo yum upgrade
Loaded plugins: extras_suggestions, langpacks, priorities, update-motd
jenkins
| 2.9 kB   00:00:00
jenkins/primary_db
|  43 kB   00:00:00
No packages marked for update

$
```

Since Java is a prerequisite for the installation of Jenkins, open-source OpenJDK (Java Development Kit) version 11 can be installed to meet this requirement, as shown in Example 3-7. In this example, the **amazon-linux-extras** command refers to the Amazon Linux Extras package repository that is provided by AWS for Amazon Linux 2 running on this instance.

Example 3-7   *Java Installation*

```
$ sudo amazon-linux-extras install java-openjdk11 -y
Installing java-11-openjdk
#output omitted#
Installing:
 java-11-openjdk              x86_64 1:11.0.16.0.8-1.amzn2.0.1    amzn2extra-java-
   openjdk11 235 k
#output omitted#
Transaction Summary
================================================================================
===============
Install  1 Package (+32 Dependent packages)
#output omitted#
Installed:
  java-11-openjdk.x86_64 1:11.0.16.0.8-1.amzn2.0.1

#output omitted#
$
```

Now that the prerequisites for Jenkins are met, Jenkins can be installed by using the **yum** command, as shown in Example 3-8.

Example 3-8 *Jenkins Installation on the EC2 Instance*

```
$ sudo yum install jenkins -y
Loaded plugins: extras_suggestions, langpacks, priorities, update-motd
Resolving Dependencies
--> Running transaction check
---> Package jenkins.noarch 0:2.361.2-1.1 will be installed
--> Finished Dependency Resolution

Dependencies Resolved

================================================================================
===============
 Package              Arch              Version              Repository
   Size
================================================================================
===============
Installing:
 jenkins              noarch            2.361.2-1.1          jenkins
   89 M

Transaction Summary
================================================================================
===============
Install  1 Package
Total download size: 89 M
Installed size: 89 M
Downloading packages:
jenkins-2.361.2-1.1.noarch.rpm
|  89 MB  00:00:02
Running transaction check
Running transaction test
Transaction test succeeded
Running transaction
  Installing : jenkins-2.361.2-1.1.noarch
  Verifying  : jenkins-2.361.2-1.1.noarch
1/1
Installed:
  jenkins.noarch 0:2.361.2-1.1
Complete!
```

After successful installation of Jenkins, the service must be enabled by issuing the
following command:

```
$ sudo systemctl enable jenkins
Created symlink from /etc/systemd/system/multi-user.target.wants/
jenkins.service to /usr/lib/systemd/system/jenkins.service.
```

When service is enabled, it also starts when the instance boots up. Next, the Jenkins service must be started by issuing the **systemctl start jenkins** command and then checking its status, as shown in Example 3-9.

Example 3-9 *Starting Jenkins*

```
$ sudo systemctl start jenkins
$ sudo systemctl status jenkins
 jenkins.service - Jenkins Continuous Integration Server
   Loaded: loaded (/usr/lib/systemd/system/jenkins.service; enabled; vendor preset:
   disabled)
   Active: active (running) since Fri 2022-10-14 10:29:48 UTC; 7s ago
 Main PID: 29032 (java)
   CGroup: /system.slice/jenkins.service
           └─29032 /usr/bin/java -Djava.awt.headless=true -jar /usr/share/java/jen-
   kins.war --web...
Oct 14 10:29:19 ip-10-10-10-229.ec2.internal jenkins[29032]: This may also be found
   at: /var/li...d
Oct 14 10:29:19 ip-10-10-10-229.ec2.internal jenkins[29032]: ***********************
   ***********...*
Oct 14 10:29:19 ip-10-10-10-229.ec2.internal jenkins[29032]: ***********************
   ***********...*
Oct 14 10:29:19 ip-10-10-10-229.ec2.internal jenkins[29032]: ***********************
   ***********...*
Oct 14 10:29:48 ip-10-10-10-229.ec2.internal jenkins[29032]: 2022-10-14
   10:29:48.837+0000 [id=3...n
Oct 14 10:29:48 ip-10-10-10-229.ec2.internal jenkins[29032]: 2022-10-14
   10:29:48.869+0000 [id=2...g
Oct 14 10:29:48 ip-10-10-10-229.ec2.internal systemd[1]: Started Jenkins Continuous
   Integratio...r.
Oct 14 10:29:48 ip-10-10-10-229.ec2.internal jenkins[29032]: 2022-10-14
   10:29:48.979+0000 [id=4...r
Oct 14 10:29:48 ip-10-10-10-229.ec2.internal jenkins[29032]: 2022-10-14
   10:29:48.979+0000 [id=4...l
Oct 14 10:29:48 ip-10-10-10-229.ec2.internal jenkins[29032]: 2022-10-14
   10:29:48.984+0000 [id=4...s
Hint: Some lines were ellipsized, use -l to show in full.
```

During the installation of Jenkins, an administrator password is created. This password is required during the initial logon to the Jenkins service via a web browser in the subsequent step. Write down or copy this password at this stage. The following output shows the password for this installation:

```
$ sudo cat /var/lib/jenkins/secrets/initialAdminPassword
cf011199344c41c39e55cc16ffaa871a
```

Accessing Jenkins on the Web for the First Time

Now that the Jenkins service is running, the NetDevOps engineer (or an administrator) can access it on a web browser by connecting to the URL http://<ip_address>: 8080. Subsequent configurations of the Jenkins service are performed from the web browser as captured in the following steps.

Once the NetDevOps engineer accesses the web page http://<ip_address>: 8080, an initial "Getting Started" web page is displayed.

On the initial Getting Started web page, the user is prompted to enter the one-time administrator password generated and copied from file (/var/lib/jenkins/secrets/initialAdminPassword) in the previous step via SSH access to the EC2 instance.

Figure 3-4 shows the screenshot of this web page prompting the user to enter the password.

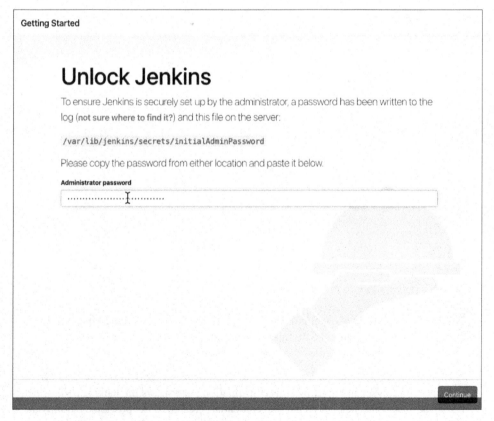

Figure 3-4 *The Jenkins "Getting Started" page – initialAdminPassword*

After successful authentication, plugins must be installed on this Jenkins server. The plugins allow it to integrate with other tools such as GitHub, LDAP, and so on and to provide additional functionality natively on the server such as Pipeline Stage View, keeping local credentials, SSH build agents, and more.

Select the **Install suggested plugins** option to install the previously mentioned and various other plugins at this stage, as shown in Figure 3-5. Additional plugins can be installed later via the Plugin Manager on the Jenkins administration web page.

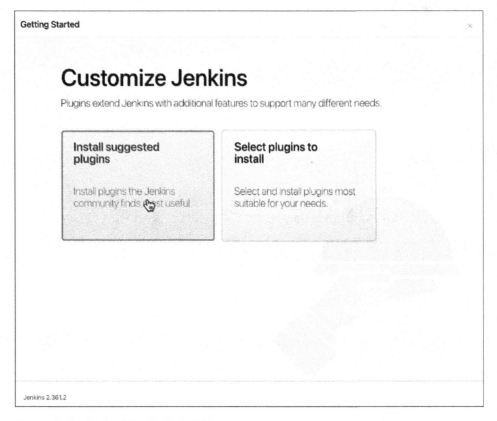

Figure 3-5 *Jenkins Plugin Installation*

Then, an administrator account must be created, as shown in the **Create First Admin User** page shown in Figure 3-6. In this setup, an administrator account with ID of "admin" and a password is created, as shown in Figure 3-6.

A confirmation page about the installation of the Jenkins server is shown on the next page. As you can see in Figure 3-7, this confirmation page shows the Jenkins URL, which is used to access this Jenkins server. The credentials created in the previous step must be used to access the Jenkins server via the Jenkins URL using a web browser. Click the **Save and Finish** button at the bottom of this page to complete the initial configuration and installation.

Getting Started

Create First Admin User

Username:

admin

Password:

....

Confirm password:

....

Full name:

admin

E-mail address:

|

Jenkins 2.361.2   Skip and continue as admin   Save and Continue

Figure 3-6 *Jenkins Administrator Account Creation*

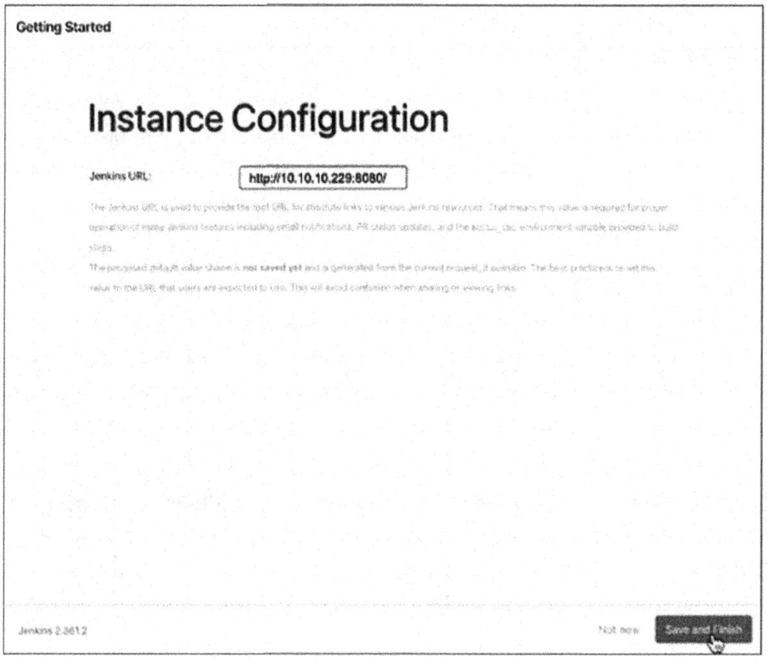

Getting Started

Instance Configuration

Jenkins URL: http://10.10.10.229:8080/

The Jenkins URL is used to provide the root URL for absolute links to various Jenkins resources. That means this value is required for proper operation of many Jenkins features including email notifications, PR status updates, and the BUILD_URL environment variable provided to build steps.

The proposed default value shown is not saved yet and is generated from the current request, if possible. The best practice is to set this value to the URL that users are expected to use. This will avoid confusion when sharing or viewing links.

Jenkins 2.361.2   Not now   Save and Finish

Figure 3-7 *Jenkins Instance Configuration*

This completes the installation of a standalone Jenkins server. As an alternative, installation of Jenkins as a virtual machine, on another Linux distribution, can also be performed using the same guidelines.

Plugins

The software delivery lifecycle uses many tools. To allow the flexibility for integrating these tools, Jenkins uses the concept of plugins. Such integrations of the Jenkins server allow you to retrieve information and share data with those tools. The orchestration logic on Jenkins allows it to perform actions based on information received from these tools using the plugins, and the plugins can also allow Jenkins to send information to these tools. Further details on orchestration logic are covered in the "Pipeline" section of this chapter.

Hundreds of plugins have been developed and are shared by the open-source community. If a plugin for a tool is not available, it can be developed. Hence, the plugin architecture provides flexibility to use existing plugins and allows to you develop new plugins if there is no existing plugin for a given tool. Also, if there is a need to extend the functionality of an existing integration, the existing plugins can be enhanced.

There are various scenarios and use cases for how the plugins can be utilized by Jenkins for integration to tools. Plugins allow integration with version control systems, infrastructure providers, platforms, and so on, and they help to deliver on various scenarios utilizing those products with Jenkins. At the time of writing of this book, a complete list of Jenkins plugins is available at https://plugins.jenkins.io/.

Use Cases for Plugins

Integration of Jenkins with source code management (SCM) or a version control system (VCS) such as git is one of the use cases of the plugins. Multiple plugins can provide this git integration: "git" and "GitHub" are a couple of plugins commonly used for this purpose. The plugin named git allows Jenkins to perform various git operations, such as fetch, pull, check out a branch, and more on a repository in git-based VCSs such as GitHub, GitLab, and so on. The plugin named GitHub allows you to integrate Jenkins with GitHub projects. When new code or changes are pushed to the GitHub repository, upon receiving notification (also called a webhook) from the GitHub repository, this Jenkins plugin can initiate a build of a job on Jenkins without any delay. This plugin also provides other capabilities, such as creating a hyperlink to the GitHub repository on the Jenkins job/build status page. Use cases in this chapter cover additional usage of these git plugins.

Another example for a plugin use case is the Docker plugin, which allows the Jenkins controller to instantiate and launch an agent within a Docker container. This provides flexibility to launch agents on the fly, execute a job (or jobs) by using those agents, and then terminate those agents by stopping and terminating the Docker container.

What about a scenario where someone wants to utilize a public cloud provider infrastructure to launch Jenkins agents? Well, not a problem. The Amazon EC2 plugin can be used to start agents as EC2 instances on AWS. Like Jenkins agents running as a Docker container, these EC2 instances can be terminated when they are not required.

In NetDevOps, tools such as Ansible, Terraform, and testing frameworks are typically used. There are multiple methods to integrate and use these tools within a Jenkins pipeline. Let's look at some of these methods:

- One option is to simply use shell (aka bash) commands on the Jenkins server (or on the agent) to invoke actions and execute an Ansible playbook, Terraform script, or a test suite.

- Another option is to use a Docker container with the required NetDevOps tools (Ansible, Robot framework, and so on) as part of pipeline execution.

- If available, a plugin for the tool can also be considered a viable option. At the time of writing, Jenkins plugins for Ansible, Terraform, and the Robot framework are available. As an example, the Ansible plugin allows for the configuration of Ansible playbooks, hosts, credentials, and so on natively on the Jenkins server as part of the pipeline creation. Furthermore, the plugin allows you to invoke the Ansible playbook directly from this Jenkins instance as part of the build execution.

The choice of using one of these (or other) methods can be made based upon the flexibility and restrictions of the respective plugin. For example, the Ansible plugin can provide flexibility by using credentials directly from Jenkins credentials store. Similarly, with the Ansible plugin, the Jenkins environment variables can also be accessed within the Ansible playbook. At the time of writing, the details for each plugin are available at https://plugins.jenkins.io. On each Jenkins plugin web page, it is advisable that you examine the releases (frequency of version updates, release dates), issues and resolutions, and source code updates on GitHub prior to choosing a path for utilizing a plugin or considering an alternate option.

Management and Installation of Plugins

The plugins can be easily installed on the Jenkins server UI. As mentioned earlier, the Jenkins UI is accessible using a web browser via http://{ip_address_of_jenkins}:8080. By default, the Jenkins open-source community has an "update site" hosted on the public Internet. By default, each Jenkins server searches for and downloads the plugins from this site. This update site is also referred to as "Update Center."

Navigate through the following steps for managing plugins:

Step 1.   After successful authentication on the Jenkins UI, the main page called **Dashboard** is displayed in the web browser. On the left pane of **Dashboard**, click the **Manage Jenkins** option.

Step 2.   On the **Manage Jenkins** page, there are two options to access the Plugin Manager and view more details about the plugins:

- Click **Go to plugin manager.**

- Scroll down to the **System Configuration** section and click **Manage Plugin.**

Step 3.   The **Plugin Manager** page provides information about the plugins in multiple tabs:

- **Update tab:** This tab provides the information about any updates available to plugins that are already installed on Jenkins.

- **Available tab:** This tab provides plugin information and allows you to search for the plugins available for installation on the Jenkins server. The inventory of plugins is provided from the update site (aka Update Center). This tab allows to search for and select the desired plugin and then initiate the installation by clicking the **Install without restart** or **Download now and install after restart** button. During the installation of a plugin, all the dependencies are automatically installed as well.

- **Installed tab:** This tab provides the information about the plugins that are already installed on the Jenkins server. Recall that during the installation of Jenkins in the previous section, we selected **Install suggested plugins.** This tab shows all the plugins installed at that stage and subsequently.

- **Advanced tab:** This tab provides additional configuration settings for installing plugins. These settings include configuration for any HTTP proxy server to allow the Jenkins server to access the update site on the Internet using this proxy. An additional option is to deploy the plugin as a file upload from the administrator's workstation or from a web server. This provides flexibility for installing the plugin, in addition to using the update site. Any change to the update site's URL is also allowed on this tab.

Step 4.   It is recommended to uninstall any plugins not required anymore. The benefit of removing undesired plugins is that this offloads memory and CPU usage from the server. The uninstall step is performed under the **Installed** tab of **Plugin Manager.** The uninstall option for a plugin is only allowed if it's safe to uninstall it and there are no dependencies for it.

Step 5.   Under the **Installed** tab of **Plugin Manager,** you can disable a plugin by toggling the **Enable** button. Just like the uninstall option, the toggle button (to disable) will be enabled for a plugin if it's safe to uninstall it (that is, if there are no conflicts with other plugins).

Next, let's cover orchestration logic by using the pipelines in Jenkins.

Pipelines

The primary use of Jenkins is to define and orchestrate the execution of tasks across a variety of software delivery lifecycle tools. In the context of NetDevOps, the primary use of Jenkins is to automate and orchestrate the building, testing, and deployment of network configurations and software. This orchestration is done by creating a pipeline. In a distributed deployment of Jenkins, the execution of tasks for a pipeline is performed by the Jenkins agent, while the configurations are performed on the Jenkins controller. In the case of a nondistributed deployment, the pipeline execution is done by the Jenkins controller itself.

As explained previously in this chapter, a pipeline can be defined directly in the Jenkins UI. Alternatively, the pipeline can be defined in a file named *Jenkinsfile*. Typically, Jenkinsfile is used to create a pipeline. Like other code, this file is typically saved on a VCS such as the GitHub repository. The benefits of change history, traceability, past file versions, and so on are all realized by storing this file on a VCS. Thus, collaboration among multiple team members in the NetDevOps project is also achieved by keeping this file, along with other code, on a VCS as well.

Let's look at some additional details about pipeline configuration. Regardless of the mechanism used for creating a pipeline—that is, using the Jenkins UI or via a Jenkinsfile—the pipeline contains one or more *stages*. Each stage can contain one or more *steps*. These steps are basically the instructions for Jenkins to perform tasks (that is, a step defines what Jenkins should do).

These steps are executed sequentially. In other words, after the successful completion of a step, the next step is executed. If the execution for any of the steps fails, the pipeline fails as well.

There are two syntax options for configuring or creating a pipeline in the Jenkins UI or as a Jenkinsfile on a VCS:

- Option 1: Scripted pipeline using Groovy language syntax

- Option 2: Declarative pipeline using declarative syntax

Note   The "Declarative Pipelines" and "Scripted Pipelines" sections in this chapter provide details about the syntax and examples of these pipelines.

Using a declarative language is considered an easier way to define the pipeline, whereas the Groovy language provides most functionality and flexibility.

As mentioned earlier, regardless of the syntax used, if the pipeline is saved in a Jenkinsfile, then this file is typically also saved and maintained in an SCM or VCS. Also, Jenkins is integrated to an SCM using plugins. For example, a Jenkinsfile can be stored in a GitHub repository. The GitHub and git plugins are used in Jenkins to integrate with

GitHub. Configuration on the Jenkins pipeline allows you to trigger the *build* of this pipeline (that is, trigger a job or project) when an event (such as new code being pushed) occurs on that GitHub repository. Use cases in later sections of this chapter cover this in more detail.

The Jenkins UI has a pipeline syntax generator that can be used to learn and generate code for declarative and scripted pipelines. The scripted pipeline code can be generated on the **Snippet Generator** page, whereas the declarative pipeline code can be generated on the **Declarative Directive Generator** page. On each of those pages, a sample step can be selected from the drop-down menu to generate the respective pipeline code. This pipeline syntax page will dynamically load the required directives based on the sample step selected from the drop-down menu. The pipeline code is then generated by clicking the **Generate Pipeline script** button. This is a very helpful utility and is accessible on the Jenkins UI on the pipeline configuration page or directly at http://{IP_address jen-kins}:8080/pipeline-syntax/.

As discussed earlier, Jenkins interacts with multiple systems such as GitHub repositories, cloud systems, and so on. These interactions often require some sort of credentials. These credentials can be stored in the Jenkins UI by navigating to **Manage Jenkins > Manage Credentials** from the **Dashboard** page. Various types of credentials can be stored here, including username and password, API tokens as secret text, SSH username with a private key, secret content in a file via secret file option, and so on. These credentials can be used during the execution of a pipeline, and some examples are covered in use cases in this chapter.

Let's look at both declarative and scripted pipelines in more detail.

Declarative Pipelines

Declarative pipeline uses declarative syntax. This syntax, as the name suggests, is expected to be abstracted in nature. In declarative languages, the desired target state is expressed at a high level rather than writing step-by-step procedures to achieve the desired state.

For NetDevOps team members who do not have past knowledge of the Groovy language and do not want to go through the process of learning it, declarative syntax offers a simpler solution for creating pipelines. However, for more experienced programmers, declarative syntax can also be considered a bit restrictive versus creating scripted pipelines using the Groovy language.

One of the benefits of using a declarative pipeline is the **Restart from Stage** option in the Jenkins UI. If a pipeline fails due to a transient error, this option allows you to start execution from any of the stages defined in that pipeline. If the pipeline is created using the Groovy language, the complete job must be executed from the beginning, and there is no option to restart the pipeline execution from a specific stage.

A predefined structure is used to create declarative pipelines. We will look in detail at declarative pipeline syntax in the following use case. Here are some details of note about this syntax:

- The declarative pipeline is enclosed within a **pipeline** block. It is the top-level block for declarative syntax.

- The **pipeline** block has various sections in the declarative syntax. Within these sections, one or more *directives* or *steps* are defined.

- The **stages** section is used to describe the main work performed within the pipeline.

- Within the **stages** section, a **stage** directive is defined. Linking back to NetDevOps, a "stage" could be Build, Test, Deploy, and so on.

- Within each stage, one or more tasks are executed. These tasks are defined in the **steps** section within the declarative pipeline. Therefore, the actual execution activities are performed within "steps." Here are a couple of examples:

  - **sh** executes a shell command or a script on a Linux system.

  - The **echo** command displays the text or string passed as an argument.

- The **agent** section of the declarative pipeline controls the location where the execution happens physically (that is, the machine where the complete pipeline or a stage is executed).

  - Agent configuration, as well as the selection of an agent, can be done at the top level of the pipeline under the **pipeline** block or at a **stage** level.

- A **post** is another type of section that executes one or more steps after successful execution of the complete pipeline or a stage.

- *Directives* can help to add logic to the pipeline. They can be used to set triggers, add environment variables, and so on in the pipeline. The following list provides a few of the directives that can be part of the declarative pipeline:

  - **environment:** This contains key-value pairs that are defined as environment variables. Credentials can be defined within the environment directive.

  - **parameters:** This is a list of values a user may be asked to provide when a pipeline is triggered.

  - **triggers:** These are directives that allow you to initiate (that is, trigger) the execution of a pipeline. There are multiple options for triggering and initiating the execution of a pipeline. Examples include defining cron-style syntax that allows a scheduled trigger based on the predefined time, polling a source control using a Poll SCM mechanism to check if there are changes in the version control system, completing an upstream job/project, and so on. More details with use cases are provided in the "Triggers" section of this chapter.

■ **when:** This directive allows you to execute a stage based on a condition.

Refer to Figure 3-8 to view the syntax of a declarative pipeline that is executed in Jenkins running on Linux system, noting the following in particular:

■ This pipeline can be executed on any of the agent nodes.

■ The pipeline has only one stage, named "Hello."

■ A single step, **echo**, is executed. This **echo** command displays the message "Hello World."

Declarative Pipeline – "hello world"

```
pipeline {
    agent any

    stages {
        stage('Hello') {
            steps {
                echo 'Hello World'
            }
        }
    }
}
```

Figure 3-8   *Declarative Pipeline "hello world"*

Let's look at the following use case to understand additional details about declarative syntax for the creation of pipelines in Jenkins and to understand the directives just explained.

Use Case: Declarative Pipeline to Validate Ansible Playbook

This use case goes through the definition of a pipeline within Jenkins for the "Use Case: Release Management for NetDevOps" covered in Chapter 1, "Why Do We Need NetDevOps?" In this use case, Jenkins is used to create a NetDevOps pipeline for a data center environment. The Jenkins pipeline is configured to trigger steps for the automated building and testing of code. It is assumed that Cisco Nexus switches are used within the data center to provide connectivity to bare-metal, virtualized servers and to the corporate intranet. Also, Ansible is used for automating the deployment and configuration management of this environment.

Ansible code is developed by a NetDevOps engineer, and this code is put in a GitHub remote repository. As you'll recall, "vlan.yml" and "hosts" files were developed in the use case in Chapter 1.

To create the declarative pipeline, access the Jenkins UI on a web browser by logging in to http://{ip_address_of_Jenkins}:8080. Upon successful logon, the **Dashboard** page is displayed.

On the left pane of the **Dashboard** page, click **New Item**. The next page shows various options to create a pipeline, including **Freestyle project**, **Pipeline**, and **Multiconfiguration project**. Select the **Pipeline** option.

On this page, the **Enter an item name** text box is displayed at the top. It allows you to specify the name of this pipeline project. Enter **ansible1** and scroll to the bottom of the page and click the OK button. This results in the pipeline being saved with the name "ansible1." This field is required and is filled in by administrators at their own discretion.

The next page shows the settings for this pipeline. These settings include the option to discard old build records, integrate GitHub projects, and more. There's also an option to configure triggers for initiating a build under the "Build Triggers" section. Ignore these settings, as this pipeline will be triggered manually.

Scroll down to the **Pipeline** section on this page. The declarative syntax of the pipeline will be defined in this section. Under **Definition**, make sure that **Pipeline script** is selected from the drop-down menu. A text box named **Script** is empty by default.

Figure 3-9 shows a partial view of this web page for further clarity.

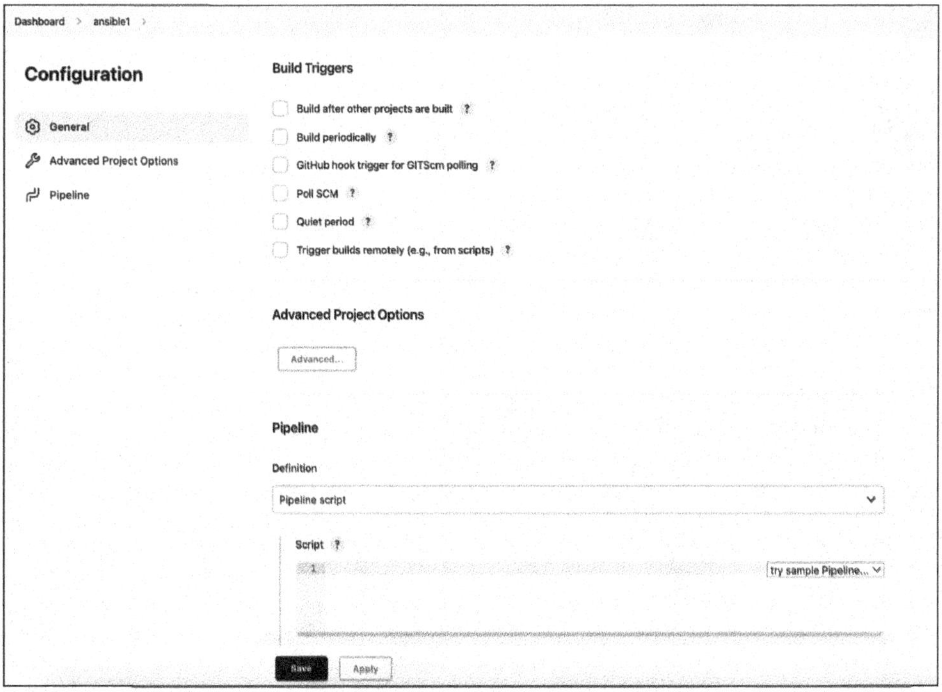

Figure 3-9 *Pipeline Configuration Page*

Let's review the pipeline logic and the syntax before the actual configuration of the pipeline in the **Script** text box:

■ As per this use case, the pipeline will execute a series of automated steps in three stages on a testing environment to validate the Ansible code.

■ The three stages in the pipeline are named Build, Test, and Clean up.

■ During the Build stage, two steps are performed:

   1. A Docker container is launched from a Docker image. This Docker image has been created in advance. More details about creating this Docker image are covered later in this section.

   2. The **git clone** command is executed to copy the Ansible code from the GitHub repository on this newly created container.

■ During the Test stage, unit tests are performed to validate the Ansible code that has been developed by the NetDevOps team member.

■ Lastly, during the Clean up stage, the Docker environment is removed from the test environment.

Figure 3-10 provides an overview of this pipeline with multiple stages.

Pipeline

Stages
Stage–Build
Step: Launch Docker container
Step: Copy Ansible code in container (git clone)
Stage–Test
Step: Run unit tests
Stage–Cleanup
Step: Remove docker container

Figure 3-10 *Jenkins Pipeline with Build, Test, and Clean up Stages*

Now that you understand the logic of the pipeline, let's go back to the **Script** text box on the **Configuration** page to define the declarative pipeline.

Example 3-10 captures the contents of declarative language syntax for the pipeline that needs to be entered in the **Script** text box (as shown in Figure 3-9).

Example 3-10   *Declarative Pipeline*

```
pipeline {
    agent any
    stages {
        stage('Build') {
            steps {
                echo 'Build stage'
                sh "docker run -dit --name ansible_git netdevops/ansible_git_v1"
                sh 'docker exec -i ansible_git /bin/sh -c "git clone https://github.
com/netdevops-1/dc-automation.git"'
            }
        }
        stage('Test') {
            steps {
                echo 'Test stage'
                sh 'docker exec -i ansible_git /bin/sh -c "ansible-playbook dc-auto-
mation/vlan.yml -i dc-automation/hosts --syntax-check"'
                sh 'docker exec -i ansible_git /bin/sh -c "ansible-playbook dc-auto-
mation/vlan.yml -i dc-automation/hosts --check"'
            }
        }
        stage('Clean up') {
            steps {
                echo 'Clean up stage'
                sh "docker rm ansible_git -f"
            }
        }
    }
}
```

Once the information in Example 3-10 has been entered in the Script text box, click **Save** to save this project. Leave the default setting of **Use Groovy Sandbox**, which allows any user to run the script without need of administrator privileges.

Note   The GitHub repository shown in the examples of this chapter will no longer exist by the time you read this book. You need to create your own repository and follow the steps through this chapter. This enables you to learn NetDevOps by working with it.

Now we are ready to run the pipeline. In this case, we will trigger and run the pipeline manually. However, before manually triggering it, let's review the details of declarative pipeline syntax and also prepare a Docker image that will be used for the execution of this pipeline.

Details of the Declarative Pipeline Syntax

The details of declarative syntax for the steps and stages executed in this declarative pipeline in Example 3-10 are explained in this section.

The syntax **agent any** indicates that the pipeline can run on any agent. In this setup, a standalone Jenkins server is used, so the execution of the job will be done on the same server.

The Build stage block starts with **stage('Build')** and has two **sh** steps. These **sh** commands invoke the default shell and execute the following commands on the Jenkins server:

■ The **docker run** shell command creates a docker container named ansible_git from the docker image netdevops/ansible_git_v1.

■ The **docker exec** shell command executes the **git clone** command within the newly created container named ansible_git. This **git** command copies the dc-automation repository from GitHub.

Note   This repository was created by a NetDevOps engineer with user ID "netdevops-1" (refer to Chapter 1). The procedure for creating a Docker image is covered in the "Steps to Create the Docker Image" section in this chapter.

During the Test stage, as captured by **stage('Test')**, two unit -tests on the Ansible playbook are performed by executing the following shell (**sh**) steps:

■ The syntax of the Ansible playbook is checked by issuing the first **sh** command with the **–syntax-check** flag.

■ A dry run of the Ansible playbook is performed by issuing the second **sh** command with the **–check** flag.

During the Clean up stage, as captured by **stage('Clean up')**, this newly created Docker container in the Build stage is removed. The **docker rm** command with the **force** (**-f**) option is executed on the shell to remove this running container.

Let's now look at the steps to create a Docker image for this use case.

Steps to Create the Docker Image

The prerequisite for creating the Docker container is that the Docker daemon must be installed on this Jenkins server running the AWS Linux 2 image. Initiate an SSH connection to the Jenkins instance and then install Docker by running the following **yum** command:

```
$ sudo yum install docker
```

After successful installation of Docker, it can be enabled to start on system boot, and then you can run it with **systemctl start**, as shown in the following commands:

```
$ sudo systemctl enable docker.service
$ sudo systemctl start docker.service
#OUTPUT OMITTED#
```

All users who need permission to run Docker commands must be added to the "docker" group on this Linux instance. Both "ec2-user" and "jenkins" users are added to this group by issuing the following commands:

```
$ sudo usermod -aG docker ec2-user
$ sudo usermod -aG docker jenkins
```

You can log out of the SSH session and then initiate a new SSH session to the Jenkins server for new group assignments to take effect. An alternate option is to use the command **sudo su** ec2-user.

The Docker version can be confirmed by issuing the following command:

```
$ docker -v
Docker version 20.10.17, build 100c701
$
```

Now a Docker image can be created on this Jenkins server. To build a Docker image, you create a Dockerfile on this server. The contents of this Dockerfile are shown as per execution of the **more** command in Example 3-11. The contents of this Dockerfile have the following instructions:

- As per the **FROM** instruction of this Dockerfile, the base image of Alpine is used for this Docker container. Alpine is a lightweight Linux distribution that is commonly used as the base image for Docker containers. It has a small footprint, which makes it well-suited for use in containers where disk space and memory are limited.

- Three **RUN** commands are executed on this base image. These **RUN** commands install Ansible, git, and the Cisco NXOS Ansible module collection, along with the prerequisite software packages/libraries.

- In addition, the Dockerfile also sets an environmental variable (as per the **ENV** command) to disable SSH host key checking. This setting is required for Ansible to ignore host key checking by the underlying tools Ansible uses to connect to the Nexus switches.

Example 3-11   *Dockerfile Content*

```
$ more Dockerfile
FROM alpine:3.11
RUN apk add ansible gcc python3-dev libc-dev libffi-dev openssl-dev py3-pip git
  libssh-dev
RUN pip3 install --upgrade paramiko ansible-pylibssh
RUN ansible-galaxy collection install cisco.nxos
ENV ANSIBLE_HOST_KEY_CHECKING=False
$
```

Next, the **docker build** command is used to create the Docker image from the Dockerfile. Partial snippets of the execution of this command are shown in Example 3-12. The "." at the end of the **docker build** command specifies the current directory as the build context. This command builds a Docker image and installs the Ansible and git packages, as per the instructions in the Dockerfile. Further, the **-t** option tags the resulting Docker image with the name "netdevops/ansible_git_v1."

Example 3-12   *Docker Image Creation*

```
$ docker build -t netdevops/ansible_git_v1 .
Sending build context to Docker daemon  3.072kB
Step 1/5 : FROM alpine:3.11
3.11: Pulling from library/alpine
79e9f2f55bf5: Pull complete
Digest: sha256:bcae378eacedab83da66079d9366c8f5df542d7ed9ab23bf487e3e1a8481375d
Status: Downloaded newer image for alpine:3.11
 ---> a787cb986503
Step 2/5 : RUN apk add ansible gcc python3-dev libc-dev libffi-dev openssl-dev py3-
  pip git libssh-dev
 ---> Running in 5e2d6fa40841
fetch http://dl-cdn.alpinelinux.org/alpine/v3.11/main/x86_64/APKINDEX.tar.gz
fetch http://dl-cdn.alpinelinux.org/alpine/v3.11/community/x86_64/APKINDEX.tar.gz
(1/52) Installing libbz2 (1.0.8-r1)

#output omitted#

(52/52) Installing python3-dev (3.8.10-r0)
Executing busybox-1.31.1-r11.trigger
Executing ca-certificates-20191127-r2.trigger
OK: 383 MiB in 65 packages
Removing intermediate container 5e2d6fa40841
 ---> 1b9ecf95a615
```

```
Step 3/5 : RUN pip3 install --upgrade paramiko ansible-pylibssh
 ---> Running in a7e9359b5490
Collecting paramiko
  Downloading paramiko-2.11.0-py2.py3-none-any.whl (212 kB)
Collecting ansible-pylibssh
#output omitted#
Successfully installed ansible-pylibssh-1.0.0 paramiko-2.11.0
Removing intermediate container a7e9359b5490
 ---> 6fc044ad4ffa
Step 4/5 : RUN ansible-galaxy collection install cisco.nxos
 ---> Running in 5105698f8137
Process install dependency map
Starting collection install process
Installing 'cisco.nxos:3.1.1' to '/root/.ansible/collections/ansible_collections/
  cisco/nxos'
Installing 'ansible.netcommon:3.1.1' to '/root/.ansible/collections/ansible_collec-
  tions/ansible/netcommon'
Installing 'ansible.utils:2.6.1' to '/root/.ansible/collections/ansible_collections/
  ansible/utils'
Removing intermediate container 5105698f8137
 ---> d4789084252d
Step 5/5 : ENV ANSIBLE_HOST_KEY_CHECKING=False
 ---> Running in 23403959f221
Removing intermediate container 23403959f221
 ---> c3ddd8417709
Successfully built c3ddd8417709
Successfully tagged netdevops/ansible_git_v1:latest
$
```

The **docker images** command in Example 3-13 displays information about images currently available on this host. It provides information such as repository and image name, tag, and image ID. In this case, the output of this command confirms the availability of the newly created image, along with the Alpine image downloaded from the Docker hub (that is, the default Docker repository).

Example 3-13 *Verifying Docker Images*

```
$ docker images
REPOSITORY                TAG       IMAGE ID       CREATED          SIZE
netdevops/ansible_git_v1  latest    c3ddd8417709   16 seconds ago   380MB
alpine                    3.11      a787cb986503   10 months ago    5.62MB
$
```

This Docker image is now ready and can be used for the execution of the declarative and scripted pipelines in this chapter.

Building the Declarative Pipeline

In Jenkins, a build is one run of a project (in other words, each execution of a project is considered a build). As mentioned earlier, the execution of a project is also referred to as a job. In this use case, the build for this project/pipeline will be initiated manually. This manual build is performed using the following steps:

Step 1.   After you save the pipeline, the **Status** page shows up. From the left navigation pane, click **Build Now** to start this build. Figure 3-11 shows the navigation pane.

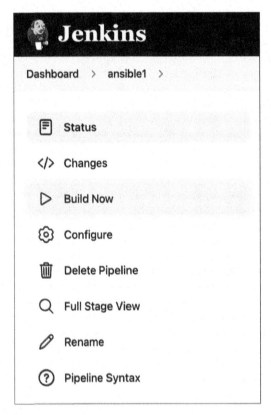

Figure 3-11   *Starting Build Now for the Declarative Pipeline*

Once you select **Build Now**, the **Status** page shows the execution of each stage.

Figure 3-12 shows the Stage view from the Jenkins UI after successful execution of the build for the declarative pipeline ansible1. Note the following in this figure:

■ Three stages (Build, Test, and Clean up) are executed in this pipeline.

■ The duration for each of these three stages for Job #16 is also shown.

- The number 16 means that this pipeline has been executed 15 times previously by the administrator. Upon execution of each job, this number increments.

- The logs for each stage can be viewed by clicking the appropriate icon.

Figure 3-12 *Build Execution of Declarative Pipeline*

Step 2.   Additional details of all the stages and steps can be viewed by looking at the "console output" of the job. To view this output, either click the job number (#16 in Figure 3-12 under Stage view) or expand the **Build History** from the left navigation pane and click the job number. On the next page, click **Console Output** from the navigation pane on the left side. Example 3-14 shows the successful execution for job number 16.

Example 3-14 *Console Output on Jenkins*

```
Started by user admin
[Pipeline] Start of Pipeline
[Pipeline] node
Running on Jenkins in /var/lib/jenkins/workspace/ansible1
[Pipeline] {
[Pipeline] stage
[Pipeline] { (Build)
[Pipeline] echo
Build stage
[Pipeline] sh
+ docker run -dit --name ansible_git netdevops/ansible_git_v1
d7558f51e714cc733b0a12edeff36c859218c31105b437abff9fde321653d2d2
```

```
[Pipeline] sh
+ docker exec -i ansible_git /bin/sh -c 'git clone https://github.com/netdevops-1/
  dc-automation.git'
Cloning into 'dc-automation'...
[Pipeline] }
[Pipeline] // stage
[Pipeline] stage
[Pipeline] { (Test)
[Pipeline] echo
Test stage
[Pipeline] sh
+ docker exec -i ansible_git /bin/sh -c 'ansible-playbook dc-automation/vlan.yml -i
  dc-automation/hosts --syntax-check'
playbook: dc-automation/vlan.yml
[Pipeline] sh
+ docker exec -i ansible_git /bin/sh -c 'ansible-playbook dc-automation/vlan.yml -i
  dc-automation/hosts --check'
PLAY [create new VLANs] ********************************************************
TASK [Gathering Facts] ********************************************************
ok: [sandbox-nxos-1.cisco.com]
ok: [131.226.217.151]
TASK [provision VLAN] ********************************************************
ok: [131.226.217.151] => (item=101)
ok: [sandbox-nxos-1.cisco.com] => (item=101)
ok: [131.226.217.151] => (item=102)
ok: [sandbox-nxos-1.cisco.com] => (item=102)
PLAY RECAP ********************************************************
131.226.217.151            : ok=2    changed=0    unreachable=0    failed=0
  skipped=0    rescued=0    ignored=0
sandbox-nxos-1.cisco.com   : ok=2    changed=0    unreachable=0    failed=0
  skipped=0    rescued=0    ignored=0
[Pipeline] }
[Pipeline] // stage
[Pipeline] stage
[Pipeline] { (Clean up)
[Pipeline] echo
Clean up stage
[Pipeline] sh
+ docker rm ansible_git -f
ansible_git
[Pipeline] }
[Pipeline] // stage
[Pipeline] }
[Pipeline] // node
[Pipeline] End of Pipeline
Finished: SUCCESS
```

The previous use case provides the details for creating a declarative pipeline using declarative syntax in Jenkins.

Scripted Pipelines

Scripted pipelines use the Groovy language, which provides more flexibility and functionality. Groovy is an object-oriented programming language. The syntaxes of Java and Groovy are quite similar to each other. Being a scripted language, Groovy also requires a learning curve and hence can result in some complexity for administrators or NetDevOps team members involved in creating and maintaining pipelines.

Here are some details about using Groovy for scripted pipelines:

- Just like in a declarative pipeline, the agents, stages, and shell commands using **sh**, **post**, and so on are defined in the scripted pipeline.

- The Groovy scripted syntax provides the option to use **if/else** conditional statements. This allows administrators to have more control and more easily define the conditional logic for the execution of the pipelines. For example, **if** and **else** conditions can be used to easily define the execution logic for a certain type of branch name.

- Error and exception handling can also be defined via Groovy exception handling support. The syntax supports the use of **try**, **catch**, and **throw** for handling exceptions and errors.

Let's look at the following use case to understand the scripted pipeline using Groovy syntax.

Use Case: Scripted Pipeline to Validate Ansible Playbook

We will now look at the same use case covered previously in the "Use Case: Declarative Pipeline to Validate Ansible Playbook" section to develop a scripted pipeline using Groovy syntax.

The goal, requirements, and steps that need to be executed for this scripted pipeline are exactly the same as for the declarative pipeline. In this use case, scripted language syntax will be used to achieve those steps instead of the declarative language syntax.

This time, a new **Pipeline** project named "ansible1_script" within the Jenkins UI will be created using the same steps. The only difference is that in this project, on the **Configuration** web page under **Pipeline > Definition > Script**, scripted syntax will be used for the pipeline, as shown in Example 3-15.

Example 3-15 *Scripted Pipeline*

```
node {
stage('Build') {
    echo 'Build stage'
    sh "docker run -dit --name ansible_git netdevops/ansible_git_v1"
    sh 'docker exec -i ansible_git /bin/sh -c "git clone https://github.com/netde-
    vops-1/dc-automation.git"'
}
stage('Test') {
    echo 'Test stage'
    sh 'docker exec -i ansible_git /bin/sh -c "ansible-playbook dc-automation/vlan.
    yml -i dc-automation/hosts --syntax-check"'
    sh 'docker exec -i ansible_git /bin/sh -c "ansible-playbook dc-automation/vlan.
    yml -i dc-automation/hosts --check"'
}
stage('Clean up') {
    echo 'Clean up stage'
    sh "docker rm ansible_git -f"
}
}
```

The scripted pipeline syntax starts with the **node** block, which refers to the actual machine (agent) where the pipeline will be executed. Since this is a nondistributed setup, no label is provided for the node. The **node** block for this single-node setup could also be configured as **node('built-in')**, where the *built-in* label refers to the controller node. You can see the node information on the Jenkins UI by navigating to **Dashboard > Manage Jenkins > Manage Nodes and Clouds.**

Like in the declarative pipeline, the **stage** block is used to conceptually define one or more groups. The tasks are executed in these groups. In this use case, Build, Test, and Clean up stages are defined by using **stage('Build')**, **stage('Test')**, and **stage('Clean up')** syntax, respectively.

Within each of the stage blocks, one or more tasks are executed. The stages and their actual steps (**echo** and **sh** commands) have already been explained in the previous use case. For reference, the steps are as follows:

- **echo** displays the text message during the execution of the job.

- **sh** executes the respective shell commands defined in the pipeline.

Similarly, the creation of the Docker image was also explained in the previous use case.

Like in the declarative pipeline, this project is also triggered manually by clicking **Build Now** (under **Dashboard > ansible_script**).

Refer to Figure 3-13 to see the "build history" when this job is run manually from the Jenkins UI. The figure shows the successful execution of job #2 for the Build, Test, and

Clean up stages, respectively. As expected, the result of Build for this scripted pipeline is very similar to the declarative pipeline.

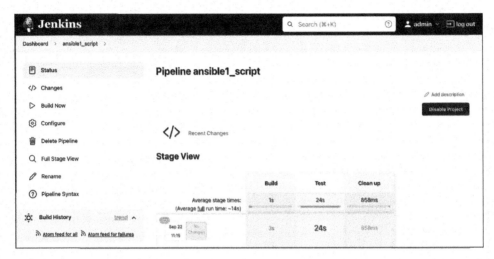

Figure 3-13 *Jenkins Build for Scripted Pipeline*

Furthermore, on the Jenkins UI, you can select **Console Output** to see additional details of all the stages and steps executed in this job. Example 3-16 shows this console output for this job.

Example 3-16 *Console Output on Jenkins*

```
Started by user admin
[Pipeline] Start of Pipeline
[Pipeline] node
Running on Jenkins in /var/lib/jenkins/workspace/ansible1_script
[Pipeline] {
[Pipeline] stage
[Pipeline] { (Build)
[Pipeline] echo
Build stage
[Pipeline] sh
+ docker run -dit --name ansible_git netdevops/ansible_git_v1
4603632fc8e9ab00dd2cfd8ccbf3d5a46c01744f7b1cd3cb2960b1ec6353aad5
[Pipeline] sh
+ docker exec -i ansible_git /bin/sh -c 'git clone https://github.com/netdevops-1/
  dc-automation.git'
Cloning into 'dc-automation'...
[Pipeline] }
[Pipeline] // stage
[Pipeline] stage
```

```
[Pipeline] { (Test)
[Pipeline] echo
Test stage
[Pipeline] sh
+ docker exec -i ansible_git /bin/sh -c 'ansible-playbook dc-automation/vlan.yml -i
  dc-automation/hosts --syntax-check'

playbook: dc-automation/vlan.yml
[Pipeline] sh
+ docker exec -i ansible_git /bin/sh -c 'ansible-playbook dc-automation/vlan.yml -i
  dc-automation/hosts --check'

PLAY [create new VLANs] *******************************************************

TASK [Gathering Facts] ********************************************************

ok: [131.226.217.151]
ok: [sandbox-nxos-1.cisco.com]

TASK [provision VLAN] *********************************************************
ok: [sandbox-nxos-1.cisco.com] => (item=101)
ok: [131.226.217.151] => (item=101)
ok: [sandbox-nxos-1.cisco.com] => (item=102)
ok: [131.226.217.151] => (item=102)

PLAY RECAP ********************************************************************
131.226.217.151            : ok=2    changed=0    unreachable=0    failed=0
  skipped=0    rescued=0    ignored=0
sandbox-nxos-1.cisco.com   : ok=2    changed=0    unreachable=0    failed=0
  skipped=0    rescued=0    ignored=0

[Pipeline] }
[Pipeline] // stage
[Pipeline] stage
[Pipeline] { (Clean up)
[Pipeline] echo
Clean up stage
[Pipeline] sh
+ docker rm ansible_git -f
ansible_git
[Pipeline] }
[Pipeline] // stage
[Pipeline] }
[Pipeline] // node
[Pipeline] End of Pipeline
Finished: SUCCESS
```

This use case covered the details for the scripted pipeline in Jenkins, and it shows the Groovy syntax in comparison to the declarative syntax used earlier.

Triggers

As covered in the previous use cases, the build for the pipeline is performed manually. However, it is reasonable to expect that NetDevOps teams will desire to start a build as soon as there are changes to the actual code. This is a core point of continuous integration/continuous delivery/deployment, and the benefits of this approach are obvious, as covered in detail in Chapter 1. To achieve this goal, you use a mechanism named triggers in Jenkins. If, for example, a pipeline is integrated with a VCS, you can trigger (or initiate) a build in Jenkins when a NetDevOps team member commits the code in the repository on the VCS.

Here are some of the trigger options configurable in Jenkins:

- Build after other projects are built
- Build periodically
- Poll SCM
- Trigger builds remotely (for example, from scripts)
- GitHub hook trigger for GITScm polling

As shown previously in Figure 3-9, these options are available on the **Configuration** page under the **Build Triggers** section.

Let's look at these options in detail in the following sections.

Build After Other Projects Are Built

This option allows project execution to be started after the build of another project is completed. You can think of other projects that are being watched as the "source projects," while the project where this trigger is enabled is basically the "destination project."

Multiple source projects (that is, projects being watched) can be selected as part of this trigger setting to initiate the build of the destination project.

Jenkins provides further flexibility to NetDevOps team members to check the status of the build of the source project and to act on the destination project, as per their needs. There may be use cases where the build of the destination project must only be done if the build of the source project didn't have any errors. Or there might be use cases where the build trigger of the destination project must be done even if the build of the source project failed.

There are multiple configurable options within the Jenkins UI that allow for the configuration of these settings. These options are configured on the destination project and include the following:

- **Trigger only if the build is stable:** This means to trigger the build on the destination project if the build was successful on the source project and no errors were reported.

- **Trigger even if the build is unstable:** This means to trigger the build on the destination project if the build was successful on the source project, even though some of the publishers, such as Testing framework, may have reported failed tests.

- **Trigger even if the build fails:** This means to trigger the build on the destination project even if the build on the source project had a fatal error.

- **Always trigger, even if the build is aborted:** This means to trigger the build on the destination project if the build on the source project had timed out or an administrator stopped it manually.

Build Periodically

This option allows you to configure cron-like functionality to schedule build jobs periodically. Cron is a job scheduler utility available in Linux and Unix operating systems. As mentioned earlier, NetDevOps teams naturally prefer to execute a pipeline when there are changes to the code. However, there are valid use cases for periodic execution. For example, a periodic build may be used when there are limited resources to test the pipeline, so this option may be used to trigger the build of a pipeline at a specific time. Build Periodically may be used to trigger a pipeline that retrieves configurations of network devices and then compares those with a baseline configuration for audit and compliance purposes. It may be used to trigger a pipeline that collects performance data (latency, delay, packet loss, and so on) directly from the network devices or by using tools that collect performance data from the network.

If this option is selected on the **Configuration** page of a pipeline in the Jenkins UI, then a "schedule" to trigger periodic builds must be added. The syntax of the cron schedule in Jenkins is as follows:

```
MINUTE HOUR DOM MONTH DOW
```

The following list details the different parts of the syntax:

- **MINUTE** is the minute in the hour and is configured as a number in the range of 0–59.

- **HOUR** is the hour of the day and is configured as a number in the range of 0–23.

- **DOM** is the day of the month and is configured as a number in the range of 1–31.

- **MONTH** is the month of the year and is configured as a number in the range of 1–12.

- **DOW** is the day of the week and is configured as a number in the range of 0–7. Both 0 and 7 are considered Sunday.

- Finally, an asterisk (*) indicates all valid values for a field.

For example, the following syntax will trigger a build every 20 minutes:

```
H/20 * * * *
```

Poll SCM

As mentioned earlier in this chapter, SCM stands for source code management. Git and CVS are examples of SCM systems. When Jenkins is configured with the **Poll SCM** setting, it polls the SCM at the specified intervals. If any updates are made to the SCM since the previous build, Jenkins initiates a new build for the project.

Like the **Build Periodically** setting, Jenkins is configured with a schedule for the polling period. The **Schedule** field uses the same syntax explained in the "Build Periodically" section.

As mentioned earlier, use of a push mechanism from the SCM is considered an optimal and better mechanism to detect updates on SCM to trigger builds on Jenkins. This push mechanism is explained in the following section.

Trigger Builds Remotely

Jenkins enables the triggering of a project build by allowing administrators to configure a special URL for the project. As part of this URL, an authentication token is also configured. This authentication token can be a text string that becomes part of the URL.

As the name of this trigger option indicates, once this URL is accessed via a web browser, script, or other mechanisms, the build of the project is triggered on Jenkins.

The URL syntax is as follows:

```
https://{IP_address_of_Jenkins}:8080 /job/ansible1_script/
build?token=TOKEN_NAME
```

The **TOKEN_NAME** in the URL is the predefined token that has been configured if this option is enabled for a project on the Jenkins server.

GitHub Hook Trigger for GITScm Polling

The **Build Periodically** and **Poll SCM** settings covered previously provide the ability to trigger a project build manually or at a prescheduled time. Triggering a project build based on events in GitHub can be done with this setting. This capability is provided by the GitHub plugin, and it is one of the plugins automatically installed on Jenkins as part of "suggested plugins."

Various events in GitHub can trigger a build in Jenkins. These events in GitHub include a commit to repository on GitHub, the creation or deletion of a branch or tag, the addition of comments on a commit, the deletion of a repository, and more.

For this mechanism, GitHub needs to be configured to send an HTTP POST message to the Jenkins server. Such an HTTP POST is called a webhook. If the GitHub SaaS service is used, this means that the Jenkins server must be accessible on the public Internet, so the webhook (that is, the HTTP POST message) from GitHub SaaS can reach the Jenkins server. In this sort of deployment model, the Jenkins server is expected to be protected and secured by blocking traffic from the Internet from reaching it. Use of a whitelist is one solution in this case (that is, allowing traffic from only specific IP addresses). This option is used in this chapter, and it allows access to the Jenkins server from a specific range of GitHub IP addresses. Another strategy is to use webhook relay or forwarder mechanism. A webhook relay acts as an intermediary device between an SCM (such as GitHub) and the Jenkins server. If there are still constraints, technical or otherwise, that prevent such connectivity from GitHub to the Jenkins server, then one of the previously mentioned poll mechanisms can be used to trigger a project build.

The following use cases go into detail about GitHub webhook integration. As explained earlier, the Jenkins server used in these use cases is installed on a public cloud infrastructure, as an AWS EC2 instance, and there is network connectivity from GitHub to Jenkins. Also, the security rules within AWS security groups associated with the AWS EC2 instance must allow traffic (HTTP ingress messages) from GitHub. The list of GitHub IP addresses can be retrieved from the GitHub meta API. At this time of writing, this list is available at https://api.github.com/meta.

Use Case: GitHub Webhook and Jenkins

Let's go through a use case to extend the existing "ansible_script" project on Jenkins for webhook integration to GitHub. As you'll recall, this project/job was created earlier in the Jenkin UI in the "Scripted Pipeline" section of this chapter. It uses locally defined scripted language syntax for the pipeline. In this use case, the build for this project will be triggered when a commit or update is done on the GitHub repository.

Figure 3-14 provides a high-level flow diagram for the operations on Jenkins and webhook from GitHub.

Here are the steps in the flow diagram shown in Figure 3-14:

Step 1. A commit to the GitHub repository is performed by a NetDevOps engineer. For example, the NetDevOps engineer makes changes to the Ansible playbook (vlan.yml file) and then pushes the changes to the GitHub repository.

Step 2. As per the GitHub configuration, a webhook (HTTP POST) is sent from GitHub to the Jenkins controller.

Step 3. This webhook message triggers the execution of the project in Jenkins. This project has a pipeline script configured locally on the Jenkins server UI.

Step 4.   Jenkins polls the GitHub repository and checks if there is an update to the repository since the last build. Assuming there is a change, Jenkins proceeds to Step 5.

Step 5.   The Jenkins server executes the stages and steps as defined on the pipeline.

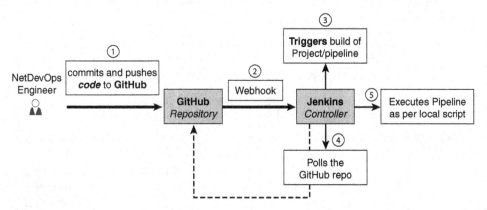

Figure 3-14   *Flow Diagram of Jenkins and Webhook from GitHub*

We will use the GitHub repository https://github.com/netdevops-1/dc-automation.git from the previous sections of this chapter and in Chapter 1.

> **Note**   You can follow the procedure documented in this section to test the webhook integration by creating your own GitHub repository. The git software package needs to be installed on the Jenkins server as well. The installation of git is performed with the following command by accessing the Jenkins server using SSH:
>
> ```
> $ sudo yum install git -y
> ```

After successful installation of git, the following configurations need to be performed on Jenkins UI and on GitHub to trigger a build in Jenkins—when a commit to a repository is done on GitHub and for GitHub to send a webhook to Jenkins:

Step 1.   On GitHub, enable a webhook on the git repository and add the Jenkins server as recipient for the webhook. Also, verify the existing personal access token (PAT) or create a new one.

Step 2.   On Jenkins, add the GitHub server with appropriate credentials (GitHub username and respective PAT).

Step 3.   On Jenkins, update the configuration of the existing "ansible_script" project to trigger a build upon receiving the webhook.

Step 1   GitHub: Webhook and PAT

On GitHub, the following configurations are required to send webhook notifications when a commit is done on the repository:

Step 1.1.   Navigate to **GitHub** repository on a web browser. In this use case, the repository https://github.com/netdevops-1/dc-automation is being used. You can navigate to the appropriate GitHub repository you have created.

Step 1.2.   Select **Settings** on that repository page. Next, under the **General** navigation pane, on the left side of this page, scroll down and click **Webhooks**.

Step 1.3.   On the right side of the web page, click **Add webhook**. Under **Payload URL**, enter **http://{ip address of jenkins}:8080/github-webhook/**. This is the default URL in Jenkins for accepting HTTP POST. In this setup, the URL http://44.208.200.59:8080/github-webhook/ is configured and points to the Jenkins server's public IP address. Other settings are left at the default value. Next, click **Add webhook** to enable the webhook for this repository.

Note   The default setting for **Which events would you like to trigger this webhook?** of **Just the push event** means that whenever code is pushed to this repository, GitHub will send a webhook to the previously specified payload URL (for example, a NetDevOps team member issuing a **git push**).

Step 1.4.   The Jenkins server also requires access to the GitHub repository. For this purpose, a new PAT can be created by navigating to **Settings** under the User drop-down menu (upper-right corner) on any GitHub page. The GitHub profile **Settings** can also be accessed directly from https://github.com/settings/profile.

Step 1.5.   On the **Settings** page, scroll down and click **Developer settings** in the left pane. Then click **Personal access tokens**, select **Tokens (classic)**, and then select **generate new token (classic)**. On the next page, you can add a note to reflect the purpose of this PAT, such as "Integration to Jenkins." Leave the default expiration of 30 days. However, make sure to select the scopes of **repo, admin:repo_hook**, and **admin:org_hook** on this page. Then click **Generate token** and copy the token that's generated.

This token will be required during the configuration of Jenkins in the next step.

Step 2   Jenkins: GitHub Server and Its Credentials

In Jenkins, the following configurations must be performed to add the GitHub server with the appropriate PAT credentials created in "Step 1   GitHub: Webhook and PAT" so that the Jenkins server can access the GitHub repository.

Step 2.1.   After logging on to Jenkins, navigate to **Dashboard > Manage Jenkins > Configure System** (under **System Configuration** section).

Step 2.2.   Scroll down to the **GitHub** section and click **Add GitHub Server.**

Step 2.3.   In the **Name** text box, use the name **github_saas** (note: this can be any name you like).

Step 2.4.   Leave the default setting of API URL to use the API of public GitHub.

Step 2.5.   Under **Credentials**, click the **+** (Add) button and then click **Jenkins** to add the username and the respective PAT for GitHub. Note that the username, ID, and PAT are created in https://www.github.com. For this use case, the username and ID of "netdevops-1" and its respective PAT are entered. If you are replicating this setup, you must use your own username, ID, and PAT, as appropriate for your setup. On the **Add Credentials** page, the following settings are used:

- Domain = **Global credentials (unrestricted).**

- Kind = **Secret text.**

- Scope = **Global (Jenkins, nodes, items, all child items, etc.).**

- Secret = *enter personal access token* (that is, copy and paste the PAT generated from GitHub.com).

- ID = **netdevops-1.**

- Description = **netdevops-1.**

- Click **Add.**

- Make sure to select this newly created account from the **Credentials** drop-down menu.

Step 2.6.   Click **Test Connection** to verify that GitHub account credentials (using PAT) are correctly entered.

Step 2.7.   Select the **Manage hooks** checkbox.

Step 2.8.   Click **Save** on the bottom of the page to save the GitHub server settings.

Figure 3-15 shows the final configuration of the GitHub server in Jenkins.

Figure 3-15   *GitHub Server Configuration in Jenkins*

Step 3   Jenkins: Configure Trigger on the Project

In Jenkins, the existing pipeline project must be configured to start a build upon receiving a webhook. Note that you may create a new pipeline or other type of project, such as freestyle project, as well. In this use case, the existing pipeline project is modified as per the following steps:

Step 3.1. After logging on to the Jenkins **Dashboard**, navigate to the existing **ansible1_ script** project by clicking it.

Step 3.2. On the left pane, click **Configure**.

Step 3.3. On the next page, scroll down to the **Build Triggers** section and enable **GitHub hook trigger for GITScm polling** by clicking the checkbox next to it.

Step 3.4. Scroll down further to the **Pipeline** section on this configuration page.

Step 3.5. The existing "script" needs to be changed and two additional settings must be added (the complete script is shown in Example 3-17). The two new settings are as follows:

■ The property to trigger the build of the pipeline is configured with **pipelineTriggers()**. In this case, this property is configured to trigger the build when a **githubPush()** (that is, webhook from GitHub) is received by Jenkins.

■ When Jenkins receives the webhook, the GitHub plugin validates whether the repository defined within the pipeline matches the source repository of the webhook. To succeed in this validation, a git "checkout" is configured in this specific scripted pipeline. Note: when the validation is successful, the GitHub plugin initiates a poll of the GitHub repository. If updates are found on the repository, it triggers a build in Jenkins. This poll activity is performed using the Git plugin. Furthermore, in **checkout**, the parameter **credentialsId** instructs Jenkins to use the credentials of **netde-vops-1** for authentication to GitHub. Recall that these credentials, which use a PAT, were added to Jenkins in "Step 2   Jenkins: GitHub Server and Its Credentials."

Step 3.6. In the **Script** text box, the complete script now includes all the text shown in Example 3-17. Note that besides the **pipelineTriggers** and git **checkout**, the rest of the script is the same as that covered earlier in the "Pipeline" section of this chapter.

Example 3-17 *Pipeline Script*

```
properties([pipelineTriggers([githubPush()])])
node {
checkout([$class: 'GitSCM', branches: [[name: '*/master']], extensions: [], userRe-
    moteConfigs: [[credentialsId: 'netdevops-1', url: 'https://github.com/netdevops-1/
    dc-automation.git/']]])
stage('Build') {
    echo 'Build stage'
    sh "docker run -dit -name ansible_git netdevops/ansible_git_v1"
    sh 'docker exec -I ansible_git /bin/sh -c""git clone https://github.com/netde-
vops-1/dc-automation.gi"''
}
stage''Tes'') {
    echo''Test stag''
    sh''docker exec -i ansible_git /bin/sh -c""ansible-playbook dc-automation/vlan.
yml -i dc-automation/hosts--syntax-chec"''
    sh''docker exec -i ansible_git /bin/sh -c""ansible-playbook dc-automation/vlan.
yml -i dc-automation/hosts--chec"''
}
stage''Clean u'') {
    echo''Clean up stag''
    sh""docker rm ansible_git -f"
}
}
```

Step 3.7. After you complete the updates, as per Example 3-17, in the "Script" text box, click **Save** at the bottom of the **Configuration** page to update this project.

A manual build of the pipeline on the Jenkins server needs to be performed once. This is required so that the GitHub webhook trigger is registered by Jenkins. This manual build is accomplished with the following steps:

- After logging on to Jenkins, navigate to the existing **ansible1_script** project from the **Dashboard**.

- Click **Build Now** on the left pane. After completion of the build, make sure that the build is successful.

Now let's test that the webhook trigger in Jenkins works properly. To validate it, some updates to the GitHub repository need to be done. These updates can be done as per the following steps:

- First, a "git push" is performed by a NetDevOps team member, after making some changes to the Ansible playbook vlan.yml. The GitHub ID of this team member is netdevops-1, and the steps shown in Example 3-18 are executed on the development environment of this NetDevOps team member.

Example 3-18 *Updates to GitHub Repository*

```
$ git remote -v
origin https://github.com/netdevops-1/dc-automation.git (fetch)
origin https://github.com/netdevops-1/dc-automation.git (push)


$
$ git status
On branch master
Your branch is up to date with 'origin/master'.
Changes not staged for commit:
  (use "git add <file>..." to update what will be committed)
  (use "git restore <file>..." to discard changes in working directory)
  modified:   vlan.yml
no changes added to commit (use "git add" and/or "git commit -a")
$
$ git add vlan.yml
$
$ git commit -m "github webhook test"
[master 217988b] github webhook test
 1 file changed, 1 insertion(+), 1 deletion(-)


$
```

```
$ git push --set-upstream origin master
Enumerating objects: 5, done.
Counting objects: 100% (5/5), done.
Delta compression using up to 8 threads
Compressing objects: 100% (3/3), done.
Writing objects: 100% (3/3), 289 bytes | 289.00 KiB/s, done.
Total 3 (delta 2), reused 0 (delta 0), pack-reused 0
remote: Resolving deltas: 100% (2/2), completed with 2 local objects.
To https://github.com/netdevops-1/dc-automation.git
   9f386a1..217988b  master -> master
Branch 'master' set up to track remote branch 'master' from 'origin'.


$
$
```

- Let's verify that the update on the GitHub repository triggered the build in Jenkins. On the Jenkins server, navigate to **Dashboard** and then click the **ansible1_script** project. On the next page of this project, click the latest build to check whether it was triggered via a webhook.

- The partial output from this build triggered by a webhook is shown in Example 3-19. The very first line of this output, **Started by GitHub push by netdevops-1**, confirms the reason for the build. Further, the git **commit** message (**Commit message: "github webhook test"**) multiple lines down in Example 3-19 confirms the message entered by netdevops-1 for the commit in the previous step.

Example 3-19 *Console Output in Jenkins*

```
Started by GitHub push by netdevops-1
[Pipeline] Start of Pipeline
[Pipeline] properties
[Pipeline] node
Running on Jenkins in /var/lib/jenkins/workspace/ansible1_script
[Pipeline] {
[Pipeline] checkout
The recommended git tool is: NONE
using credential netdevops-1
> git rev-parse --resolve-git-dir /var/lib/jenkins/workspace/ansible1_script/.git #
  timeout=10
Fetching changes from the remote Git repository
 > git config remote.origin.url https://github.com/netdevops-1/dc-automation.git/ #
  timeout=10
Fetching upstream changes from https://github.com/netdevops-1/dc-automation.git/
```

```
> git --version # timeout=10
> git --version # 'git version 2.37.1'
> git fetch --tags --force --progress -- https://github.com/netdevops-1/dc-automa-
  tion.git/ +refs/heads/*:refs/remotes/origin/* # timeout=10
> git rev-parse refs/remotes/origin/master^{commit} # timeout=10
Checking out Revision 217988b088d25a976c8ac3f97ad676950e8e3301 (refs/remotes/origin/
  master)
> git config core.sparsecheckout # timeout=10
> git checkout -f 217988b088d25a976c8ac3f97ad676950e8e3301 # timeout=10
Commit message: "github webhook test"
> git rev-list --no-walk 9f386a1f54dcc8fb42440e301c100b5142e1cb69 # timeout=10
[Pipeline] stage
[Pipeline] { (Build)
[Pipeline] echo
Build stage
[Pipeline] sh
+ docker run -dit --name ansible_git netdevops/ansible_git_v1
ddb6ca766cb5dc64532b255594b1f504f711ce26257f1b824a828777d594f5d6
[Pipeline] sh
+ docker exec -i ansible_git /bin/sh -c 'git clone https://github.com/netdevops-1/
  dc-automation.git'
Cloning into 'dc-automation'...
[Pipeline] }
[Pipeline] // stage
[Pipeline] stage
[Pipeline] { (Test)
[Pipeline] echo
Test stage
[Pipeline] sh
+ docker exec -i ansible_git /bin/sh -c 'ansible-playbook dc-automation/vlan.yml -i
  dc-automation/hosts --syntax-check'
playbook: dc-automation/vlan.yml
[Pipeline] sh
+ docker exec -i ansible_git /bin/sh -c 'ansible-playbook dc-automation/vlan.yml -i
  dc-automation/hosts --check'
PLAY [create new VLANs] ************************************************
TASK [Gathering Facts] ************************************************
ok: [sandbox-nxos-1.cisco.com]
ok: [131.226.217.151]
TASK [provision VLAN] ************************************************
ok: [sandbox-nxos-1.cisco.com] => (item=101)
ok: [131.226.217.151] => (item=101)
ok: [sandbox-nxos-1.cisco.com] => (item=102)
ok: [131.226.217.151] => (item=102)
```

```
PLAY RECAP ***********************************************************************
131.226.217.151            : ok=2     changed=0     unreachable=0     failed=0
  skipped=0     rescued=0     ignored=0
sandbox-nxos-1.cisco.com   : ok=2     changed=0     unreachable=0     failed=0
  skipped=0     rescued=0     ignored=0
[Pipeline] }
[Pipeline] // stage
[Pipeline] stage
[Pipeline] { (Clean up)
[Pipeline] echo
Clean up stage
[Pipeline] sh
+ docker rm ansible_git -f
ansible_git
[Pipeline] }
[Pipeline] // stage
[Pipeline] }
[Pipeline] // node
[Pipeline] End of Pipeline
Finished: SUCCESS
```

The output shown in Example 3-19 validates that a webhook is sent by GitHub when the repository is updated. Also, when this webhook is received by Jenkins, it triggers a build of the project and executes the pipeline.

> **Tip**   On GitHub, you can use view webhook events that are sent to Jenkins. On GitHub, navigate to **Settings** of the git repository. Next, under the **General** navigation pane on the left side of this page, scroll down to click **Webhooks.** Then, on right pane, select the webhook configured in this section. The **Recent Deliveries** tab shows all the requests sent by GitHub.

Use Case: Jenkinsfile in Git and Webhook

Let's go through a use case where, instead of writing and keeping a scripted pipeline in the Jenkins UI, we create a "Jenkinsfile" that's kept in the same GitHub repository along with the rest of the code. The benefits of keeping the Jenkinsfile in GitHub are the same as keeping any other file in GitHub—collaboration, version control, history, and so on. This allows multiple NetDevOps team members to collaborate and maintain a pipeline effectively.

Just like the previous use case, we configure a trigger to build a pipeline upon receiving a webhook from GitHub, and any commit on the GitHub repository triggers the build on this pipeline.

Figure 3-16 provides an overview of the operations for the webhook along with the Jenkinsfile on GitHub.

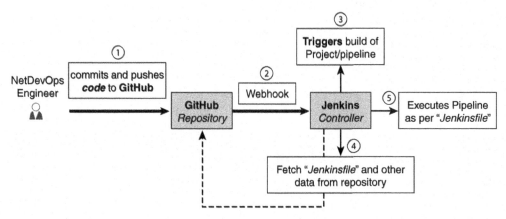

Figure 3-16   *Flow Diagram of Jenkinsfile in GitHub with Webhook*

Here are the steps shown in Figure 3-16:

Step 1.   A commit to GitHub repository is performed.

Step 2.   A webhook (HTTP POST) is sent from GitHub to the Jenkins controller because of this commit.

Step 3.   The webhook triggers execution of a project in Jenkins. This project needs to use the **Pipeline Script from SCM** option under **Configuration > General Pipeline > Definition** for the project. Per this option, the Jenkinsfile is downloaded from the GitHub repository.

Step 4.   Jenkins downloads the Jenkinsfile and the rest of the code from GitHub repository.

Step 5.   Jenkins executes the stages and steps defined in this Jenkinsfile.

The following configuration steps need to be performed on the Jenkins UI and on GitHub to trigger a build in Jenkins and for Jenkins to download the Jenkinsfile from GitHub. As mentioned earlier, the pipeline steps are executed based on the content of this Jenkinsfile:

Step 1.   In Jenkins, add a GitHub server with the appropriate credentials (personal access token). Note: This one-time configuration is performed within the "Global" settings of the Jenkins server. If this configuration was done in the section "Use Case: GitHub Webhook and Jenkins," then it's not required here.

Step 2.   On the GitHub repository, enable a webhook and add the Jenkins server URL to send the webhook.

Step 3.   In Jenkins, new credentials will be created. The credentials are required for authentication to GitHub.

Step 4.   In Jenkins, create a new pipeline project that uses the Jenkinsfile from GitHub (that is, the pipeline script from SCM). A build is triggered when the webhook from GitHub is received.

Step 1   Jenkins: GitHub Server and Its Credentials

Step 1 was already configured in the section "Use Case: GitHub Webhook and Jenkins."

Step 2   GitHub: Webhook

The existing GitHub repository https://github.com/netdevops-1/dc-automation, which has a webhook enabled as per the section "Use Case: GitHub Webhook and Jenkins" is used here, so no further configuration is necessary.

Note   You will need to enable the webhook in your own GitHub repository.

Step 3   Jenkins: Create New Credentials

For this use case, to integrate Jenkins with GitHub and store a Jenkinsfile in GitHub, a new credential (that is, username and password) must be created in Jenkins. The new credential will be used in the project created in "Step 4   Jenkins: Create Project with Pipeline Script from SCM," later in this section.

Step 3.1.   After logging on to the Jenkins UI, navigate to **Dashboard > Manage Jenkins**.

Step 3.2.   Scroll down and click **Manage Credentials** under **Security**. Here, existing credentials will be displayed in the right pane. Click any of the **(global)** instances under the **Domain** column on the right pane. The next page will display all the global credentials that exist on the Jenkins server.

Step 3.3.   On the **Global credentials** page, click **+ Add Credentials** in the left pane to add new credentials using the following settings:

■ Kind = **Username with Password**.

■ Scope = **Global (Jenkins, nodes, items, all child items, etc.)**.

■ Username = **netdevops-1**. In this case "netdevops-1" is used since it's associated with the GitHub repository; however, you need to use the GitHub username associated with your GitHub repository.

■ Password = *enter personal access token* (that is, copy and paste the PAT generated on GitHub.com for this username).

- ID = **netdevops-1-creds.**

- Description = **netdevops-1-creds.**

- Click **Create.**

This will result in the creation of new credentials (username and password). However, the password will still be a PAT, as it is required for authentication to GitHub.

Note   In this step, you will need to create and use the PAT for your username on GitHub.

Step 4   Jenkins: Create Project with Pipeline Script from SCM

For this use case, a new project will be created in Jenkins that will read the Jenkinsfile from GitHub.

In the Jenkins UI, perform the following configuration steps:

Step 4.1.   After logging on to Jenkins, navigate to the existing **ansible1_script** project from the **Dashboard.**

Step 4.2.   On the right pane, select **Disable Project**, and then make sure the message "This project is currently disabled" appears. The reason for disabling this pipeline is that it has a trigger to build a pipeline based on the webhook from the same GitHub repository, and both pipelines are the same. They both try to run a Docker container with the same name, and this will result in an error as the same name cannot be given to two Docker containers.

Step 4.3.   From the Jenkins **Dashboard**, click **New Item.**

Step 4.4.   On the next page, follow these steps:

1. Enter the name **ansible1_script Jenkinsfile** for this project.

2. Select **Pipeline.**

3. Click **OK** at the bottom of the page to save this project.

Step 4.5.   On the next configuration page, scroll down to the **Build Triggers** section and enable **GitHub hook trigger for GITScm polling** by clicking the checkbox next to it.

Step 4.6.   Scroll down further to the **Pipeline** section on this configuration page.

Step 4.7.   From the **Definition** drop-down menu, select **Pipeline from SCM** and then select the following settings:

- SCM = **Git.**

- Repository URL = **https://github.com/netdevops-1/dc-automation.git.**

- Credentials = **netdevops-1/****** (netdevops-1-creds)**.

- Leave other settings at their defaults.

Note   You must use your own GitHub repository URL and credentials in this step.

Step 4.8.   Click **Save** at the bottom of the page to save this project.

Figure 3-17 shows a partial screenshot of the configuration of this pipeline.

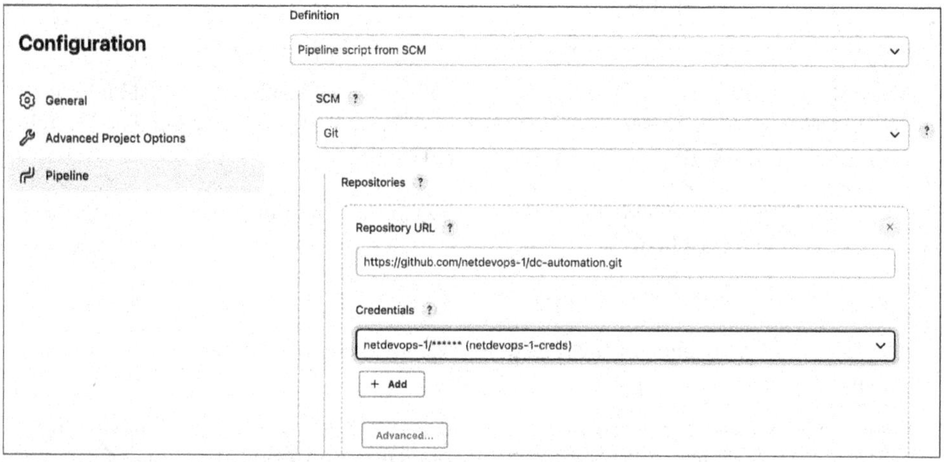

Figure 3-17   *Jenkins Pipeline with Jenkinsfile in GitHub*

Now let's add a file named Jenkinsfile to the GitHub repository https://github.com/net-devops-1/dc-automation. There are multiple ways to add this file, including a git commit/push from the NetDevOps team member, and those details are not shown here.

The content of the Jenkinsfile is shown in Example 3-20.

Example 3-20   *Jenkinsfile*

```
properties([pipelineTriggers([githubPush()])])
node {
checkout([$class: 'GitSCM', branches: [[name: '*/master']], extensions: [], userRe-
  moteConfigs: [[credentialsId: 'netdevops-1', url: 'https://github.com/netdevops-1/
  dc-automation.git/']]])
stage('Build') {
    echo 'Build stage'
    sh "docker run -dit --name ansible_git netdevops/ansible_git_v1"
    sh 'docker exec -i ansible_git /bin/sh -c "git clone https://github.com/netde-
  vops-1/dc-automation.git"'
}
```

```
stage('Test') {
    echo 'Test stage'
    sh 'docker exec -i ansible_git /bin/sh -c "ansible-playbook dc-automation/vlan.
  yml -i dc-automation/hosts --syntax-check"'
    sh 'docker exec -i ansible_git /bin/sh -c "ansible-playbook dc-automation/vlan.
  yml -i dc-automation/hosts --check"'
}
stage('Clean up') {
    echo 'Clean up stage'
    sh "docker rm ansible_git -f"
}
}
```

Once the Jenkinsfile is added to the GitHub repository, we'll trigger a manual build of the pipeline on the Jenkins server by using the following steps. This manual build needs to be done once, so the GitHub webhook is registered by Jenkins.

■ After logging on to Jenkins, navigate to the existing **ansible1_script Jenkinsfile** project from the **Dashboard.**

■ Click **Build Now.** Make sure that the build is successful.

Now let's trigger the build of the project when some updates are performed on the GitHub repository.

Example 3-21 shows the execution of commands by a NetDevOps team member with a GitHub ID of netdevops-1. These commands show that an Ansible playbook named vlan. yml is modified and then this file is pushed to the GitHub repository.

Example 3-21   *Updates to GitHub Repository*

```
$ git add vlan.yml
$
$ git commit -m "Jenkinsfile in GitHub and webhook"
[master 9c7bc9c] Jenkinsfile in GitHub and webhook
 1 file changed, 1 insertion(+), 1 deletion(-)
$ git push
Enumerating objects: 5, done.
Counting objects: 100% (5/5), done.
Delta compression using up to 8 threads
Compressing objects: 100% (3/3), done.
Writing objects: 100% (3/3), 301 bytes | 301.00 KiB/s, done.
Total 3 (delta 2), reused 0 (delta 0), pack-reused 0
remote: Resolving deltas: 100% (2/2), completed with 2 local objects.
To https://github.com/netdevops-1/dc-automation.git
   3070aa0..a69c00b  master -> master
$
$
```

Let's verify that updates on the GitHub repository triggered the build in Jenkins. On the Jenkins server, navigate to **Dashboard** and then click the **ansible1_script Jenkinsfile** project. On the next page of this project, click the latest build to check if it was triggered via a webhook.

Example 3-22 shows a partial console output from this build that is triggered upon receiving a webhook. It is indicated by the very first line "Started by GitHub push by netdevops-1." Furthermore, the git commit message (**Commit message: "Jenkinsfile in GitHub and webhook"**) confirms the last commit that triggered the automatic build of this project.

Example 3-22 *Jenkins Console Output*

```
Started by GitHub push by netdevops-1
Obtained Jenkinsfile from git https://github.com/netdevops-1/dc-automation.git
[Pipeline] Start of Pipeline
[Pipeline] properties
[Pipeline] node
Running on Jenkins in /var/lib/jenkins/workspace/ansible_script1 Jenkinsfile
[Pipeline] {
[Pipeline] checkout
Selected Git installation does not exist. Using Default
The recommended git tool is: NONE
using credential netdevops-1
 > git rev-parse --resolve-git-dir /var/lib/jenkins/workspace/ansible_script1 Jen-
   kinsfile/.git # timeout=10
Fetching changes from the remote Git repository
 > git config remote.origin.url https://github.com/netdevops-1/dc-automation.git/ #
   timeout=10
Fetching upstream changes from https://github.com/netdevops-1/dc-automation.git/
 > git --version # timeout=10
 > git --version # 'git version 2.37.1'
using GIT_ASKPASS to set credentials
 > git fetch --tags --force --progress -- https://github.com/netdevops-1/dc-automa-
   tion.git/ +refs/heads/*:refs/remotes/origin/* # timeout=10
 > git rev-parse refs/remotes/origin/master^{commit} # timeout=10
Checking out Revision a69c00b4605aecfb788923ae1218d9509cc4cc4c (refs/remotes/origin/
   master)
 > git config core.sparsecheckout # timeout=10
 > git checkout -f a69c00b4605aecfb788923ae1218d9509cc4cc4c # timeout=10
Commit message: "Jenkinsfile in GitHub and webhook"
 > git rev-list --no-walk 3070aa0571b21d07556bf82767ff0c5f25a0ac21 # timeout=10
[Pipeline] stage
[Pipeline] { (Build)
[Pipeline] echo (show)
[Pipeline] sh (show)
```

```
[Pipeline] sh (show)
[Pipeline] }
[Pipeline] // stage
[Pipeline] stage
[Pipeline] { (Test) (show)
[Pipeline] // stage
[Pipeline] stage
[Pipeline] { (Clean up) (show)
[Pipeline] // stage
[Pipeline] }
[Pipeline] // node
[Pipeline] End of Pipeline
Finished: SUCCESS
```

This use case shows the use of a Jenkinsfile in GitHub, along with a webhook trigger to build a project in Jenkins.

Alternatives

Various alternative CI/CD products are offered commercially and via the open-source community, including the following:

- GitLab
- CircleCI
- Travis CI
- Drone CI

GitLab is another platform commonly used for CI/CD. It differs from Jenkins in a variety of ways. One of those differences is that VCS capabilities are also built in to GitLab natively. Hence, users of GitLab can host repositories natively on it. GitLab also offers additional capabilities, such as visibility, insights, release planning, integrated workflows, and so on. In addition, GitLab provides flexible deployment models with both self-managed and SaaS (cloud-delivered). The self-managed version of GitLab can be installed on various Linux distributions, Kubernetes, cloud providers, and so on, while the SaaS option provides flexibility to get going in a simple and straightforward way. For SaaS deployments, a GitLab runner application can be installed on the on-premises infrastructure. Runners coordinate with GitLab (SaaS) and execute the CI/CD build (that is, jobs) defined in the GitLab pipeline. You may think of a runner as the agent or proxy for GitLab (SaaS)—it executes steps per the instructions it receive from GitLab. The results of the runner executions are sent back to GitLab. Therefore, all the management, visibility, insights, and so on are performed via the SaaS platform.

CircleCI is another purpose-built CI/CD platform, just like Jenkins. It offers on-premises deployment and SaaS consumption model options. CircleCI integrates with a variety of VCSs, such as GitHub, GitLab SaaS, and more. Getting detailed insights into the workflows, jobs, and projects are some of the functionalities provided by CircleCI. These help to improve the productivity of NetDevOps team members by giving detailed insights. For the SaaS offering, a runner can be used to integrate with SaaS. The concept is very similar to GitLab runners. CircleCI runners help to extend the coverage of pipeline execution to on-premises environments as well.

Drone CI is another platform for CI/CD that executes the build of a pipeline inside Docker containers. The container-based architecture allows easy scaling and deployment. It integrates with multiple VCSs, including GitHub, GitLab, and more. In Drone, a pipeline is defined in a file. This file has a declarative syntax using YAML, which is simple and considered to be human-friendly. Therefore, NetDevOps team members can easily create new pipelines and understand the existing ones. This file is kept in the root directory of the git repository, and the webhook to Drone triggers the execution of the pipeline. Manual or scheduled execution of the pipelines (that is, builds) can be done. Drone has a server and runner architecture. The runners poll the server for any pending tasks in the pipeline, which are then executed.

Summary

In this chapter, we looked at the details of implementing CI/CD pipelines with Jenkins. We did a deep-dive into the architecture and installation of Jenkins. We looked at the details of declarative and scripted pipelines as well as covered the syntax of both pipelines.

We went over use cases to demonstrate the configuration and development of pipelines. We also showed how the integration of Jenkins with version control systems provides flexibility, speed, agility, and so on for NetDevOps use cases. We covered plugins and various trigger mechanisms to build Jenkins pipelines.

In the next chapter, we will deep-dive into the implementation of NetDevOps pipelines with Jenkins. You can always revisit this chapter to see details about Jenkins.

Review Questions

You can find answers to these questions in Appendix A, "Answers to Review Questions."

1. Jenkins offers which of the following deployment options?

   a. On-premises only

   b. SaaS only

   c. Self-managed (on-premises or cloud)

   d. SaaS and on-premises

2. Which pipeline syntaxes does Jenkins support?

   a. Declarative and scripted pipelines

   b. Declarative only

   c. Scripted pipeline

   d. Freestyle pipeline

3. Jenkins supports which type of architecture?

   a. Distributed architecture with a controller and agents

   b. Centralized architecture only

   c. Distributed architecture with a controller and runners

   d. Software-defined architecture with a controller

4. Is the syntax for the following declarative pipeline valid?

```
---
pipeline {
    agent any
    stages {
        stage('Hello') {
            steps {
                echo 'Hello World'
            }
        }
    }
}
```

   a. Yes

   b. No

5. Jenkins plugins can be installed from the UI.

   a. True

   b. False

6. If you want to trigger a pipeline on Jenkins when a commit is done on GitHub, then what needs to be configured on GitHub to notify an update?

   a. HTTP PUT

   b. PATCH

   c. HTTP POST on GitHub

   d. Webhook on GitHub

7. If you want to trigger a build on Jenkins from a script, what is the best "Build Trigger" option to use on the pipeline?

   a. Trigger builds remotely

   b. Build periodically

   c. Build after other projects are built

   d. GitHub hook trigger for GITScm polling

8. Declarative pipelines use the Groovy language and hence provide more flexibility and functionality than scripted pipelines.

   a. True

   b. False

9. What is considered the best practice for building pipelines with a Jenkinsfile?

   a. Integrate Jenkins with GitHub using plugins. Define a pipeline using a Jenkinsfile and save this file in the GitHub repository.

   b. Create a freestyle project and define the pipeline steps in this project.

   c. Define a pipeline in the Jenkinsfile. Save it in a NetDevOps team member's workstation and collaborate with team members via email.

   d. The Jenkinsfile is always kept on the Jenkins server. It cannot be saved in the GitHub repository.

10. How can Jenkins integrate with tools like automated testing (Robot, Selenium), configuration management (Ansible, Puppet), monitoring, and so on?

   a. Jenkins integration can be done by developing custom software code.

   b. SDKs on Jenkins can be used for such integrations.

   c. Jenkins integrations with such tools can be done using plugins.

   d. Jenkins does not allow integration with other tools.

## Chapter 4

How to Implement NetDevOps Pipelines with Jenkins

In this chapter, you will find practical implementations of Jenkins pipelines applied to networking. This chapter builds on what you learned in Chapter 3, "How to Implement CI/CD Pipelines with Jenkins," to implement the use cases presented in Chapter 2, "Getting Started with NetDevOps." We'll start with examples and demonstrations of the most commonly used stages, including the following:

- Retrieving code from source control

- Testing and linting code

- Pausing for user input

- Rolling back in the case of failure

- Chaining different pipelines

We'll finish by combining these individual stages into pipelines that address the most common NetDevOps use cases, such as network provisioning, configuration, data collection, and compliance verification.

Throughout this chapter, you will find code snippets you can apply directly to your environment—not only for Jenkins pipelines but also for automation tools such as Ansible and Terraform.

Common Stages

Just like with many other tools and programming languages, a common set of instructions is present in the majority of pipeline implementations. For example, the **import** statement in the Python programming language allows the Python interpreter to load the necessary modules to execute the code and is present in nearly all Python scripts. Another example is issuing the command **configure terminal** after connecting to a device's command-line interface (CLI) and before configuring most Cisco network devices.

This section focuses specifically on Jenkins pipelines—the must-know stages that are the most predominant for NetDevOps use cases.

Retrieving Code from Source Control

The first stage in a pipeline almost always pulls code from a source control repository. This is commonly referred to as "checking out code" or "cloning the repository." In Chapter 1," Why Do We Need NetDevOps?", we already covered the need for and the benefits of source control, so in this chapter we'll assume your code lives there.

In order to check out code from a Git repository to your Jenkins worker node, you will need the Git plugin. This plugin is automatically installed if you installed the recommended plugins when performing the first-time setup of Jenkins, as covered in Chapter 3.

Using the plugin is simple: you just have to use the **git** function inside the steps of a stage and specify a URL, as shown in Example 4-1.

Example 4-1   *Git Plugin in a Declarative Pipeline*

```
pipeline {
    agent any

    stages {
        stage('Clone the repository') {
            steps {
                git (url: ' https://github.com/netdevops-1/dc-automation.git')
            }
        }
    }
}
```

However, this is the simplest case, representing a public Git repository without authentication or multiple branches. In the majority of the cases, you will want to specify a branch and a mechanism of authentication, and you can do so by using the parameters **crendentialsId** and **branch**, as shown in Example 4-2. This sample Jenkins pipeline consists of a single stage with a single step that clones a Git repository from the URL https://github.com/example/example.git. The branch specified is "development" and the credentials for accessing the code repository are stored under the ID 12345-1234.

Example 4-2   *Git Plugin in a Declarative Pipeline with Authentication*

```
pipeline {
    agent any

    stages {
        stage('Clone the repository') {
            steps {
                git (branch: 'development',url: 'https://github.com/netdevops-1/dc-
    automation.git', credentialsId: '12345-1234')
            }
        }
    }
}
```

In Example 4-2, you can see that the credentials are not in clear text; rather, they are an identifier. This is offered by another Jenkins plugin called **Credentials**. It also comes installed by default, and to use it, you need to select your user in the top-right menu shown in Figure 4-1 (the user in this case is **netdevops**). Then select to **Credentials** at the bottom of the list on the left side of the page, which is also visible in Figure 4-1.

Figure 4-1   *Jenkins User Menu*

In that menu, select either your user or **System**, depending on who you want to have access to the credentials. In your user menu, select the domain, and then in the top right select **Add Credential**. Different kinds of credentials are listed, but the most commonly used are the following:

- Username and password
- Certificate
- SSH user and private key

The identifier for the credentials can be supplied by the creator or it can be randomly generated. If the input is left blank, this is the identifier required in the **credentialsId** parameter of the Git plugin.

If you execute the pipeline, expect output similar to Example 4-3. The first thing you see is the user who initiated the build (in this case, the username is netdevops). Then you can see the directory in your worker node where this build will be run (/var/lib/jenkins/workspace/Pipeline2). Finally, after many **git** commands have run automatically, you can see that we have checked out the repository. In this example, we are using a sample repository, but you should try this with your own code repository.

Example 4-3 *Jenkins Pipeline Git Clone Output*

```
Started by user netdevops
[Pipeline] Start of Pipeline
[Pipeline] node
Running on Jenkins in /var/lib/jenkins/workspace/Pipeline2
[Pipeline] {
[Pipeline] stage
[Pipeline] { (Clone the repository)
[Pipeline] git
The recommended git tool is: NONE
No credentials specified
Cloning the remote Git repository
Cloning repository https://github.com/netdevops-1/dc-automation.git
 > git init /var/lib/jenkins/workspace/Pipeline2 # timeout=10
Fetching upstream changes from https://github.com/netdevops-1/dc-automation.git
 > git --version # timeout=10
 > git --version # 'git version 2.37.1'
 > git fetch --tags --force --progress -- https://github.com/netdevops-1/dc-automa-
   tion.git +refs/heads/*:refs/remotes/origin/* # timeout=10
 > git config remote.origin.url https://github.com/netdevops-1/dc-automation.git #
   timeout=10
 > git config --add remote.origin.fetch +refs/heads/*:refs/remotes/origin/* # time-
   out=10
Avoid second fetch
 > git rev-parse refs/remotes/origin/master^{commit} # timeout=10
Checking out Revision 9c7bc9cc4d69f62fad36def5e96d991a25fe7d0b (refs/remotes/origin/
   master)
 > git config core.sparsecheckout # timeout=10
 > git checkout -f 9c7bc9cc4d69f62fad36def5e96d991a25fe7d0b # timeout=10
 > git branch -a -v --no-abbrev # timeout=10
 > git checkout -b master 9c7bc9cc4d69f62fad36def5e96d991a25fe7d0b # timeout=10
Commit message: "Jenkinsfile in GitHub and webhook"
First time build. Skipping changelog.
[Pipeline] }
[Pipeline] // stage
[Pipeline] }
[Pipeline] // node
[Pipeline] End of Pipeline
Finished: SUCCESS
```

There are other ways to clone your repository that do not require the Git plugin (for example, by executing containers inside your Jenkins worker nodes rather than in the worker node itself). This approach isolates your build artifacts from the worker node, because all the work happens inside the container. This is represented in Example 4-4. There is no best way to do this; it is a matter of preference and how you decide to set up your pipelines.

Example 4-4 *Cloning Code Repository Inside a Container*

```
pipeline {
    agent any

    stages {
        stage('Clone the repository') {
            steps {
                sh "docker run -dit --name ansible_git netdevops/ansible_git_v1"
                sh 'docker exec -i ansible_git /bin/sh -c "git clone https://github.
com/netdevops-1/dc-automation.git"'
            }
        }

    }
}
```

At this step, you have the code in your local worker node.

Linting

This is a stage you will most commonly find in code development pipelines rather than in NetDevOps ones. Nonetheless, linting is the automated checking of your source code for programmatic and stylistic errors. This is done by using a lint tool. You use this stage to enforce specific styles such as for indentation and variable names. As a result, the quality of your code base will remain high. On top of that, linters also detect syntax errors. Detecting errors early in the development process is advantageous because you do not waste time or resources on the more computational heavy stages.

Lint tools differ among the various automation tools you might be using (for example, tflint or the native fmt for Terraform and ansible-lint for Ansible).

Consider you have the simple Terraform file shown in Example 4-5. Its goal is to create a virtual machine with some specific characteristics (such as type t2x.micro and subnet-0d643f40). EC2 is the virtual machine service of AWS. If you look closely at the code, you can see some parts are not properly indented, as highlighted.

Example 4-5 *Terraform Configuration File Using EC2 Module*

```
module "ec2_instance" {
    source  = "terraform-aws-modules/ec2-instance/aws"
  version = "~> 3.0"

  name = "single-instance"
  ami                    = "ami-0f15e0a4c8d3ee5fe"
    instance_type          = "t2x.micro"
  key_name             = "secret"
  monitoring           = true
  vpc_security_group_ids = ["sg-005fcb1e73b7a827a"]
  subnet_id            = "subnet-0d643f40"

  tags = {
    Terraform   = "true"
    Environment = "dev"
  }
}
```

However, the preceding code is perfectly valid for Terraform because it does not mandate a specific indentation style. This is where Terraform format linter can help.

If you save the code of Example 4-5 and execute the following command, you will see what changes the format linter recommends, as shown in Example 4-6.

Example 4-6 *Terraform fmt diff Output*

```
$ terraform fmt -check -diff
aws.tf
--- old/aws.tf
+++ new/aws.tf
@@ -1,11 +1,11 @@
 module "ec2_instance" {
-    source  = "terraform-aws-modules/ec2-instance/aws"
+  source  = "terraform-aws-modules/ec2-instance/aws"
   version = "~> 3.0"

   name = "single-instance"

   ami                    = "ami-0f15e0a4c8d3ee5fe"
-    instance_type          = "t2x.micro"
+  instance_type          = "t2x.micro"
   key_name             = "ivobonito"
   monitoring           = true
   vpc_security_group_ids = ["sg-005fcb1e73b7a827a"]
}
```

The **terraform fmt** command will rewrite Terraform configuration files to conform to an established format and style. However, the -check flag causes **terraform fmt** to run in check mode, which means it will check to see if the Terraform code in the current directory and its subdirectories is correctly formatted and will return an error if it is not. The -diff flag displays a unified diff of the changes to the Terraform code that would be made if the **terraform fmt** command were run without the -check flag. This allows you to see the changes that would be made without actually changing the code.

You can choose to apply the recommended changes by simply removing the -check and -diff flags. Terraform will automatically apply the new format to the same file.

However, there are more subtle errors in Example 4-5 that **terraform fmt** does not catch because it only focuses on file format and indentation. **tflint**, on the other hand, is a linter with a ruleset focused on possible errors and best practices about cloud resources. You must install it; it does not come with the vanilla version of Terraform.

Example 4-7 shows an execute of **tflint** on the same Terraform file. It highlights that the instance type we are trying to create does not actually exist, and it also recommends that we set a required version for our Terraform, which is a Terraform best practice.

Example 4-7 *tflint Execution Output*

```
$ tflint
2 issue(s) found:

Warning: terraform "required_version" attribute is required (terraform_required_ver-
  sion)

  on  line 0:
   (source code not available)

Reference: https://github.com/terraform-linters/tflint-ruleset-terraform/blob/
  v0.2.1/docs/rules/terraform_required_version.md

Error: "t2x.micro" is an invalid value as instance_type (aws_instance_invalid_type)

  on azure.tf line 12:
   3:    instance_type = "t2x.micro"

Reference: https://github.com/terraform-linters/tflint-ruleset-terraform/blob/
  v0.2.1/docs/rules/terraform_required_providers.md}
```

In a Jenkins pipeline, the lint stage is typically after cloning the repository and before executing the automation code, as shown in Example 4-8.

Example 4-8 *Jenkins Declarative Pipeline with Specific Linting Stage*

```
pipeline {
    agent any

    stages {
        stage('Clone repository') {
            steps {
                cleanWs()
                git (branch: 'main',
                url: 'https://github.com/example/example.git')
            }
        }
        stage('Lint') {
            steps {
                sh 'tflint'
            }
        }
        stage('Terraform apply') {
            steps {
                sh 'terraform apply -auto-approve'
            }
        }
    }
}
```

Choosing a specific lint tool is important, depending on what you are trying to achieve, but on top of that, if you decide to add a linting tool to a Jenkins pipeline stage, you will also need to understand what type of exit code the tool outputs, as this differs from tool to tool. The exit code will influence whether your pipeline continues or aborts.

Tip Jenkins uses the returned exit code of the script to determine the outcome of the build: 0 means successful, whereas 1 means failed.

To verify the exit code of the last executed program in a Unix operating system, run the command **echo $?**

As mentioned, the most common targets of linting tools are the automation tool's artifacts; however, the Jenkinsfile that represents a pipeline can also be a target for linting. There is a Jenkins linter integrated into your Jenkins instance. You can use it by running the following command, substituting *JENKINS_PORT* and *JENKINS_HOST* with your Jenkins instance's values:

```
ssh -p JENKINS_PORT JENKINS_HOST declarative-linter < Jenkinsfile
```

Testing

Testing can be performed using two methods: static code testing and dynamic testing. Static code testing consists of executing an analysis tool on your code that examines the code without actually running it. This is fairly similar to a lint tool; however, typically the goal is to identify risks (for example, security risks such as open ports) or to identify company policy violations (such as VLAN numbering instead of syntax or best practices errors).

Dynamic testing is not new to NetDevOps. In the networking domain, it is common to test after configuration changes, although sometimes these tests are manually executed by an operator. The tests typically come in the form of executing scripts that verify a specific behavior. In the context of NetDevOps, these scripts can collect **show** commands to assert some condition, connect to a device to verify reachability, generate traffic to stress an interface, or a combination of any of these actions.

Suppose you have Terraform code that creates a security group that allows ingress traffic on ports 22 and 80 and egress traffic in all ports, and you have an EC2 instance with 50GB of disk space associated with the security group, as shown in Example 4-9.

Example 4-9   *Terraform Configuration File Using EC2 Module*

```
resource "aws_security_group" "iac-sg" {
  name = "Sec-Group"
  vpc_id = "vpc-5234832d"

  // Allows port 22 ingress
  ingress {
    from_port = 22
    protocol = "tcp"
    to_port = 22
    cidr_blocks = ["0.0.0.0/0"]
  }

  // Allows port 80 ingress
  ingress {
    from_port = 80
    protocol = ""
    to_port = 80
    cidr_blocks = ["0.0.0.0/0"]
  }
  // Allows all ports egress
  egress {
    from_port      = 0
    to_port        = 0
```

```
    protocol        = "-1"
    cidr_blocks     = ["0.0.0.0/0"]
  }

  lifecycle {
    create_before_destroy = true
  }
}


resource "aws_instance" "project-iac" {
  ami = "ami-0c1bea58988a989155"
  instance_type = "t2.micro"
  subnet_id = "subnet-0d643f40"
  key_name = "key"


  vpc_security_group_ids = [
    aws_security_group.iac-sg.id
  ]
  root_block_device {
    delete_on_termination = true
    iops = 200
    volume_size = 50
    volume_type = "gp2"
  }
  tags = {
    Name = "VM1"
    Environment = "DEV"
  }

  depends_on = [ aws_security_group.iac-sg ]
}
```

To statically verify your Terraform code for potential security risks or misconfigurations, you can use **tfsec**. It does not come with the default installation of Terraform; you must install it separately.

Example 4-10 shows an execution of **tfsec** using its default configuration in a Terraform file (azure.tf). It highlights nine potential problems, including having a security group opened to the Internet and the root device volume unencrypted. **tfsec** also proposes information resources on each specific finding that can help you address the results. Your results might be different if you are using a newer **tfsec** version.

Example 4-10   *tfsec Execution Output*

```
$ tfsec
Result #1 CRITICAL Security group rule allows ingress from public internet.

 azure.tf:10

   1     resource "aws_security_group" "iac-sg" {
   .
  10 [      cidr_blocks = ["0.0.0.0/0"]
  ..
  31    }


        ID aws-ec2-no-public-ingress-sgr
    Impact Your port exposed to the internet
Resolution Set a more restrictive cidr range

More Information
- https://aquasecurity.github.io/tfsec/v1.27.5/checks/aws/ec2/no-public-ingress-
sgr/
- https://registry.terraform.io/providers/hashicorp/aws/latest/docs/resources/
security_group_rule#cidr_blocks

#OUTPUT OMMITED#
Result #5 HIGH Root block device is not encrypted.

 azure.tf:34-56

  34  ┌ resource "aws_instance" "project-iac" {
  35  |    ami = "ami-0c1bea58988a989155"
  36  |    instance_type = "t2.micro"
  37  |    subnet_id = "subnet-0d643f40"
  38  |    key_name = "ivobonito"
  39  |
  40  |
  41  |    vpc_security_group_ids = [
  42  └       aws_security_group.iac-sg.id
  ..


        ID aws-ec2-enable-at-rest-encryption
    Impact The block device could be compromised and read from
Resolution Turn on encryption for all block devices
```

```
More Information
- https://aquasecurity.github.io/tfsec/v1.27.5/checks/aws/ec2/enable-at-rest-
encryption/
- https://registry.terraform.io/providers/hashicorp/aws/latest/docs/resources/
instance#ebs-ephemeral-and-root-block-devices
```

```
#OUTPUT OMMITED#

  timings

  disk i/o              37.885µs
  parsing               339.592µs
  adaptation            173.54µs
  checks                23.145753ms
  total                 23.69677ms


  counts

  modules downloaded    0
  modules processed     1
  blocks processed      2
  files read            1


  results

  passed                1
  ignored               0
  critical              3
  high                  2
  medium                0
  low                   4


1 passed, 9 potential problem(s) detected.
```

Some findings of **tfsec**, or some other static analysis tool, might not be suited for your environment; for example, you might want all your volumes unencrypted. Because customizing is a common requirement, all these tools offer ways to ignore default rules and to add your own custom ones. This type of customization is helpful to not fail your Jenkins build because when the static analysis tool finds a non-compliant rule, default or not, it exits with a code different from 0, failing your Jenkins pipeline execution.

For dynamic tests, there is no generic tool. Although tools like Terratest exist, you generally have to create your own scripts for the specific outcome you want to test.

In Chapter 6, "How to Build Your Own NetDevOps Architecture," you can see an example of a dynamic testing script for a network configuration pipeline.

Here are some common dynamic tests:

- Connect to device and verify configurations.

- Connect to device and verify operational data using **show** command output.

- Reachability test (for example, using **ping** or **telnet** with a specific port).

- Performance test (for example, using **iperf**).

> **Note**   Some environments, such as the AWS cloud, have automated reasoning tools that verify a behavior without actually running any code. Instead, they use formal verification that automatically generates and checks mathematical proofs that verify the correctness of systems. The VPC Reachability Analyzer and AWS Network Manager route analyzer are examples of these tools.

The more critical the infrastructure, the more extensive the testing should be. In a pipeline, static testing is done before deploying, whereas dynamic testing is done after deploying, as shown in Example 4-11. In this example, validation.py represents a Python script that performs post-configuration verifications such as VLANs in the UP state and an expected operating system version after a software upgrade.

Example 4-11   *Jenkins Declarative Pipeline with Static and Dynamic Testing*

```
pipeline {
    agent any

    stages {
        stage('Clone repository') {
            steps {
                cleanWs()
                git (branch: 'main',
                url: 'https://github.com/example/example.git')
            }
        }
        stage('Static tests') {
            steps {
                sh 'tfsec'
            }
        }
        stage('Terraform apply') {
```

```
        steps {
            sh 'terraform apply -auto-approve'
        }
    }
    stage('Validation tests') {
        steps {
            sh 'python3 validation.py'
        }
    }
  }
}
```

When you're developing your own dynamic testing scripts, make sure you return the expected exit codes to interact with the Jenkins pipeline execution.

Rolling Back on Failure

Depending on the automation tool you use, you might have to reverse some configurations if they fail. Some automation tools like Terraform automatically roll back actions in the case of a failure; they are "atomic" in the sense that either all actions succeed or all actions are reverted. However, other tools like Ansible do not work this way, and it is possible that the first commands succeed but the last ones do not, and you end up with some sort of inconsistent or corrupt configuration.

Another use case for rollbacks is when the automation successfully completes but the testing phase reveals unexpected results. This could be the result of infinite sets, such as improper configuration values, or even software bugs. Therefore, the easiest way to reduce downtime is to roll back and then examine the logs.

The concept of a rollback is not new in the networking domain. Before maintenance windows and/or configuration changes, network engineers typically produce new configurations as well as their counterpart—rollback configurations. Example 4-12 shows the configuration of a new BGP neighbor as well as a rollback configuration.

Example 4-12 *New eBGP Neighbor and Corresponding Rollback in a Cisco IOS-XE Router*

```
R1# conf t
R1(config)#router bgp 65002
R1(config-router)#neighbor 172.16.0.2 remote-as 65002

R1#conf t
R1(config)#router bgp 65002
R1(config-router)#no neighbor 172.16.0.2 remote-as 65002
```

When using Jenkins, you can more rapidly roll back in the case of failure, thus minimizing downtime. This is true for when the automation script fails and when the testing stage shows unexpected results. You can do this using the **post** section. You can add a **post** section to a stage or to the entire pipeline. Example 4-13 shows a **post** section that will always run at the end of the pipeline, independent of the status; in this case, it cleans the workspace. It also shows another **post** section that will only run if the stage "First" fails, and it rolls back the configuration using an Ansible playbook. At this time, the content of those playbooks is not important, as they require domain knowledge of what is being automated as well as knowledge of the automation tool. What is important to learn and remember here is how the **post** section can be used.

Example 4-13   *The post Sections in a Declarative Pipeline*

```
pipeline {
    agent any

    stages {
        stage('First') {
            steps {
                git (branch: 'main',
                    url: 'https://github.com/netdevops-1/dc-automation.git')
                sh 'ansible-playbook dc-automation/vlan.yml -i dc-automation/hosts'
            }
            post {
                failure {
                    sh 'ansible-playbook dc- automation/delete_vlan.yml -i dc-auto-
mation/hosts'
                }
            }
        }
    }
    post {
        always {
            cleanWs (cleanWhenNotBuilt: false,
                deleteDirs: true,
                disableDeferredWipeout: true,
                notFailBuild: true,
                patterns: [[pattern: '.gitignore', type: 'INCLUDE']])
        }
    }
}
```

There are multiple conditions you can use inside a **post** section; you have been introduced to **always** and **failure**, but there are more:

- **changed:** Only run the steps in **post** if the current pipeline's run has a different completion status from its previous run.

- **aborted:** Only run the steps in **post** if the current pipeline's run has an "aborted" status, usually due to the pipeline being manually aborted. This is typically denoted by gray in the web user interface (UI).

- **success:** Only run the steps in **post** if the current pipeline or stage's run has a "success" status, typically denoted by blue or green in the web UI.

- **cleanup:** Run the steps in this **post** condition after every other **post** condition has been evaluated, regardless of the pipeline or stage's status.

- **always:** Run the steps in the **post** section regardless of the completion status of the pipeline or stage's run.

- **failure:** Only run the steps in **post** if the current pipeline or stage's run has a "failed" status, typically denoted by red in the web UI.

- **fixed:** Only run the steps in **post** if the current pipeline's run is successful and the previous run failed or was unstable.

Tip   If you want to test your failure scenarios, you can use Jenkins' **error** step:

```
error('This will throw an error')
```

The error step will signal an error and fail your stage. You can use the **post** section for more actions than just rolling back; for example, you can use it to always run your cleanup step instead of having it in a separate stage.

Pausing for Input

Often, you will need to receive user input during a pipeline execution. This can be for different reasons, but by far the most common is an approval workflow. For example, you might have a single pipeline that deploys configuration changes to a development environment and then deploys them to your production environment. In between these two deployment stages, you might want to review the logs and manually approve the changes.

The input step allows you to achieve this behavior. It pauses the pipeline execution and allows a user to interact and control the flow of the build. In a declarative pipeline, you add the input step as shown in Example 4-14. The **message** parameter is the only mandatory parameter, and it customizes the message shown to the user. Other available customization parameters include **ok**, which customizes the shown "proceed" message, and

parameters, which allows you to ingest information from the user and make it available throughout the lifecycle of the pipeline stage.

Example 4-14 *The input Step in a Declarative Pipeline*

```
pipeline {
    agent any

    stages {
        stage('Input Stage') {
            input {
                message "Should we continue?"
                ok "Yes, we should."
                parameters {
                    string(name: 'ENV', defaultValue: 'DEV', description: 'Which
environment to deploy to')
                }
            }
            steps {
                echo "Deploying to ${ENV}."
            }
        }
    }
}
```

When executing the pipeline, the user can provide input either in the console output, as shown in Figure 4-2, or directly in the stage view, as shown in Figure 4-3.

Should we continue?

ENV

Which environment to deploy to

DEV

Yes, we should.   Abort

Figure 4-2 *Input in the Console Output Menu*

You can restrict who approves an input step by using the **submitter** parameter. It accepts both user IDs and groups. However, bear in mind that, independent of this parameter, Jenkins administrators are able to respond to the input. Example 4-15 shows how you can extend Example 4-14 to only allow the user Ivo to continue the deployment.

Figure 4-3   *Input in the Stage View Menu*

Example 4-15   *The Input Step in a Declarative Pipeline Restricted by User*

```
pipeline {
    agent any

    stages {
        stage('Input Stage') {
            input {
                message "Should we continue?"
                ok "Yes, we should."
                submitter "Ivo"
                parameters {
                    string(name: 'ENV', defaultValue: 'DEV', description: 'Which
environment to deploy to')
                }
            }
            steps {
                echo "Deploying to ${ENV}."
            }
        }
    }
}
```

Cleaning Up

Executing Jenkins pipelines that both pull resources (for example, checking out a code repository) and create resources (for example, a software artifact) progressively consumes disk space on your worker nodes.

This is not such a major hurdle for NetDevOps as it is for software projects because the code repositories for infrastructure as code (IaC) are typically small; nonetheless, it is a good practice to delete Jenkins workspaces after the builds. You could connect to your worker nodes directly and manually delete them; however, a Jenkins plugin is available that helps you with this: Workspace Cleanup.

Verify your environment by connecting to a worker node, navigating to your default workspace path, and issuing an **ls** command, like so:

```
$ cd /var/lib/jenkins/workspace
$ ls
Pipeline2  Pipeline1
```

Your terminal should output one folder per each pipeline you have executed.

Instead of manually deleting these folders, this plugin makes cleaning up really simple—all you have to do is invoke the function **cleanWS** inside the execution steps, as shown in Example 4-16.

Example 4-16   *Workspace Cleanup Plugin in a Declarative Pipeline*

```
pipeline {
    agent any

    stages {
        stage('Clone the repository') {
            steps {
                cleanWs()
                git (url: 'https://github.com/example/example.git')
            }
        }
    }
}
```

Although the previous example shows cleaning the environment before the build (meaning the first thing you do when you start), you can also clean your environment after the build is complete by using the same function in the **post** section rather than in the **steps** section of a pipeline. In Example 4-17, **cleanWS** is always called after the build, independent of the resulting status. Furthermore, you can see the following configuration parameters:

- **disableDeferredWipeout:** Indicates to delete the workspace immediately instead of asynchronously.

- **notFailBuild:** During the workspace cleanup, various issues can happen; for example, a file cannot be deleted because it's still open and locked by some other process. By default, when such problems happen, the build is marked as failed. If this option is checked, workspace cleanup never marks the build as failed.

- **patterns:** By default, this job's entire workspace will be deleted. You can make this more selective by specifying some file patterns (using Apache Ant PatternSet syntax) to select only a subset of the workspace.

In this case, delete the workspace immediately, excluding .propsfile, but do not fail the build in case some file cannot be deleted.

Example 4-17 *Workspace Cleanup Plugin in post Actions*

```
pipeline {
    agent any

    stages {
        stage('Clone the repository') {
            steps {
                git (url: 'https://github.com/example/example.git')
            }
        }
    }
    post {
        // Clean after build
        always {
            cleanWs(cleanWhenNotBuilt: false,
                    disableDeferredWipeout: true,
                    notFailBuild: true,
                    patterns: [[pattern: '.gitignore', type: 'INCLUDE'],
                               [pattern: '.propsfile', type: 'EXCLUDE']])
        }
    }
}
```

Again, there is no widely accepted best practice; it depends on your preference and situation. However, some situations, such as if you want to troubleshoot one of the artifacts built locally, can force you into cleaning at the beginning and not at the end.

Chaining Pipelines

Pipelines are managed as code; therefore, having specific pipelines per task allows for better code manageability. However, many NetDevOps tasks are complicated because they are a composite of smaller tasks chained together. Instead of copy/pasting code into one big pipeline, best practices dictate to have several parameterized pipelines chained together by an overlay pipeline (that is, a pipeline that orchestrates the execution of other pipelines). To achieve this, you can use the **build** step, which triggers a building of another pipeline.

Imagine you have two pipelines already built—one called vlan_pipeline that creates a VLAN in some specific switches, and another called compliance_pipeline that verifies security compliance across your environment. Example 4-18 shows a declarative pipeline that calls each of these pre-existing pipelines sequentially. The vlan_pipeline is called with the specific VLAN you want to create through the use of parameters, as explained in Chapter 3.

Example 4-18 *Using the build Step to Chain Different Pipelines*

```
pipeline {
    agent any

    stages {
        stage('First') {
            steps {
                build(job: 'vlan_pipeline', parameters: [string(name: 'VLANS',
value: "123")])
                build(job: 'compliance_pipeline')
            }
        }
    }
}
```

Executing the pipeline from Example 4-18 produces the output shown in Example 4-19.

Example 4-19 *Pipeline Chaining Execution Output*

```
Started by user netdevops
[Pipeline] Start of Pipeline
[Pipeline] node
Running on Jenkins in /var/lib/jenkins/workspace/pipeline1
[Pipeline] {
[Pipeline] stage
[Pipeline] { (First)
[Pipeline] build (Building vlan_pipeline)
Scheduling project: vlan_pipeline
```

```
Starting building: vlan_pipeline #8
[Pipeline] build (Building compliance_pipeline)
Scheduling project: compliance_pipeline
Starting building: compliance_pipeline #9
[Pipeline] }
[Pipeline] // stage
[Pipeline] }
[Pipeline] // node
[Pipeline] End of Pipeline
Finished: SUCCESS
```

You can see a disadvantage of using this technique instead having all the code in a single pipeline divided among the stages: it executes each of the pipelines individually, so execution logs are scattered among the pipelines, making troubleshooting harder. The overlay pipeline execution logs do not have a lot of information.

Single-Operation Pipelines

Pipelines can be specialized in a single task, such as provisioning virtual machines or retrieving logs from all your devices. To achieve these tasks, we combine several stages, as shown in Chapter 2.

Implementing an automation script (for example, an Ansible playbook to configure a Cisco router or a Terraform file to provision virtual machines) always requires tool and domain knowledge. However, any automation script can be integrated into the following single-operation pipelines. Make sure you test them with your own automation scripts. If you want to learn how to develop these automation scripts, the book *Network Automation Made Easy* (Cisco Press, 2022) provides in-depth guidance and easy-to-follow examples.

Provisioning

There are many different provisioning tools and many different things to provision. However, this section focuses on the most commonly used tool, Terraform, and the most common target, a cloud environment.

Example 4-20 presents a Jenkins implementation of a provisioning pipeline. It clones a repository and does some static verifications. If these static verifications succeed, it then executes the provisioning script in a developer environment. This is followed by more verifications—this time, dynamic testing. If those verifications also succeed, it proceeds to execute the provisioning script in the production environment; otherwise, it destroys the changes made to the development environment. Finally, it tests the production environment post-changes.

Example 4-20 *Jenkins Declarative Pipeline for Provisioning*

```
pipeline {
    agent any

    stages {
        stage('Clone repository') {
            steps {
                git (branch: 'main',
                    url: 'https://github.com/example/example.git')
            }
        }
        stage('Static tests') {
            steps {
                sh 'tfsec'
            }
        }
        stage('Dev Terraform apply') {
            steps {
                dir('dev') {
                    sh 'terraform apply -auto-approve'
                }
            }
        }
        stage('Dev Validation tests') {
            steps {
                sh 'python3 validation.py dev'
            }
            post {
                failure {
                    dir('dev') {
                        sh 'terraform destroy -auto-approve'
                    }
                }
            }
        }
        stage('Prod Terraform apply') {
            steps {
                dir('prod') {
                    sh 'terraform apply -auto-approve'
                }
            }
        }
```

```
stage('Prod Validation tests') {
        steps {
            sh 'python3 validation.py prod'
        }
    }
}
post {
    always {
        cleanWs(cleanWhenNotBuilt: false,
                deleteDirs: true,
                disableDeferredWipeout: true,
                notFailBuild: true)
    }
}
}
```

There are many ways to deploy to two different environments (for example, dev and prod) in the same Jenkins pipeline. In Example 4-20, we are using a structure that consists of two folders, as shown in Example 4-21. This allows us complete control over each environment, meaning changes in one environment do not affect the state of the other environment. However, there is code duplication because the terraform file, main.tf, exists in both folders.

Example 4-21   *Terraform One-Folder-per-Environment Approach*

```
$ tree
.
├── dev
│   ├── main.tf
│   └── terraform.tfvars
├── prod
│   ├── main.tf
│   └── terraform.tfvars
└── validation.py
```

The alternative is to have a single main.tf Terraform file to avoid code duplication. However, this approach does not allow us to easily destroy resources from each environment separately. Example 4-22 shows this folder structure.

Example 4-22   *Terraform One-Variable-File-per-Environment Folder Approach*

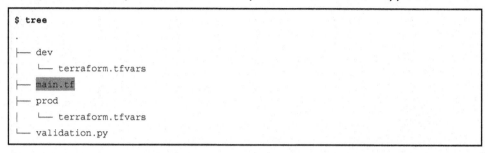

```
$ tree

.
├── dev
│   └── terraform.tfvars
├── main.tf
├── prod
│   └── terraform.tfvars
└── validation.py
```

Tip   Advanced Terraform users might want to look into using Terraform Workspaces, which refer to having separate instances of state data inside the same Terraform working directory.

Another possible implementation of having two different environments is to have different pipelines per environment and to chain them using the **build** step, as shown previously in this chapter. There is not a well-accepted best practice, but using different folders is the easiest approach.

Configuration

Configuration can range from configuring virtual machines post-provisioning, to configuring Cisco network devices such as routers and switches, to configuring software products post-installation. In this section, we focus on using Ansible to configure Cisco network devices.

Unlike in the "Provisioning" section of this chapter, where we used a single pipeline for both development and production environments, this section shows you how to use an overlay pipeline that orchestrates the execution of another pipeline twice—once for the development environment and once for the production environment. This approach allows you to have a pipeline with fewer stages because they are reused with different variables.

Note   In a setup where an overlay pipeline executes other pipelines, the terms "parent" and "child" pipelines are often used.

Example 4-23 shows the folder structure of the code. It consists of several folders. The folder "configurations" contains the desired configuration for the network device, NXOS-1.txt. Another folder, "environments," contains other nested subfolders per environment (dev and prod), which contain the Ansible inventory file and variables for each of the target devices. There is a "helpers" folder for anything not related to Ansible as well as a "playbooks" folder where the Ansible playbooks live.

Example 4-23 *Ansible Folder Structure*

```
$ tree
.
├── configurations
│   └── NXOS-1.txt
├── environments
│   ├── dev
│   │   ├── group_vars
│   │   │   └── all.yml
│   │   └── inventory.py
│   └── prod
│       ├── group_vars
│       │   └── all.yml
│       └── inventory.py
├── helpers
│   └── ccat.py
└── playbooks
    ├── retrieve_outputs.yml
    ├── retrieve_running_config.yml
    └── vlans.yml
```

Example 4-24 shows the "child" Jenkins pipeline for configuration. It receives an input parameter, **ENV**, that is used to determine in which environment, dev or prod, the configuration is deployed. Then it clones the repository and performs some static testing on the configuration to be applied. This example uses the Cisco Config Analysis Tool (CCAT), a Python tool that analyzes configuration files for Cisco devices and performs a list of checks to make sure they are hardened. If the configuration passes the static security checks, the pipeline runs an Ansible playbook that retrieves and saves locally the running-config of the device to a file named backup_config. After this, it executes another playbook that retrieves the **show** command's output and parses it to verify functionality; in this case, whether the VLANs and interfaces are in the UP state. If this is true, the next stage executes an Ansible playbook that replaces the old configuration with the new one. Lastly, it reverifies, with the same playbook, whether the VLANs and interfaces are still in the UP state. If they are, the pipeline finishes cleaning up the workspace. If they are not, it rolls back to the previous known-good configuration by overwriting the configuration file used by the Ansible playbook, with the **–extra-vars** flag pointing to the saved configuration file from the third stage, "Retrieve, validate and save running-config," and then reverifies the network device status.

In Chapter 6, you can see examples of Ansible playbooks, both for the configuration and testing stages.

Example 4-24 *Jenkins Declarative Child Pipeline for Configuration*

```
pipeline {
    agent any

    parameters {
        string(name: 'ENV')
    }

    stages {
        stage('Clone repository') {
            steps {
                git (branch: 'main',
                url: 'https://github.com/example/example.git')
            }
        }
        stage('Static tests') {
            steps {
                sh 'python3 ccat.py configurations/NXOS-1.txt'
            }
        }
        stage('Retrieve, validate and save Running-Configuration') {
            steps {
                sh "ansible-playbook playbooks/retrieve_running_config.yml -i
environments/${params.ENV}/hosts"
            }
        }
        stage('Retrieve and validate show commands') {
            steps {
                sh "ansible-playbook playbooks/retrieve_outputs.yml -i
environments/${params.ENV}/hosts"
            }
        }
        stage('Deploy new Configurations') {
            steps {
                sh "ansible-playbook playbooks/vlans.yml -i environments/${params.
ENV}/hosts"
            }
        }
        stage('Retrieve and validate new Configuration') {
            steps {
                sh "ansible-playbook playbooks/retrieve_outputs.yml -i
environments/${params.ENV}/hosts"
            }
```

```
        post {
            failure {
                sh "ansible-playbook playbooks/vlans.yml -i
environments/${params.ENV}/hosts -e \"config_file=backup_config\""
                sh "ansible-playbook playbooks/retrieve_outputs.yml -i
environments/${params.ENV}/hosts"
            }
        }
    }
}

    post {
        always {
            cleanWs(cleanWhenNotBuilt: false,
                    deleteDirs: true,
                    disableDeferredWipeout: true,
                    notFailBuild: true)
        }
    }
}
```

To implement the configuration pipeline according to the best practices, you first need to deploy it in a development environment. For that, you can create the parent pipeline as shown in Example 4-25. This pipeline only has two stages: the first one executes the Example 4-24 pipeline in the development environment, and the second one waits for input from a specific user to proceed and then, if that input is positive, deploys to the production environment using the same pipeline from Example 4-24.

Example 4-25 *Jenkins Declarative Parent Pipeline for Configuration*

```
pipeline {
    agent any

    stages {
        stage('Deploy to Dev') {
            steps {
                build(job: 'replace_config', parameters: [string(name: 'ENV', value:
"dev")])
            }
        }
        stage('Deploy to Prod') {
            input {
                message "Do you want to deploy to Production"
```

```
                ok "Yes, deploy to Production"
                submitter "Ivo"
            }
            steps {
                build(job: 'replace_config', parameters: [string(name: 'ENV', value:
    "prod")])
            }
        }
    }
}
```

The way the Example 4-25 pipeline implements the concept of development and production environments is through the use of input variables on the child pipeline, as shown in Example 4-26. They are linked to the folder structure in Example 4-23. Each of these folders has an Ansible inventory file with different network devices and credentials.

There are other ways to implement a multi-environment pipeline while using Ansible as the automation tool. In particular, you can use a single inventory file with host groups and use those in the playbook execution, as shown in Example 4-26. However, using named folders with different inventory files is one of the most widely used options.

Example 4-26 *Ansible Inventory File with Groups*

```
$ cat inventory
all:
  hosts:
    IOS-01.example.com:
  children:
    dev:
      hosts:
        NXOS-01.example.com:
        NXOS-02.example.com:
    prod:
      hosts:
        NXOS-11.example.com:
        NXOS-12.example.com:
        NXOS-13.example.com:

$ cat vlans.yml
---

  - name: create new VLANs
    hosts: dev

## OUTPUT OMMITED ##
```

Data Collection

Storing data from your network, either on a scheduled or on-demand basis, is becoming increasingly more important because of all the ways you can turn this data into business insights. For example, network metrics, in a time series format, can be used to create predictive maintenance mechanisms using machine learning. But even if you are not in a machine learning stage yet, data collection pipelines can help your operators access curated information quicker while keeping records of when the information was collected and by whom, allowing you to limit access to the devices.

These pipelines are simple because their complexity usually lies within the automation that scrapes and parses the device data. Example 4-27 shows a pipeline that executes every 30 minutes using a cron trigger and uses Python scripts to collect, parse, and export curated device information. The post-cleanup workspace task is very important in pipelines that save a lot of information locally, such as data collection pipelines.

Example 4-27 *Jenkins Declarative Pipeline for Data Collection*

```
pipeline {
    agent any
    triggers {
        cron('H/30 * * * *')
    }

    stages {
        stage('Clone repository') {
            steps {
                git (branch: 'main',
                    url: 'https://github.com/example/example.git')
            }
        }
        stage('Collect Data') {
            steps {
                sh 'python3 collect.py'
            }
        }
        stage('Process and Aggregate') {
            steps {
                sh 'python3 process.py'
            }
        }
        stage('Export Data') {
            steps {
```

```
                    sh 'python3 export.py'
                }
            }
        }
        post {
            always {
                cleanWs(cleanWhenNotBuilt: false,
                        deleteDirs: true,
                        disableDeferredWipeout: true,
                        notFailBuild: true)
            }
        }
    }
}
```

The gather and processing stages are often merged into a single stage if the automation script performs both functions. Also, you should favor short-running scripts to long-running ones so that you can take advantage of checkpointing—even if the script fails, part of its work will already be saved.

The Jenkins cron syntax follows the syntax as the cron utility, previously mentioned in Chapter 3. As a review, the expression to represent every day at 6 a.m. is (0 6 * * *), while the expression to represent only the first day of the month at 6 a.m. is (0 6 1 * *). Jenkins extends the typical cron syntax; a new operator when using cron in Jenkins is **H**, which allows you to space jobs across time, producing an even load on the system. In the previous example, we ran the Jenkins job every day at 6 a.m., but what if we have multiple jobs at that time? A better way would be to use the expression (H H * * *), which would still run the jobs once a day but spaced out instead of right at 6 a.m.

Both Python and Ansible are good tools to use to scrape and parse information and to export information. Although the previous example also uses a Python script, in networking, FTP is more commonly used.

Compliance and Reporting

For compliance or validation use cases, where you want to make sure a set of rules is being followed in your network, you must first create the ruleset that specifies the compliance rules. This type of rule system requires domain knowledge and is specific to each use case. Nonetheless, rule systems are available online for specific compliance standards, such as PCI DSS, that you only need to adapt to your automation tool of choice.

To apply your ruleset, you first need to gather network information, as shown in Example 4-28 in the stage "Gather Data." Depending on the automation tool you are using, you might want to co-locate the verification with the information-gathering stage. In this example, two separate stages are used because the data collection stage utilizes a different, specific data collection pipeline.

This separate data collection pipeline, named get_config, retrieves and saves information. You could replace the first stage with access to that saved data instead of an execution of the data collection pipeline. This approach would be more scalable—instead of the same data being collected for each pipeline, data is gathered once and used for multiple ends.

After you have the data, you can run any automation tool that checks the data for compliance (in this case, represented in the "Verify Compliance" stage by a Python script). If the compliance verification fails, the user is prompted for an input to accept an automatic remediation action. This is very complex to implement for all scenarios; however, in more simplistic scenarios, you can have the automation ready to counteract and return the device to a compliant status. For example, if your compliance script checks for SSHv1 on a router, the remediation can be to force the router to SSHv2. Likewise, in the cloud, you can check for open security groups to the Internet and remediate them to a more restrictive configuration. Nonetheless, this must be coded on a case-by-case basis. After the automation tool attempts to remediate the situation, it reruns the compliance verification script.

If the verification passes, a report is generated, which always happens independent of the status of the compliance verification because you always want the report. Generating reports using Ansible or Terraform is very cumbersome. Python is more suited for this task. Regardless of the tool, generating Word or PowerPoint documents is hard to automate. For automated reporting, formats like Markdown are the preferred choice—they have an easy-to-learn syntax, and they can be version-controlled, together with your automation source code, in a version control repository. MkDocs is an example of a command-line tool that helps you automatically create documentation from Markdown files.

The pipeline in Example 4-28 runs at 6 a.m. every day.

Example 4-28   *Jenkins Declarative Pipeline for Compliance Reporting*

```
pipeline {
    agent any
    triggers {
        cron('0 6 * * *')
    }

    stages {
        stage('Clone repository') {
            steps {
                git (branch: 'main',
                    url: 'https://github.com/example/example.git')
            }
        }
        stage('Gather Data') {
            steps {
```

```
                build(job: 'get_config')
            }
        }
        stage('Verify compliance') {
            steps {
                sh 'python3 compliance.py'
            }
            post {
                failure {
                    input (message: "Do you want to attempt an automatic fix?",
    ok: "Yes, please fix it")
                    sh 'python3 automatic_remediation.py'
                    sh 'python3 compliance.py'
                }
            }
        }
    }

    post {
        always {
            sh 'python3 generate_report.py'

            cleanWs(cleanWhenNotBuilt: false,
                deleteDirs: true,
                disableDeferredWipeout: true,
                notFailBuild: true)
        }
    }
}
```

A pipeline that only performs reporting is similar; however, it wouldn't have the compliance verification stage. You can create all kinds of reporting pipelines, but compliance reporting pipelines are by far the most common type.

Combined Pipelines

Combined pipelines are pipelines that have complex functions such as troubleshooting and migrations. They are usually composed of multiple, parameterized single-operation pipelines or many stages of individual operations. This type of pipeline can be long, with many stages, and these stages either call other parameterized pipelines or implement all the logic themselves.

Migrations

Migrations pipelines are created for specific migrations and typically do not exist in a general form, just like migrations activities in the networking domain. For example, migrating from an old network architecture to a newer one, migrating a specific data center to the cloud, and merging a newly acquired branch to the main architecture are all specific activities.

In networking, this type of pipeline is composed of the orchestration of data-gathering and configuration stages. Creating this type of pipeline requires the engineers to have domain knowledge, not only about the configurations to be applied at what stage and the rollback configurations, but also about the influence of those configurations on the network devices. Many migrations involve device downtime, meaning the device becomes unreachable, and therefore the automations will not be able to interact with it. Retries or planned pauses are often required to make migration pipelines work.

Example 4-29 shows a migration pipeline that executes another configuration replacement pipeline, like the one in Example 4-24, and then tries three times to verify the changes made. It tries three times to exemplify a change that requires a reboot, such as a Cisco IOS software upgrade, or a convergence event, such as routing protocol convergence. In the case that all three tries fail, it rolls back the configuration to the initial one using the same configuration pipeline.

Note   Network migrations are complex activities, and Jenkins pipelines can help you orchestrate the whole process. However, they will still require you to prepare all the correct configurations.

Example 4-29   *Jenkins Declarative Pipeline for Device Configuration Migration*

```
pipeline {
    agent any

    stages {
        stage('Clone repository') {
            steps {
                git (branch: 'main',
                    url: 'https://github.com/example/example.git')
            }
        }
        stage('Replace config') {
            steps {
```

```
                    build(job: 'replace_config', parameters: [string(name: 'CONFIG',
        value: "NX-OS1")])
            }
        }
        stage('Example') {
            options {
                retry(3)
            }
            input {
                message "Continue?"
            }
            steps {
                sh 'python3 verify.py'
            }
            post {
                failure {
                            build(job: 'replace_config', parameters: [string(name: 'CON-
        FIG', value: "backup_NX-OS1")])
                }
            }
        }
    }
}
```

Although the previous example only targeted a single environment, you should adapt this example to target at least two—development and production—if you intend to use it.

Migration pipelines can take advantage of Jenkins' ability to run stages in parallel (for example, to execute a configuration change in two or more devices at the same time). You can do this by using the **parallel** keyword, as shown in Example 4-30. It changes the network device's TACACS key at the same time it changes the key on the TACACS server (in this case, Cisco ISE).

Example 4-30 *Jenkins Declarative Pipeline with Parallel Stages*

```
pipeline {
    agent any

    stages {
        stage('Configure new TACACS key') {
            parallel {

                stage('Configure on network devices') {
```

```
                    steps {
                        sh "ansible-playbook playbooks/tacacs.yml -i environments/
    hosts"
                    }
                }

                stage('Configure on Cisco ISE') {
                    steps {
                        sh "ansible-playbook playbooks/ISE_tacacs.yml -i environ-
    ments/hosts"
                    }
                }
            }
        }
    }
}
```

You can also use the **parallel** section to run steps in parallel.

Troubleshooting

Troubleshooting is a very knowledge-dependent activity. The troubleshooter requires domain knowledge in the technology, device manufacturer syntax, overall troubleshooting steps, among other things. Examples of common troubleshooting tasks include reachability testing through the use of ping/traceroute tools, analyzing system logs, verifying network devices configurations, and analyzing bandwidth limits.

You can create many different troubleshooting NetDevOps pipelines, but the two most common are troubleshooting self-fix and troubleshooting aider.

For the troubleshooting self-fix category, the Jenkins pipeline architecture is similar to the one shown in Example 4-28 for compliance. These pipelines consist of a first stage that gathers data, a second stage that parses and verifies the data for issues, and a third and final stage that attempts to fix any of the identified issues. For this to work, you need to create your own knowledge base that consists of a set of commands to gather data, a set of known outputs that signify issues, and a set of commands or instructions that can fix those issues. As mentioned in the "Compliance and Reporting" section of this chapter, constructing this knowledge base is a complicated task that often requires a lot of research and investment.

A troubleshooting aider pipeline is the recommended approach when it comes to NetDevOps pipelines for troubleshooting. This type of pipeline aims to reduce the burden on the operator when it comes to troubleshooting, rather than trying to fix the issue on its own. It can reduce the burden in multiple ways:

■ **Abstract the command syntax differences on each device type/vendor:** An operator only needs to know the pipeline inputs, and the pipeline will translate those to whatever syntax is required per device type/vendor. This reduces the knowledge required by the operator.

■ **Minimize the amount of information shown:** A pipeline can collect a large number of known, useful verbose outputs, parse them, and show to the operator a less verbose version of the collected information.

■ **Create and compare baselines across devices:** A pipeline can, in near real time, not only show the operator metrics of the specific device or devices being troubleshooted but also a comparison of those metric to known-good devices. This minimizes the effort and time taken on the operator to identify issues.

The usual architecture of troubleshooting aider pipelines is similar to that of data collection pipelines, as shown in Example 4-24. It includes a stage that gathers data, using any automation tool of choice, configured with well-known and well-accepted troubleshooting commands, followed by a stage that parses and either saves this information in a file or database or prints the output on the Jenkins job console. At this stage, or in a separate one, the automation can also try to highlight what it considers to be anomalous without attempting a fix. Again, this requires a knowledge base of what is expected, or not, from the collected outputs.

The difference between data collection pipelines and troubleshooting pipelines is that data collection pipelines are usually run on a schedule, whereas troubleshooting pipelines are triggered on-demand. Furthermore, the uses for data collection pipelines are wider than just troubleshooting (for example, building historical time-series databases, as we have seen in a previous section).

Troubleshooting is an evolving use case, and you will find different NetDevOps approaches to it. Some networking products, such as newer network controllers like Cisco DNA Assurance, which is part of Cisco DNA Center, are beginning to have automated troubleshooting resolution workflows embedded into them that propose fixes based on collected device command outputs. This is a product-driven approach to creating a NetDevOps pipeline.

Summary

In this chapter, you learned how to construct Jenkins declarative pipelines using stages, steps, and plugins to implement the common NetDevOps use cases explained in Chapter 2:

■ Configuration

■ Provisioning

■ Data collection

- Compliance and reporting

- Migration

- Troubleshooting

With this knowledge, you can now orchestrate your own use cases, even if they are not covered in this chapter directly. At the end, NetDevOps pipelines are always a combination of one or more single actions. If you are not familiar with some of the automation tools used in this chapter, such as Ansible, Python, and Terraform, Chapter 6 will show you an end-to-end implementation including the code necessary for the automation piece.

Many of the examples of this chapter used a development network. In Chapter 5, "How to Implement Virtual Networks with EVE-NG," you will learn how to create a virtual network using EVE-NG, a multivendor network emulation software platform. You can use this technique to replace your static development network devices and provision a virtual network in the stage before you need to use it in your pipelines.

Review Questions

You can find answers to these questions in Appendix A, "Answers to Review Questions."

1. In Jenkins, which step do you use to pause a pipeline and receive user input?
   a. input
   b. parameters
   c. submitter
   d. message

2. Which of the following credential types is not natively supported by Jenkins?
   a. Username with password
   b. Certificate
   c. GPG key
   d. SSH user and private key

3. In Jenkins, which step do you use to trigger another pipeline?
   a. build
   b. start
   c. sh
   d. step

4. Which of the following conditions do you set in your **post** section if you want it to run only in the first successful build after failed ones?
   a. always
   b. fixed
   c. failure
   d. changed

5. In a Jenkins pipeline execution, which exit code does not result in a failed build?

   a. 1

   b. 0

   c. -1

   d. 2

6. Which tool can you use to detect overly permissive security rules in Terraform files?

   a. tflint

   b. tf fmt

   c. tfsec

   d. tf validate

7. What is the preferred way to simulate a failure in a Jenkins pipeline execution?

   a. Use the built-in **error** function.

   b. Execute a command that does not exist using the **sh** function.

   c. Connect to an unresponsive device.

   d. Use an empty stage.

8. Under which sections can you add the **options** directive with a retry? (Choose two.)

   a. pipeline

   b. steps

   c. stages

   d. stage

9. Which of the following cron expressions represents "every 30 minutes"?

   a. cron('H/30 * * * *')

   b. cron('H(0-29)/10 * * * *')

   c. cron('30 9-16/2 * * 1-5')

   d. cron('* 30 * * *')

10. Does Jenkins automatically clean the workspaces for you after execution?

   a. Yes

   b. No

## Chapter 5

How to Implement Virtual Networks with EVE-NG

One of the biggest hurdles in networking is the lack of testing, and at its heart is the difficulty of finding suitable network environments for testing. In this chapter, we will look at EVE-NG for simulation of networks in virtual environments. Such virtual environments assist in verifying and testing implementations of new or modified configurations to network devices in virtual topologies. This chapter will walk through the steps to create and configure virtual topologies. In addition, the chapter will cover the following topics:

- What is EVE-NG?

- Installation of EVE-NG in a cloud computing environment

- Understanding instantiation of virtual devices and topologies on EVE-NG

- Walkthrough of the creation of virtual topologies with external IP networks

- Alternatives to EVE-NG

We will focus on these details so you can deploy EVE-NG after reading through this chapter.

What Is EVE-NG?

EVE-NG stands for Emulated Virtual Environment–Next Generation. It provides capabilities for emulation of network devices in a virtualized environment. The virtualized devices not only include network devices such as switches, routers, and firewalls but also servers to emulate Linux servers. These virtualized devices are virtual representations of physical devices and can be interconnected to form a topology within EVE-NG via just a few clicks. Furthermore, the interconnected network devices within EVE-NG can be extended and interconnected to external physical or virtual network devices, applications, and tools.

The emulation of network devices in a controlled environment (that is, a virtualized network topology) can help in many ways:

- Validating the security and reliability of the network
- Evaluating the effect of changes to the network
- Performing functional testing of features on a network
- Identifying defects and issues in advance and reducing risk
- Executing performance testing
- Confirming the behavior of APIs exposed by network devices
- Confirming the behavior of network devices prior to rolling out changes in production
- Executing automation as part of NetDevOps pipelines
- Training and education

The use of network testing with EVE-NG or any other tool as part of NetDevOps development lifecycles and pipelines provides flexibility, speed, and agility. It helps to reduce downtime by validating all the features under test, prior to production rollout, which in turn increases the overall reliability and efficiency of the network.

As part of the NetDevOps pipeline, a virtualized network topology can be launched within EVE-NG. The pipeline can be used to automate activities in EVE-NG. The use cases in the NetDevOps pipeline can be executed in this simulated network environment. Examples of use cases for virtualized topology in EVE-NG include the configuration of devices using Ansible or another configuration management tool, execution of test cases on network devices using pyATS or the Robot framework, and the testing of APIs for network devices.

An important and powerful feature of EVE-NG is the support for multivendor network devices. It supports the simulation of network devices from Cisco, Juniper, Checkpoint, Palo Alto Network, F5, and more. EVE-NG also allows administrators to add devices that were not earlier supported or have not been tested.

EVE-NG allows us to design and create a virtual network topology as per our own needs by using a graphical user interface (GUI). The web GUI is used for activities such as launching devices, creating virtual network topologies by connecting those devices, saving configurations of devices, setting startup configurations for devices, enabling boot-up mechanisms, and so on. The use of a GUI for administration provides flexibility and an easier learning curve. Hence, we can more quickly simulate network topologies.

EVE-NG exposes the activities performed via its web GUI through APIs. Those APIs can be used to perform activities as part of the NetDevOps pipeline. Examples of activities where APIs can be used include starting an existing (pre-saved) virtualized network topology on EVE-NG and creating a new virtualized network topology for the execution of automation tasks on network devices. More details on APIs are provided later in this chapter.

Although we focus on network testing as a key reason for and use case of utilizing EVE-NG, it provides the means to learn about products from multiple vendors, without the need for a large capital expenditure on the procurement of the actual hardware.

So how do we use EVE-NG?

Two versions of EVE-NG software are available. The Community edition can be installed by anyone for free. A paid version known as the Professional edition of EVE-NG is also available. As expected, the Professional version provides additional features as well as support. The Community version supports 63 nodes (that is, networking devices) in a lab, whereas the Professional version can support 1024 networking devices. The Professional edition supports Docker containers and, unlike the Community edition, has Wireshark pre-integrated as a Docker container. The Professional edition also supports multiple startup configurations for a lab, which allows administrators to boot the lab from different startup configurations.

A comparison of the features between the Community and Professional editions is available on the EVE-NG website. At the time of writing, the official documentation of EVE-NG is available at the following URL, where more details about the differences between EVE-NG Community and Professional editions are available:

https://www.eve-ng.net/index.php/features-compare/

Table 5-1 is a snippet of the differences between these two editions.

Table 5-1 *EVE-NG Features Comparison*

Feature	Community	Professional
Price	Free	Not free
Lab Timer for training purposes	Not available	Available
User can run more than one lab	Not available	Available
TCP ports automatically chosen for telnet session to the networking devices	Fixed 128 ports per pod	Dynamic ports in the range of 1–65000
Local Wireshark capture	Available	Not available
Docker integrated Wireshark	Not available	Available
Create multiple startup configurations for a lab and the option to boot the lab from the different startup configurations	Not available	Available

We will install the Community version of EVE-NG and then create virtualized lab topologies in this chapter.

Installation of EVE-NG

The EVE-NG Community version is available in the form of OVF (Open Virtualization Format) and ISO file formats. OVF is an open-source standard for packaging and distributing software for virtual machines (VMs). EVE-NG software can be installed as a VM or directly on the bare-metal server. When EVE-NG is installed as a VM itself, all the networking devices are installed and emulated as nested VMs. This sort of setup works fine for lab testing and learning purposes in a small-scale lab. As the number of networking nodes instantiated within EVE-NG VM increases, performance bottlenecks can result. Hence, installation of EVE-NG software on a bare-metal server is considered an optimal best practice since it can scale much better than EVE-NG running as a VM.

The EVE-NG software distributed as an ISO file can be installed on a bare-metal server. Intel Virtualized Technology with Extended Page Tables (Intel VT-x/EPT) must be enabled to run and emulate networking devices. Intel VT-x is required for Intel systems to run virtualization with Kernel-based Virtual Machine (KVM). Extended Page Tables (EPT) technology further allows the virtualization of physical memory. KVM is an open-source virtualization technology that allows for running virtual machines on Linux. More details on this topic are covered later in this chapter.

Installation of EVE-NG as a VM is supported on a variety of hypervisors as well as in a cloud environment. Intel CPU supporting Intel VT-x/EPT technology is one of the prerequisites for the underlying hardware platform. Here are some of the supported environments for installing and running EVE-NG:

- Virtualized EVE-NG on a PC or laptop

- Virtualized EVE-NG on VMware Player 15.0 or later

- Virtualized EVE-NG on VMware ESXi 6.5 or later

- Bare=metal EVE-NG on Ubuntu Server 20.04

- Virtualized EVE-NG on Google Cloud Platform (GCP)

Whether EVE-NG is installed as a VM or as a bare metal, the correct sizing of the host machine, including CPU, memory, and hard disk, is important to utilize and run EVE-NG efficiently. It is recommended that you calculate the proper resources for the networking devices that will be created and tested within virtual environments in EVE-NG. Such validation can alleviate any performance issues and help you to choose the correct underlying host platform for EVE-NG. At the time of writing, a resource calculator in the form of an Excel file is provided at the following website:

https://www.eve-ng.net/index.php/download/

In this calculator (that is, Excel file), the CPU and RAM for devices are already documented. The total CPU and RAM usage can thus be calculated based on the number of devices in the networking scenarios that will run in the virtual environment.

The software for the Community and Professional editions of EVE-NG can also be downloaded from the above EVE-NG website.

Installation of EVE-NG on Google Cloud Platform

This chapter documents the procedure to install the Community version of EVE-NG on Google Cloud Platform (GCP). At the time of writing, AWS does not support nested virtualization, unlike GCP. Therefore, EVE-NG is not supported on AWS, so we'll cover its installation on GCP. During the installation of EVE-NG, various packages are installed from the public EVE-NG repositories, so an Internet connection and DNS resolution are required for this instance.

Figure 5-1 captures the high-level topology for installing EVE-NG as a VM in GCP.

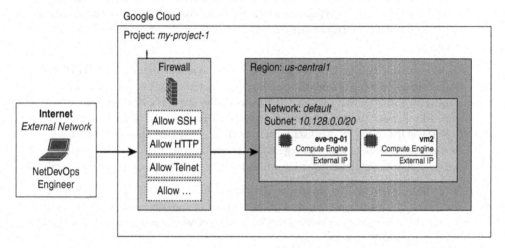

Figure 5-1 *Google Cloud Topology*

As shown in Figure 5-1, two Linux virtual machine (VM) instances are launched within GCP. A Terraform configuration file will be used to instantiate this topology on GCP. Before looking at the Terraform configuration, let's review the high-level topology and the requirements for launching EVE-NG on GCP.

In this topology, EVE-NG will be installed on one instance with a hostname of eve-ng-01. It is launched using an Ubuntu image that has nested virtualization enabled. A second instance, with a hostname of vm2, is instantiated to validate IP traffic to the EVE-NG instance. This instance, vm2, is launched using a base Debian Linux distribution image.

In this setup, VM instances eve-ng-01 and vm2 are launched in the GCP region us-central1 and in the same GCP zone. VM instances are also launched in the default network within GCP. This default network has an internal IP address network/subnet of

10.128.0.0/20 in the GCP region us-central1. Therefore, both instances use DHCP and are assigned internal IP addresses from this IP range. The instances are also assigned external IP addresses that allow communication with the Internet. Note that there is no requirement to instantiate these instances in the same GCP network, zone, and region.

After instantiation of the EVE-NG instance, SSH, HTTP, and telnet access to the EVE-NG instance is required. SSH access to the EVE-NG instance is required for a variety of reasons, including software package installation, EVE-NG software installation, uploading network device images that will be emulated within EVE-NG, and server maintenance.

EVE-NG provides an option to access the console of networking devices, simulated in the virtualized topology, by using telnet. Therefore, telnet access to the EVE-NG instance is required.

As mentioned earlier, EVE-NG provides a GUI for administration, and it is accessible via a web browser. Hence, HTTP access to the EVE-NG instance is required to manage it, including the ability to launch virtualized network devices and to create network topologies.

The firewall rules within GCP must be configured to allow inbound SSH, HTTP, and telnet traffic to EVE-NG from the NetDevOps engineers' workstations. The source IP address for these firewall rules can be hard-coded to a specific IP or to a range of IP addresses. In this topology, the traffic from the range of source IP addresses (that belong to NetDevOps engineers' workstations) to both the eve-ng-01 and vm2 instances is allowed. The source IP address range is dependent on your actual network topology. In this case, the source IP subnet is known and will be configured in the GCP firewall rules.

Once the network devices are emulated within EVE-NG, console access to those devices is required for further configuration. EVE-NG provides an option to access the console of each device using telnet on NetDevOps engineers' workstations and via the HTML5 protocol on a web browser.

The telnet-based console access is referred to as "native console." Access to the console port for each network device is required for initial configuration. The console ports for these emulated devices are accessible on TCP port ranges 32768–40000. Each emulated device is allocated a TCP port for native console access using the following formula:

Console port number for node = 32,768 + (128 * pod ID) + 1

A pod ID is a number that is associated with each user account. It can be retrieved after logging in to the EVE-NG web interface. This web interface is accessible by connecting to http://<ip_address> and selecting **Management > User Management**. The pod number associated with each user ID is shown on this page. By default, admin is the first user account within EVE-NG. Therefore, a pod ID of 0 (zero) is assigned to admin. Therefore, the console port of the first device emulated within a network topology in the EVE-NG Community version by the admin user is accessible via telnet on port number 32769.

For native console access of devices using telnet, firewall rules on GCP must allow ingress telnet traffic on these ports. As indicated earlier, native console access requires a telnet client and software installed on the administrator's desktop.

As mentioned earlier in this chapter, the EVE-NG administration page is available via a web browser. The web administration page provides an option for console access to devices using HTML5.

Custom Image on GCP Console

You must have a Google Cloud account for creating an instance on GCP. If you don't have one, you can create an account and then verify that your access works properly on the Google Cloud console using https://console.cloud.google.com/ on a web browser. At the time of writing, GCP provides a free $300 credit that can be used to install EVE-NG.

To instantiate the topology shown in Figure 5-1 within GCP, several steps must be performed.

First, access the Google Cloud console on a web browser using your appropriate Google account. Then select an existing project or create a new one within the Google Cloud console. In this use case, a new project named **my-project-1** is created on the Google Cloud console. When a new project is created in GCP, a project ID is auto-generated by default, or you can create your own. This project ID is a unique identifier for the project and is used in Terraform scripts.

Next, within the Google Cloud console, click **Activate Cloud Shell** to launch a cloud shell session.

Once the Cloud Shell Terminal opens, execute **gcloud** commands, as shown in Example 5-1. Upon execution of the first **gcloud** command, a pop-up message may appear asking you to authorize Cloud Shell. Click the **Authorize** button to proceed.

Example 5-1 *Google Cloud Shell*

```
fchaudhr@cloudshell:~ (my-project-1-382123)$ gcloud config list
[accessibility]
screen_reader = True
[component_manager]
disable_update_check = True
[compute]
gce_metadata_read_timeout_sec = 30
[core]
account = fchaudhr@cisco.com
disable_usage_reporting = True
project = my-project-1-382123
[metrics]
environment = devshell
Your active configuration is: [cloudshell-29264]


fchaudhr@cloudshell:~ (my-project-1-382123)$
```

As discussed earlier, nested virtualization must be enabled on the EVE-NG instance. In GCP, one of the methods to enable nested virtualization is to create a custom image with a special nested virtualization license key. An instance is then instantiated using this custom image. Refer to the **gcloud compute images create** command in Example 5-2 to create an Ubuntu 20.04 image using this special license key. After successful creation of this custom image, a "STATUS: READY" message appears in the cloud shell terminal, as shown in Example 5-2.

Example 5-2 *Create Nested Virtualization Image on GCP*

```
fchaudhr@cloudshell:~ (my-project-1-382123)$ gcloud compute images create
  ubuntu-2004-lts-nested --source-image-family=ubuntu-2004-lts --source-image-
  project=ubuntu-os-cloud --licenses https://www.googleapis.com/compute/v1/projects/
  vm-options/global/licenses/enable-vmx
Created [https://www.googleapis.com/compute/v1/projects/my-project-1-382123/global/
  images/ubuntu-2004-lts-nested].
NAME: ubuntu-2004-lts-nested
PROJECT: my-project-1-382123
FAMILY:
DEPRECATED:
STATUS: READY
fchaudhr@cloudshell:~ (my-project-1-382123)$
```

If you are using the free tier of GCP and get a billing-related error upon executing the **gcloud compute images create** command, you can verify that billing is properly enabled for your project at https://console.cloud.google.com/billing/projects.

The EVE-NG instance can now be launched by using this custom image with nested virtualized enabled.

Terraform Configuration File

To launch the EVE-NG instance on GCP, you use Terraform. Terraform can be installed locally on NetDevOps engineers' workstations running Windows, Mac, or Linux, or it can be used as a Docker container running locally on the workstations. The steps to install Terraform are not covered in this chapter.

Create a local directory named **virtual_network** on the NetDevOps engineers' workstations using the **mkdir** command and then switch directory by using the **cd** command:

```
$ mkdir virtual_network
$ cd virtual_network
```

Refer to Example 5-3 and Example 5-4 for the contents of a Terraform configuration file named gcp.tf in this directory. The Terraform configuration file can have any name, but it must end with a .tf extension. The file contains configurations in Terraform syntax called

HCL. There can be more than one .tf file in the directory, and Terraform uses instructions from those files in same directory to create the infrastructure. The details of Terraform configuration in gcp.tf follow.

To build and manage infrastructure on a target system, Terraform relies on plugins called "providers." As shown in Example 5-3, the Terraform file gcp.tf starts with configurations related to the GCP provider. The Terraform module indicated which provider it intends to use via a **required_providers** block. This results in installing the GCP provider during initialization.

Further, as per Example 5-3, the provider block within the Terraform script is used to define the credentials required to authenticate API calls to GCP. The default project and region of the GCP infrastructure are configured as the project ID (for the respective project in GCP) and **us-central1** in this block. As per these attributes, the instances are launched within the specified GCP project ID (with a project name of my-project-1) and region.

Google Cloud uses Service Account credentials for authentication purposes. On the GCP console, navigate to the **IAM & Admin** service and then to **Service Accounts**. Here, select **Create Service Account** to create a new account. This new account must be further configured with the role of **Editor** (under **Grant this service account access**). This role provides permissions to add, list, delete, and so on for most of the GCP services, including the Google Compute Engine (GCE). To authenticate to GCP APIs, public/ private key pairs are generated on the GCP console. A key file that contains the public/ private keys in JSON format is created for this Service Account. This is done by selecting the newly created Service Account and navigating to the **Keys** tab and then selecting **Add Key** and **Create new key** as a JSON key type. However, this file is downloaded from GCP on to the NetDevOps engineer's workstation, and its path is configured within the **credentials** attribute under the provider. In this case, this file is stored in the virtual_network directory along with the gcp.tf file.

Example 5-3 *Terraform Config File (gcp.tf) – Provider Block*

```
terraform {
  required_providers {
    google = {
      source = "hashicorp/google"
    }
  }
}


provider "google" {
  credentials = file("my-project-1-ff4f56963a9d.json")
  project     = "my-project-1-382123"
  region      = "us-central1"
}
```

The Terraform provider allows you to manage infrastructure objects on the target system by using resource blocks. Example 5-4 shows various resource blocks in the gcp.tf file.

The resource block **google_compute_instance** manages the instance on the Google Cloud Compute Engine (GCE) service. There are two such blocks in the Terraform configuration file. These instantiate two instances with the names eve-ng-01 and vm2, respectively, on GCE. Here are some details of this block in the Terraform configuration file:

- In the case of the eve-ng-01 instance, the **machine_type** argument has the setting n2-standard-4, which means that this instance gets 4x Intel x86/64-based CPUs and 16GB of RAM.

- Both instances are launched in the us-central1-a zone of the region.

- The default behavior within GCP is to not deliver an IP packet to the instance when the destination IP address is different from the actual IP address of the instance. Similarly, the default behavior is to allow an outbound packet from an instance only if the source IP address of the packet is same as the actual IP address assigned to the instance in GCP. To allow the traffic to and from an instance with different source and different destination IP addresses, the **can_ip_forward** argument must be enabled. This setting allows the IP traffic from the devices instantiated within the EVE-NG network topology to the external physical and virtual network devices. More details about this scenario are covered in the "Use Case: External IP Connectivity for Lab Topology" section in this chapter.

- The eve-ng-01 instance is launched with a performance solid-state drive (SSD) persistent disk, as described by the **type = "pd-ssd"** argument under **boot_disk**.

- The eve-ng-01 instance is instantiated using the image my-project-1-382123/ubuntu-2004-lts-nested. Note that this custom image was created earlier in this chapter using Cloud Shell Terminal commands and has nested virtualization enabled. The second instance, vm2, is launched using the image for the debian-11 Linux distribution.

- Both instances are launched in the default network within the GCP project. This default network has a subnet with an internal IP address range of 10.128.0.0/20 in the GCP region us-central1. All instances created in this network are assigned IP addresses via DHCP from this subnet.

- The **tags** attribute allows you to attach firewall rules to both instances. These firewall rules are created using **google_compute_firewall** resources. These rules allow ingress traffic for HTTP, SSH, and telnet from a specified IP address range to the eve-ng-01 and vm2 instances. Besides a firewall rule for these protocols, another rule named **allow-gcp** is also created. This firewall rule allows GCP Identity-Aware Proxy (IAP) traffic on this network. GCP IAP uses TCP forwarding and allows SSH access via a web browser on the GCP console. The IP address range 35.235.240.0/20 contains all the IP addresses that IAP uses for TCP forwarding. All these firewall rules are applied and associated to the default network.

■ The presence of the **access_config** block means that this VM instance gets an external IP address assigned and is accessible from the Internet. If this block was omitted
from the Terraform configuration file, this VM instance will not be accessible from
the Internet.

Example 5-4 *Terraform Config File (gcp.tf) – Resource Blocks*

```
resource "google_compute_instance" "eve-ng-01" {
  name           = "eve-ng-01"
  machine_type   = "n2-standard-4"
  zone           = "us-central1-a"
  can_ip_forward = true
  tags = ["allow-http", "allow-ssh", "allow-telnet", "allow-gcp"]
  boot_disk {
    initialize_params {
      image = "my-project-1-382123/ubuntu-2004-lts-nested"
      type  = "pd-ssd"
      size  = "50"
    }
  }
  network_interface {
    network = "default"
    access_config {
    }
  }
}

resource "google_compute_firewall" "allow_http" {
  name    = "allow-http"
  network = "default"
  allow {
    ports    = ["80"]
    protocol = "tcp"
  }
  direction = "INGRESS"
  source_ranges = ["172.16.1.0/24"]
  target_tags = ["allow-http"]
  priority    = 1000
}

resource "google_compute_firewall" "allow_ssh" {
  name    = "allow-ssh"
```

```
  network = "default"
  allow {
    ports    = ["22"]
    protocol = "tcp"
  }
  direction = "INGRESS"
  source_ranges = ["172.16.1.0/24"]
  target_tags = ["allow-ssh"]
  priority    = 1000


}

resource "google_compute_firewall" "allow_telnet" {
  name    = "allow-telnet"
  network = "default"
  allow {
    ports    = ["32768-32790"]
    protocol = "tcp"
  }
  direction = "INGRESS"
  source_ranges = ["172.16.1.0/24"]
  target_tags = ["allow-telnet"]
  priority    = 1000
}

resource "google_compute_firewall" "allow_gcp" {
  name    = "allow-gcp"
  network = "default"
  allow {
    ports    = ["22"]
    protocol = "tcp"
  }
  direction    = "INGRESS"
  source_ranges = ["35.235.240.0/20"]
  target_tags  = ["allow-gcp"]
  priority     = 1000
}
resource "google_compute_instance" "vm2" {
  allow_stopping_for_update = true
  name                      = "vm2"
  machine_type              = "e2-small"
```

```
zone                    = "us-central1-a"
can_ip_forward          = true
tags = ["allow-http", "allow-ssh", "allow-telnet", "allow-gcp"]
boot_disk {
  initialize_params {
    image = "debian-cloud/debian-11"
    size = "40"
  }
}
network_interface {
  network = "default"
  access_config {
  }
}
}
```

The Terraform script can be executed on a NetDevOps engineer's workstation by executing the **terraform** commands shown in Example 5-5. Terraform must be initialized in the same directory before applying these configurations. Also, as per execution of **terraform init,** Terraform finds and installs the GCP provider in the virtual_network directory.

The partial output shown in Example 5-5 confirms the creation of instances and the firewalls rules on GCP. These commands must be executed in the working directory where the Terraform configuration file (gcp.tf) is saved.

Example 5-5 *Execution of Terraform*

```
$ terraform init
#OUTPUT OMITTED#

$ terraform fmt

$ terraform validate
Success! The configuration is valid.

$ terraform apply
#OUTPUT OMITTED#
Apply complete! Resources: 6 added, 0 changed, 0 destroyed.

$
```

After the **terraform** commands have been successfully executed, the instances and related configurations are performed on GCP. As a next step, the EVE-NG Community version must be installed on the eve-ng-01 instance.

EVE-NG Software Installation on Instance

After the instantiation of the instances, ssh to the eve-ng-01 instance by navigating to the Google Compute Engine (GCE) from the Google Cloud console dashboard.

On the GCE, you can find the eve-ng-01 instance under the **Instances** tab. Under **Connect**, click the **SSH** drop-down menu to initiate SSH by clicking **Open in browser window**, as shown in Figure 5-2. As a result a separate SSH-in-browser window should open.

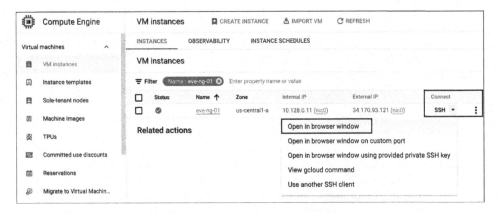

Figure 5-2 *SSH-in-Browser to EVE-NG*

The installation of EVE-NG software and other software packages is performed using the shell script within the SSH-in-browser window.

Refer to Example 5-6, which shows the commands that are executed in this SSH connection for the installation, updating, and upgrading of software packages on the eve-ng-01 instance. This installation must be done using the root privilege. An installation script named install-eve.sh is hosted on the EVE-NG official website, and its installation is started with the **wget** command. The **wget** command with the **-O** flag prints the content of the script downloaded from the website on the terminal. As a last execution step, the VM instance is restarted manually by executing the **reboot** command.

Example 5-6 *Installation of EVE-NG Software on the EVE-NG Instance*

```
fchaudhr@eve-ng-01:~$ sudo -i
root@eve-ng-01:~# wget -O - https://www.eve-ng.net/focal/install-eve.sh | bash -i
root@eve-ng-01:~# apt update
root@eve-ng-01:~# apt upgrade -y
root@eve-ng-01:~# reboot
```

After the instance has been rebooted, reconnect to the eve-ng-01 instance using the SSH-in-browser window on the GCP console.

The **EVE-NG Setup** screen appears on this SSH connection. Press **Ctrl+c** to exit from this screen and then enter **sudo -i** to get root privilege, as shown in Example 5-7.

Example 5-7   *EVE-NG Setup Screen*

```
fchaudhr@eve-ng-01:~$ sudo -i
```

At this stage, the **EVE-NG Setup** screen appears again. The guided setup prompts users to enter various settings, including the following:

- The root password.
- The hostname of the server.
- The DNS domain name.
- The IP address for the server (use DHCP for the implementation on GCP setup).
- The NTP server (optional).
- The proxy server configuration. (The VM instance connects directly to the Internet on GCP setup, so select the direct connection option.)

Upon this previous data being entered, the server proceeds to complete the installation of EVE-NG software and reboots automatically.

EVE-NG software becomes operational after the reboot. After the reboot, log back in to SSH-in-browser and validate that this instance supports hardware-accelerated KVM virtual machines by issuing the **kvm-ok** command. Refer to Example 5-8 to see the output of this, confirming that KVM support is enabled in the Linux kernel.

Example 5-8   *Confirming KVM Support on the EVE-NG Instance*

```
fchaudhr@eve-ng-01:~$ sudo -i
root@eve-ng-01:~#
root@eve-ng-01:~# kvm-ok
INFO: /dev/kvm exists
KVM acceleration can be used
root@eve-ng-01:~#
```

Next, execute the command shown in Example 5-9 to validate that the CPU of this EVE-NG server supports Intel VT-x technology. Make sure that **vmx** is found in the output of this command, which may be multiple lines long.

Example 5-9 *Confirming Intel VT-x Support on the EVE-NG Instance*

```
root@eve-ng-01:~# grep -e 'vmx' /proc/cpuinfo
flags          : fpu vme de pse tsc msr pae mce cx8 apic sep mtrr pge mca cmov pat
  pse36 clflush mmx fxsr sse sse2 ss ht syscall nx pdpe1gb rdtscp lm constant_tsc
  rep_good nopl xtopology nonstop_tsc cpuid tsc_known_freq pni pclmulqdq vmx ssse3
#OUTPUT OMITTED#
```

Another option for confirming support of the VT-x technology on the instance's CPU is shown in Example 5-10.

Example 5-10 *Confirming Intel VT-x Support*

```
root@eve-ng-01:~# lscpu | egrep -i "Model name|Virtualization"
Model name:              Intel(R) Xeon(R) CPU @ 2.80GHz
Virtualization:          VT-x
Virtualization type:     full
root@eve-ng-01:~#
```

Now EVE-NG is fully operational, and its administration interface can be accessed via a web browser for initial logon and creation of virtualized network topology.

First-Time Web Access to EVE-NG

As mentioned earlier in this chapter, EVE-NG provides a web GUI for administration purposes. The web GUI is used to create and manage a virtual lab topology, conduct user management activities, and perform administration tasks such as accessing system status, logs, and so on

The web GUI can be accessed on a web browser by going to the public IP address of the eve-ng-01 VM instance (that is, **http://{public_ip}**, where **{public_ip}** is replaced with an IP address in your respective setup). The public IP address of the eve-ng-01 instance is referred to as external IP on the GCP console under the Google Compute Engine (GCE). Keep in mind that the GCP firewall rules were configured earlier. These rules allow developers' workstation source IP addresses to access this instance via HTTP. Refer to Figure 5-3 to view this external IP address on GCP. Figure 5-3 also shows the internal IP that is assigned to the network interface card (NIC) of the eve-ng-01 instance.

First-time access to this external IP address of the EVE-NG administration page uses the default username **admin** and the password **eve**. However, before signing in, you must select the console access method of the HTML5 console from the drop-down menu on this web page.

As covered earlier in this chapter, native console access and HTML5 console access to the emulated networking devices is allowed by EVE-NG. Native console access means that telnetting to specific ports on the eve-ng-01 instance can be performed on developers' workstations to access each of the emulated networking devices. The HTML5 console method allows you to access the console from the web browser and must be selected from the drop-down menu on the initial logon page of EVE-NG, as shown in Figure 5-4.

Figure 5-3   *External IP of the eve-ng-01 Instance*

After logging into EVE-NG, navigate to the **Management > User management** page. Here, you can change the password of the admin user by clicking the **Edit** button under **Actions**. As a best practice, this default password should be changed after logging in to EVE-NG. Additional users can also be configured by clicking the **+Add user** button.

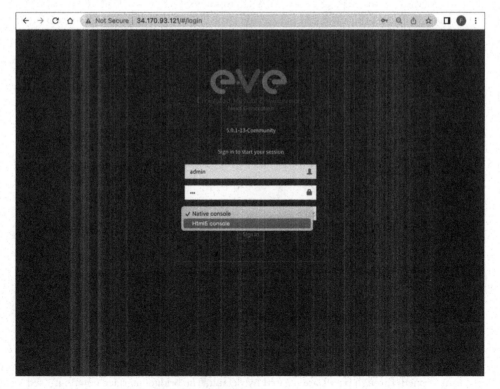

Figure 5-4   *Initial Login Web Page of EVE-NG*

Details such as system status and system logs are accessible under the **System** drop-down menu of the web administration page.

The **Main** page on the web UI allows you to add and manage labs. On this page, you can create labs. Within each lab, network lab topologies are created by adding emulated devices. By default, labs can be added on the root folder (default) under the **Main** page. EVE-NG also provides flexibility in managing labs by allowing you to create one or more folders (that is, a directory structure). You can then create and move labs within those folders. From the **Main** page, you can create a folder by providing a new folder name and clicking the **Add folder** button. The labs and folders can also be moved, deleted, exported, and imported under this page as well.

If a lab has already been created and selected, the page also displays the topology of the lab. Once you have selected an existing lab, scroll down the page and click the **Edit** or **Open** button to start devices or make any changes to the lab topology.

Now that we have explored the web administration page of EVE-NG, let's proceed with some case studies to see how networking topologies with emulated network devices are instantiated.

Use Case: Lab Using Cisco CSR 1000V

Let's go through the steps to create a new lab topology using Cisco CSR 1000V series routers. The goal of this use case is to create two CSR 1000Vs that connect to each other over GigabitEthernet interfaces and can send IP traffic to each other. At a high level, the topology of this use case is shown in Figure 5-5.

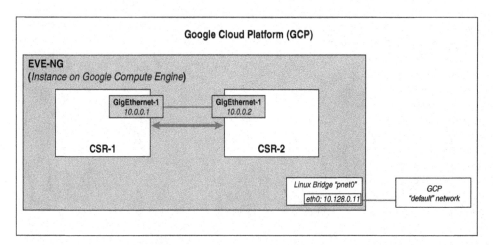

Figure 5-5   *Topology with Two CSR 1000v Routers*

During the installation of EVE-NG software, multiple Linux bridge s are created on the host (the eve-ng-01 instance in this case). At the time of writing, ten bridge interfaces, named pnet0 through pnet9, are created by default. The bridge interface (pnet0) is used for management purposes. By default, pnet0 uses the host instance's Ethernet NIC eth0 for network connectivity. In this GCP setup, pnet0 gets an IP address of 10.128.0.11 from the GCP default network by using DHCP. As shared earlier, this is the internal IP of eve-ng-01, and you may get a different IP address if you follow this procedure for installing EVE-NG on GCP. The rest of the bridge interfaces (pnet1 through pnet9) show up as cloud networks within the EVE-NG UI.

After you have created the two CSR 1000V routers within EVE-NG, the GigabitEthernet interfaces of both CSR routers must be connected to each other manually.

First, let's instantiate two CSR 1000V routers by creating a lab within EVE-NG. To begin, log on to the EVE-NG web administration page on your browser. This can be done by pointing to its external (public) IP address in GCP. Upon initial logon, the **Main** page of the EVE-NG GUI appears. On this page, hover over various buttons to see their description, such as **Select All**, **Add a new lab**, **Move to …**, **Delete**, and so on.

To create a new lab, click the **Add new lab** icon on the **Main** page. Give a new name to this lab, such as **CSRv lab1**. The **Version** field is mandatory and has a default value of 1. Description, author, and other details are optional and not required. After you click the **Save** button, a blank **Topology canvas** page opens.

Refer to Figure 5-6, which shows a blank topology canvas and the side bar on the topology canvas. The side bar is interactive and automatically expands when you move the mouse over it.

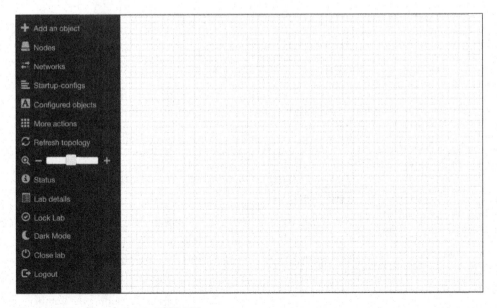

Figure 5-6 *Topology on EVE-NG*

In this topology canvas, the side bar shows the following options:

- **Add an object** allows you to add a new object such as a node, network, text box, picture, and so on. The node is the device that will be emulated in this lab topology. In this use case, CSR 1000V will be added. **Network** allows you to add a bridge or a cloud within EVE-NG. The network type of **Cloud** allows functions such as connectivity to external physical or virtual networking devices. We will look at the network type of Cloud in another use case in this chapter.

- The **Nodes** and **Networks** objects in the side bar show any devices (that is, nodes) and networks that are part of this lab topology.

- The **Startup-configs** side bar option shows the startup config for each node and whether it is enabled (button = **On**) or disabled (button = **Off**) to boot from the startup configuration.

  - As previously mentioned, if there are existing devices, these will show up under the **Nodes** side bar menu, where you can scroll to a specific node and click the **Export CFG** icon under the **ACTIONS** field. This is equivalent to exporting **show running-config** on Cisco IOS devices. Then for this specific node, set **STARTUP-CONFIG** to **Exported** from the drop-down menu. These actions result in **Startup-configs** being populated and enabled (button = **On**).

  - To view the startup config of a node, click the node name on this page.

- **More actions** is a submenu that can initiate the following actions:

  - **Start all nodes and Stop all nodes:** Initially, all the nodes/devices added to a lab topology are powered off and must be manually powered on.

  - **Wipe all nodes:** Deletes the NVRAM of the networking devices so that, at next boot, it will start from factory defaults.

  - **Export all CFGs:** Exports the running configurations of all devices. This is equivalent to exporting **show running-config** on Cisco IOS devices.

  - **Set nodes startup-cfg to exported:** This means that if the configuration of a device has been exported (either via **Export all CFGs** or the **Nodes** side bar option) then the startup configuration of all devices in this lab is enabled and set to the exported configuration.

  - **Set nodes startup-cfg to none:** This setting disables (button = **Off**) the startup configuration of all devices in this lab.

  - **Delete all startup-cfg:** This means that exported configurations of all devices will be deleted, and hence startup configs are disabled (button = **Off**) as well.

- The **Status** side bar menu shows the current state of this lab, including the number of nodes/devices running, CPU and memory usage, and so on.

To add a Cisco CSR 1000V router to this lab, click **Add an Object** and then click **Nodes** on the side bar menu. The **Add a new Node** pop-up window appears at this stage.

In the template search bar, type **Cisco** and look for **Cisco CSR 1000V (XE 16.x)** from the drop-down menu. You will find Cisco CSR, but it will be grayed out! You will not be able to add this node or any other node to the lab topology!

What's the reason for this? A freshly installed EVE-NG has no pre-installed images of any device. This means that no device can be emulated and used in the network topology. We need to add and onboard an appropriate image for Cisco CSR on this EVE-NG server. EVE-NG supports the emulation of devices using Dynamips, QEMU, and IOS on Linux (IOL). The following section provides details about adding and preparing a Cisco CSR QEMU image for EVE-NG.

Image Types on EVE-NG and Adding a CSR 1000V Image

So, what are QEMU, Dynamips, and IOL? QEMU is an open-source machine emulator. Dynamips is another type of emulation technology that was originally written to emulate Cisco routers. It emulates the actual hardware for various Cisco routers, and then IOS images compatible with that hardware can be installed on it. IOS on Linux, also referred to as IOS on Unix, is a simulator provided by Cisco and used for internal testing.

Dynamips images are available for only a few Cisco routers, such as Cisco 7200, Cisco 3725, and Cisco 1710 series. IOL images are available for Layer 2/3 switches and Layer 3 routers. IOL images, along with their license, are stored with an extension of .bin on the directory path mentioned earlier. These images must be executable.

Each of these emulation technologies has a unique image for the respective device. The required images for each device in the network topology must be added to the EVE-NG server. The transfer of an image can be done using Secure Copy Protocol (SCP).

Then the image of each device must be placed in a specific folder (that is, a directory within the EVE-NG server). The directories within the EVE-NG server for various types of images are as follows:

- QEMU images are stored in the directory **/opt/unetlab/addons/qemu/**.

- Dynamips images are stored in the directory **/opt/unetlab/addons/dynamips/**.

- IOL (IOS on Linux) images are stored in the directory **/opt/unetlab/addons/iol/bin/**.

The majority of networking devices from various vendors are supported and available as QEMU images. Hence, we will focus on the preparation and installation of a CSR 1000V QEMU image on EVE-NG. This is a multistep process since the ISO image of CSR 1000V is used to create a QEMU hard disk. This QEMU image will then be used to simulate a topology in this chapter.

Here is a summary of the steps performed for installation of a CSR QEMU image:

Step 1.　Download the ISO image of the CSR 1000V release from the Cisco website.

Step 2.　Using SCP, move the ISO image to the EVE-NG instance named eve-ng-01.

Step 3. Initiate an SSH connection to the eve-ng-01 server.

Step 4. Boot CSR from the ISO image and install to a QEMU-based hard drive.

Step 5. Move the QEMU image to a subdirectory with a specific naming syntax for CSR.

The details of these steps are provided next:

Step 1. Download the ISO image of CSR.

For step 1, you will require an account on the Cisco website that provides you software download privileges. In this case, the CSR 1000V 17.3.4a image named csr1000v-universalk9.17.03.04a.iso is downloaded from the Cisco website. This ISO file must be downloaded on a developer's workstation that has SSH access to eve-ng-01 (recall that GCP firewall rules were configured to allow this).

Step 2. Using SCP, move the ISO image to EVE-NG.

Secure copy (SCP) this ISO file from a NetDevOps engineer's workstation to the external IP address of the eve-ng-01 server. Keep in mind that GCP firewall rules must allow SSH traffic from the source IP address of this workstation. The root credentials are used for authentication of the SCP session to eve-ng-01. For SCP, freeware or commercial software with a GUI can be used. SCP can also be done by using the command-line utility. The syntax of the SCP command is as follows:

```
$ scp [source-filename] [user@]DEST-HOST:[dest-filename]
```

In this command, **[source-filename]** is the filename on the source machine, while **[dest-filename]** is the destination filename and is optional. If **[dest-filename]** is not provided, the source file is transferred with the same name to the destination host. An example of SCP command syntax for transferring a CSR image to eve-ng-01, from the appropriate directory, is as follows:

```
$ scp csr1000v-universalk9.17.03.04a.iso root@34.170.93.121:
```

Step 3. Initiate an SSH connection to EVE-NG.

After uploading the CSR image, initiate an SSH connection to the eve-ng-01 server from the NetDevOps engineer's workstation using an appropriate local application, such as Terminal on macOS or PowerShell on Windows. Again, the root credentials, which were changed earlier, are used for authentication. Here's an example of the SSH command syntax from a Terminal on macOS to the external IP of eve-ng-01 in this GCP setup:

```
$ ssh root@34.170.93.121
```

Step 4. Boot CSR from the ISO and install to disk.

Refer to Example 5-11 for the execution of commands to complete the installation of the CSR image on the eve-ng-01 server. These commands perform the following actions:

- Create a temporary directory (named "test" in this case) on eve-ng-01.

- Create an empty qcow2 image with a maximum size of 8GB for CSR by using the **qemu-img create** command.

- Start the installation of CSR using the **qemu-system-x86_64** command. Note that in this command the path to the CSR1000v ISO image is pointed out after the **-cdrom** flag. In this example, the csr1000v-universalk9.17.03.04a.iso file was transferred to this instance by using SCP in the root (~) directory.

On the next screen, scroll down to **CSR1000v Serial Console …** and press **Enter**. Refer to Figure 5-7 to see the selection of this entry. Note, if the **CSR1000v Serial Console** option is not selected, this procedure will fail.

Example 5-11   *CSR 1000V Image Installation on EVE-NG*

```
root@eve-ng-01:~# mkdir temp
root@eve-ng-01:~# cd temp
root@eve-ng-01:~/temp# /opt/qemu/bin/qemu-img create -f qcow2  virtioa.qcow2 8G
root@eve-ng-01:~/temp# /opt/qemu-2.2.0/bin/qemu-system-x86_64  -nographic
  -drive file=virtioa.qcow2,if=virtio,bus=0,unit=0,cache=none -machine type=pc-
  1.0,accel=kvm -serial mon:stdio -nographic -nodefconfig -nodefaults -rtc base=utc
  -cdrom ~/csr1000v-universalk9.17.03.04a.iso -boot order=dc  -m 4096
```

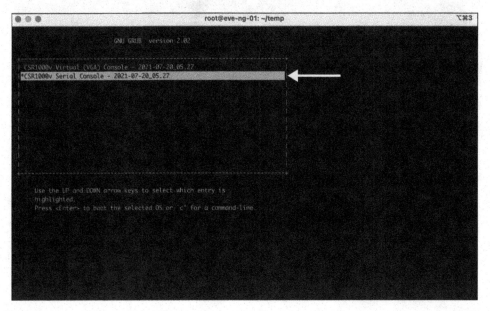

Figure 5-7   *CSR 1000v Installation*

> **Note**   After selecting Serial Console, wait for the installation of CSRv to finish.

The installation of CSR is complete when the message "Rebooting from HD" appears on the Serial Console. At this stage, press **Ctrl+a** (both keys together) and then release the keys and press c to fall back to the QEMU prompt. Then type **quit** to exit from the prompt. Refer to Figure 5-8, which shows the completion of the CSR 1000V installation.

Figure 5-8   *CSR 1000v Installation Completed*

Now the installation of the QEMU image of CSR is complete.

Step 5.   **The CSR QEMU image is saved in a specific directory path on EVE-NG.**

On the EVE-NG server, QEMU images for each device are stored in a specific directory and subdirectory with a unique naming syntax. Following are some important rules to follow for QEMU images:

■ As shared earlier in this chapter, qemu images are stored in the /opt/unet-lab/addons/qemu/ directory.

- A subdirectory or a folder must be created within the aforementioned directory. This subdirectory uses a predefined naming convention, and it must be followed strictly (this name represents the device or vendor). This subdirectory name is followed by a hyphen (-). For example, a Cisco IOS-XE–based CSR 1000V has a folder name of csr1000vng-, and Cisco Nexus 9000v has a folder name of nxos9k-.

- Additional text or a label can be provided after the hyphen. There are no special restrictions on the syntax of this label.

Refer to Example 5-12, which shows the creation of the subdirectory with the correct naming syntax, and then the QEMU image is moved to this subdirectory. Additionally, Example 5-12 shows the cleanup of the temporary directory, and then the permissions for this file and directories are also updated. This update of permissions is performed for any new image added to EVE-NG.

Example 5-12   *CSR 1000V Qemu Image Directory*

```
root@eve-ng-01:~/temp# mkdir /opt/unetlab/addons/qemu/csr1000vng-17.03.04a/
root@eve-ng-01:~/temp# ls
virtioa.qcow2
root@eve-ng-01:~/temp# mv virtioa.qcow2 /opt/unetlab/addons/qemu/csr1000vng-
    17.03.04a/
root@eve-ng-01:~/temp#
root@eve-ng-01:~/temp# cd
root@eve-ng-01:~# rm -rf temp
root@eve-ng-01:~# /opt/unetlab/wrappers/unl_wrapper -a fixpermissions
```

At this stage, the CSR 1000V image is successfully added to the eve-ng-01 server, and it can now be used in the lab topology via the web administration page. The creation of a simple topology is covered in detail in the following section.

Lab Topology Within EVE-NG

After you have added the CSR 1000V image, the lab networking topology in Figure 5-5 can be created. Navigate back to the web interface of the eve-ng-01 server on a web browser by accessing the external IP address of this VM instance. You may also select **Html5 console** on the login page of EVE-NG.

After successful authentication, navigate back to the **CSRv lab1** topology canvas. From the side bar menu, select **Add an object** and then select **Nodes**. The **Add a New Node** pop up window should appear at this stage. In the template search bar, type **Cisco** and look for Cisco CSR 1000V (XE 16.x) from the drop-down menu. This time you should be successful in selecting CSR. Refer to Figure 5-9 to see the various settings on this window and how two CSR 1000Vs can be added in this lab topology. The following settings need to be changed in this window:

- In **Number of nodes to add,** enter **2** to add two CSR nodes.

- In **Name/prefix,** enter **CSR-.** This will result in EVE-NG assigning CSR-1 and CSR-2 as the names for two nodes in the lab topology canvas.

- Leave the rest of the settings at the defaults.

Note   The image 17.03.04a shows up as the only option on the Add a New Node window. If desired, you can then modify CPU, RAM, and the number of Ethernets of these CSR 1000Vs on this screen.

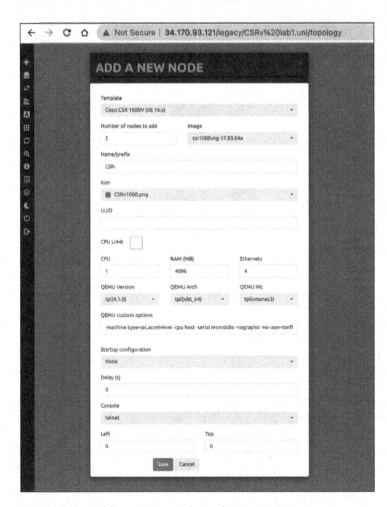

Figure 5-9   *Adding a New Node on the EVE-NG UI*

After adding two CSRs to the topology canvas, you can drag the CSRs to change their position on this canvas.

The next step is to interconnect the two CSRs with each other over their respective GigabitEthernet-1 interfaces. This can be done by using the drag-and-drop method. An orange plug with a "Connect to another node" label appears when the mouse is moved over either of the CSRs. Click this plug and then drag and drop it over the second CSR. This will result in the **Add Connection between CSR-1 and CSR-2** window to appear. In this window, choose **Gi1** interfaces from the drop-down menu on each of the CSRs and click **Save**, as shown in Figure 5-10.

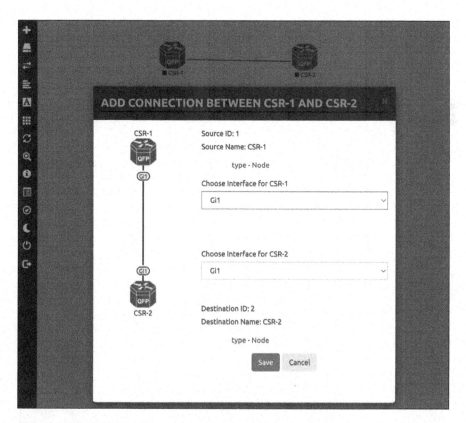

Figure 5-10 *Adding a Connection Between the Nodes*

Next, the CSR nodes must be started. To start them, right-click each one separately and click **Start**. Alternatively, select both CSRs together on the topology canvas, right-click, and select **Start Selected** from the context menu that appears.

After a few minutes, you may click **CSR-1** and **CSR-2** separately on the topology canvas, which results in launching HTML5 console access in the web browser to each of the CSRs. If HTML5 console access was not selected on the initial logon page of EVE-NG, use a telnet application on your workstation for console access to the CSRs. Additional packages, available from the eve-ng.net website, are usually required to be installed on developer workstations for launching native console access directly from the topology canvas. This can be done by using **telnet <external_ip_eve-ng> <port>** on any application on a developer workstation to access the console of the CSRs. As explained earlier in this chapter, by default, the admin user is assigned a pod ID of 0. Therefore, the consoles of CSR-1 and CSR-2 will be accessible on port numbers 32769 (**telnet {external_ip_eve-ng} 32769**) and 32770 (**telnet {external_ip_eve-ng} 32770**), respectively. CSR nodes take few minutes to boot up, so don't be alarmed if there is no message on the console initially. For example, in this lab setup on GCP, the console of CSR-1 can be accessed as follows:

```
$ telnet 34.170.93.121 32769
```

On the console of each CSR, the Cisco Initial Configuration dialog will appear. You may exit or use it to configure hostnames and GigabitEthernet-1 ports for IP connectivity. Then verify that the CSRs can pass IP traffic to each other. Refer to Example 5-13, which shows configurations of both CSRs and further verifies IP communication using the **ping** command.

Example 5-13   *CSR Configs and Validation*

```
CSR-1# show run
!
hostname CSR-1
!
interface GigabitEthernet1
 ip address 10.0.0.1 255.255.255.252
 no shutdown
!
CSR-2# show run
!
hostname CSR-2
!
interface GigabitEthernet1
 ip address 10.0.0.2 255.255.255.252
 no shutdown
!
CSR-2# ping 10.0.0.1
Type escape sequence to abort.
Sending 5, 100-byte ICMP Echos to 10.0.0.1, timeout is 2 seconds:
!!!!!
Success rate is 100 percent (5/5), round-trip min/avg/max = 1/1/2 ms
CSR-2#
```

In summary, this use case covered the steps to build a Cisco CSR 1000V QEMU image from an ISO file in EVE-NG. This use case then walked you through the steps to use this image and create a network topology with two CSR 1000V nodes. After configuration of the CSR 1000V nodes, verification of IP connectivity within EVE-NG on this topology was performed as well.

Use Case: External IP Connectivity for Lab Topology

The earlier use case covered the steps for creating a lab topology in which network devices communicate with each other within EVE-NG. Often, it is required to connect a virtual lab topology with external devices. The external devices may include physical networking devices, virtual networking devices on another server, monitoring tools, NetDevOps tools such as Ansible, and so on. So how do we achieve and provide such external IP connectivity?

Let's extend the earlier use case to provide external IP connectivity to one of the CSR routers created in the network topology on EVE-NG. This use case shows one method to achieve this connectivity. Figure 5-11 shows the high-level network topology for external connectivity.

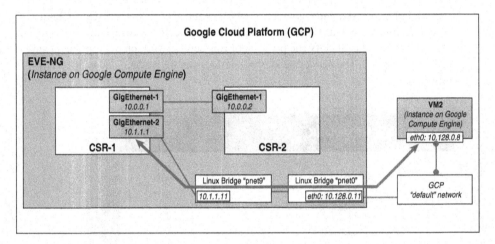

Figure 5-11 *Topology for External Connectivity*

In this topology, the GigabitEthernet-2 interface of CSR-1 will be connected to the external GCP network and route IP traffic to vm2, launched as per the earlier steps in this chapter.

Here is a summary of the additional steps performed for this external connectivity:

Step 1.   Add a cloud network in the EVE-NG lab topology canvas.

Step 2.   Connect CSR-1 to the cloud network.

Step 3.   Add the EVE-NG server IP configuration and modify the Linux kernel settings.

Step 4.   Add IP routing and modify the firewall rules on GCP.

Details for each of these steps are provided in the following sections.

Step 1   Add Cloud Network in EVE-NG Lab Topology Canvas

For this external connectivity, a network type of **Cloud** will be added on the topology canvas of the EVE-NG web administration page. Basically, this refers to a Linux bridge named pnet, described earlier in this chapter. Think of Cloud as an alias of pnet. There are ten Cloud networks on the web administration page, and each corresponds to a pnet. For example, Cloud9 corresponds to the Linux bridge named pnet9. Recall that pnet0 connects to the external network via eth0 on this eve-ng-01 instance. Cloud0 can be used for managing the traffic of EVE-NG.

In this use case, Cloud9 (that is, pnet9) will be used to provide external connectivity. To add a Cloud9 network in the lab topology, navigate to the topology canvas from the **Main** web administration page of EVE-NG. Click **Add an Object** and then select **Network** from the side bar menu. As a result, the **Add a New Network** window appears. As shown in Figure 5-12, enter any text you like for the **Name** field and select **Cloud9** from the drop-down menu. Then click **Save**. The **Left** and **Top** fields have a default value of 0. These are used to specify the position of this new network on the topology canvas and are not changed. The network and other devices can be dragged manually to any position on the canvas.

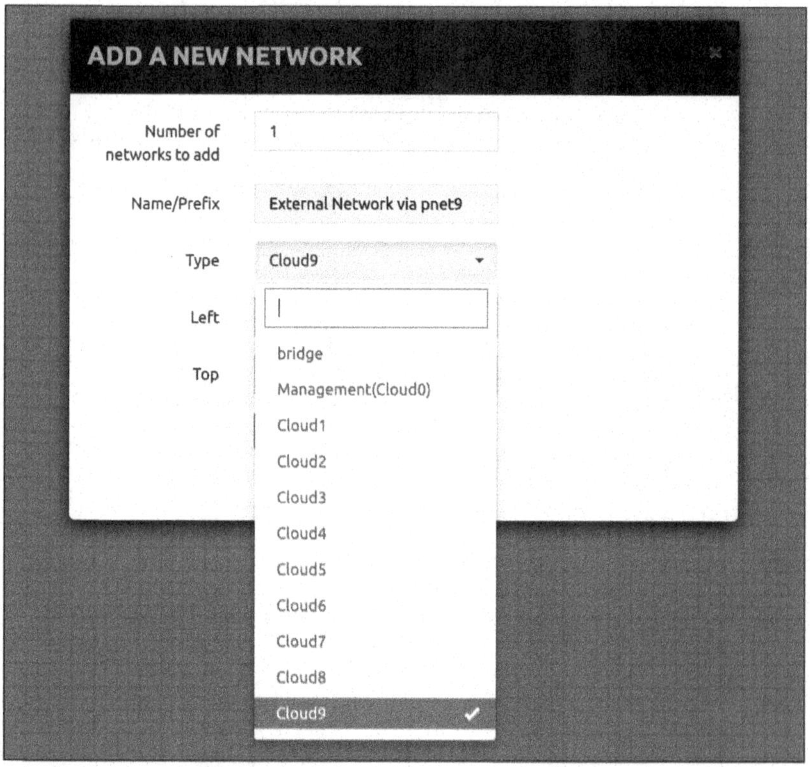

Figure 5-12 *Adding a Network on EVE-NG*

Step 2   Connect CSR-1 to Cloud Network

Next on the topology canvas, CSR-1 must be connected to this network. CSR-1 must be stopped to perform this connectivity. Hence, you need to right-click and select **Stop** on the CSR-1 node. Then click the orange plug and use the drag-and-drop method to connect CSR-1 to the newly created Cloud9 network. On the **Add connection** window, make sure the **Gi2** interface for CSR-1 is selected and then start CSR-1 (right-click and select **Start**).

Once CSR-1 has been started, access its console natively or by using the HTML5 mechanism. Refer to Example 5-14 for a partial configuration of CSR-1 required for IP external connectivity. As per this example, an IP address on GigabitEthernet2 and a static IP route are added so that the IP traffic from CSR-1 is routed to pnet9 of eve-ng-01. In this example, a default IP route pointing to the IP address of pnet9 is configured on CSR-1.

Example 5-14   *CSR-1 Configuration*

```
!
hostname CSR-1
!
interface GigabitEthernet2
 ip address 10.1.1.1 255.255.255.0
 no shutdown
!
ip route 0.0.0.0 0.0.0.0 10.1.1.11
!
```

Great. Now CSR-1 is ready to send and receive IP traffic from external devices. However, there are additional steps required on both the EVE-NG instance and GCP setup for this connectivity.

Step 3   Configure EVE-NG Server IP Address and Modify Linux Kernel Settings

One of those considerations is that the IP address (10.1.1.11) of pnet9 on eve-ng-01 has not been configured yet. This configuration needs to be done on eve-ng-01 via SSH access. Refer to Example 5-15, which shows the configuration of this IP address on the pnet9 Linux bridge. As explained earlier, the output of **ip address show pnet0** displays the internal IP of eve-ng-01. You may get a different IP address via DHCP in GCP if you follow this procedure.

Furthermore, the default behavior on the Linux kernel is to not forward IP traffic that is meant for destinations other than itself. To allow routing traffic to and from CSR-1, the IP forwarding behavior on eve-ng-01 must be changed. It is changed by modifying the kernel variable **net.ipv4.ip_forward=1**. Refer to Example 5-15, which shows this configuration change and its validation.

Additionally, the Linux kernel uses a reverse path filtering mechanism to check if the receiving packet source is routable. By default, the kernel performs source IP validation. This can be disabled for this topology as well.

Example 5-15 *EVE-NG Configs for External IP Connectivity*

```
root@eve-ng-01:~# ip address show pnet0
3: pnet0: <BROADCAST,MULTICAST,UP,LOWER_UP> mtu 1460 qdisc noqueue state UP group
  default qlen 1000
    link/ether 42:01:0a:80:00:0b brd ff:ff:ff:ff:ff:ff
    inet 10.128.0.11/32 brd 10.128.0.11 scope global dynamic pnet0
root@eve-ng-01:~# ip address add 10.1.1.11/24 dev pnet9
root@eve-ng-01:~# ip address show pnet9
12: pnet9: <BROADCAST,MULTICAST,UP,LOWER_UP> mtu 9000 qdisc noqueue state UP group
  default qlen 1000
    link/ether 66:00:ee:05:2a:07 brd ff:ff:ff:ff:ff:ff
    inet 10.1.1.11/24 scope global pnet9
root@eve-ng-01:~#
root@eve-ng-01:~# sysctl net.ipv4.ip_forward
net.ipv4.ip_forward = 0
root@eve-ng-01:~# sysctl -w net.ipv4.ip_forward=1
net.ipv4.ip_forward = 1
root@eve-ng-01:~# sysctl net.ipv4.ip_forward
net.ipv4.ip_forward = 1
root@eve-ng-01:~#
root@eve-ng-01:~# for i in /proc/sys/net/ipv4/conf/*/rp_filter; do echo 0 > "$i";
  done
root@eve-ng-01:~#
root@eve-ng-01:~# sysctl -a | grep -i rp_filter
net.ipv4.conf.all.rp_filter = 0
net.ipv4.conf.eth0.rp_filter = 0
#OUTPUT OMITTED#
```

Note that to make these changes persistent so they survive a reboot, you need to make changes (IP address on pnet9, IP forwarding, and reverse path filtering kernel) in the files on the appropriate Linux distribution. Two such files are /etc/network/interfaces and /etc/sysctl.conf. Those changes are not shown for brevity purposes.

The required configuration changes on eve-ng-01 are now complete. However, there are missing parts in the GCP setup for the complete IP traffic connectivity between the EVE-NG topology and external network devices.

Step 4   Add IP Routing and Modify Firewall Rules on GCP

One of those missing parts is IP routing in GCP. The CSR-1 interface has an IP address in the 10.1.1.0/24 subnet, and the devices on the GCP default network do not have any knowledge on how to route traffic destined for this subnet. Also, GCP firewall rules do not allow IP traffic to any VM (instance) from 10.1.1.0/24 network.

Both issues can be addressed by modifying the Terraform configuration file gcp.tf, shown earlier in Example 5-4. Refer to Example 5-16 for the modifications to this file, which include the following:

- Add a route on GCP using the **google_compute_route** resource. This resource block has a local name of **route_to_10**. As per this resource block, the traffic destined to 10.1.1.0/24 (**dest_range**) is sent to the eve-ng-01 (**next_hop_instance**) instance.

- Add a new firewall rule on GCP using the **google_compute_firewall** resource. This resource block has a local name of **allow_gcp_10**. Hence, the traffic from the source IP address range of 10.1.1.0/24 is allowed on the default network.

- Modify the **tags** attribute on the **google_compute_instance** resource for the eve-ng-01 and vm2 instances. Thus, the newly created firewall rule, which allows traffic from the source IP address range of 10.1.1.0/24, is attached to both instances.

Example 5-16 *Modifications to the Terraform Configuration File (gcp.tf)*

```
resource "google_compute_route" "route_to_10" {
  name       = "eve-ng-10-1-1"
  dest_range = "10.1.1.0/24"
  network    = "default"
  next_hop_instance      = google_compute_instance.eve-ng-01.name
  next_hop_instance_zone = "us-central1-a"
  priority               = 1000
}

resource "google_compute_firewall" "allow_gcp_10" {
  name    = "allow-gcp-10"
  network = "default"
  allow {
    protocol = "all"
  }
  direction     = "INGRESS"
  source_ranges = ["10.0.0.0/8"]
  target_tags   = ["allow-gcp-10"]
  priority      = 1000
}
resource "google_compute_instance" "eve-ng-01" {
#OUTPUT OMITTED#  tags = ["allow-http", "allow-ssh", "allow-telnet", "allow-gcp",
  "allow-gcp-10"]
#OUTPUT OMITTED#
}
```

```
resource "google_compute_instance" "vm2" {
#OUTPUT OMITTED#
  tags = ["allow-http", "allow-ssh", "allow-telnet", "allow-gcp", "allow-gcp-10"]
#OUTPUT OMITTED#
}
```

The Terraform script can be executed on a developer workstation by executing the commands shown in Example 5-17. This will apply the changes covered in Example 5-16.

Example 5-17   *Applying GCP Infrastructure Changes by Executing Terraform*

```
$ terraform validate
Success! The configuration is valid.


$ terraform apply


#OUTPUT OMITTED#
```

At this point, you can validate IP connectivity between devices emulated on EVE-NG and external networking devices. Example 5-18 shows the validation of IP connectivity from vm2 to the GigabitEthernet-2 interface of CSR-1. Note that in this GCP setup, vm2 is assigned an IP address of 10.128.0.8 by the DHCP server. You may see a different IP address assigned to your VM (instance).

Example 5-18   *Verify External IP Connectivity on vm2*

```
fchaudhr@vm2:~$ ip addr show ens4
2: ens4: <BROADCAST,MULTICAST,UP,LOWER_UP> mtu 1460 qdisc mq state UP group default
  qlen 1000
    link/ether 42:01:0a:80:00:08 brd ff:ff:ff:ff:ff:ff
    inet 10.128.0.8/32 scope global dynamic ens4
       valid_lft 75888sec preferred_lft 75888sec
    inet6 fe80::4001:aff:fe80:8/64 scope link
       valid_lft forever preferred_lft forever
fchaudhr@vm2:~$
fchaudhr@vm2:~$ ping 10.1.1.1 -c 2
PING 10.1.1.1 (10.1.1.1) 56(84) bytes of data.
64 bytes from 10.1.1.1: icmp_seq=1 ttl=254 time=1.42 ms
64 bytes from 10.1.1.1: icmp_seq=2 ttl=254 time=0.627 ms

--- 10.1.1.1 ping statistics ---
2 packets transmitted, 2 received, 0% packet loss, time 1002ms
rtt min/avg/max/mdev = 0.627/1.021/1.415/0.394 ms
fchaudhr@vm2:~$
```

This sort of IP connectivity for emulated networking devices within EVE-NG to external devices is very useful for creating NetDevOps pipelines. It allows you to use tools such as Ansible for configuration management to connect to emulated devices on EVE-NG.

APIs of EVE-NG

EVE-NG provides REST APIs for interaction with the core system. These APIs can be used for any purpose, such as creating a new lab topology by adding nodes and networks, starting or stopping specific nodes (devices) in an existing lab, starting or stopping all nodes in a lab, and so on. The availability of APIs allows you to automate the use of EVE-NG as part of a NetDevOps CI/CD pipeline. An example of a use case for the CI/CD pipeline might be that upon a commit of a new Ansible playbook in GitHub, a pipeline is kicked off. This pipeline could start nodes in an existing lab topology on EVE-NG, perform required steps (such as apply Ansible playbooks and execute automated tests on this topology), and then stop all the nodes in the topology.

The documentation for REST APIs is available on the EVE-NG website. The web GUI uses the REST APIs for all interactions on the web browser. Thus, the history of REST API requests can also be seen from the log file named access.txt by navigating from the **Main** administration page to **System** and **System Logs**. An alternate option is to view the APIs utilized in the web GUI by using **Developer Tools** in the Chrome browser while navigating through EVE-NG on the browser.

Let's explore some of the EVE-NG REST API requests using the **curl** command-line interface on a developer's workstation.

The Community version of EVE-NG uses HTTP. All API requests require an authenticated user. To log in to EVE-NG, issue the API request shown in Example 5-19. The appropriate user credentials are passed in this **POST** request. In response, the EVE-NG server confirms the successful authentication of the user and returns a cookie. As per the -c option, the cookie is saved to a file named ~/cookie1. This cookie is used for API requests in the subsequent **curl** commands by using the -b option. By default, the output of **curl** commands is shown on a single line and therefore is not readable. As shown in Example 5-19, the json_pp utility is used to "pretty print" the JSON data. This utility comes preinstalled on macOS; however, you may need to install it on your operating system.

Example 5-19 *API Request – Authentication*

```
$ curl -s -c ~/cookie1 -X POST -d '{"username":"admin","password":"password0"}'
  http://34.170.93.121/api/auth/login | json_pp
{
  "code": 200,
  "status": "success",
  "message": "User logged in (90013)."
}
```

The existing labs can be searched by issuing the API request shown in Example 5-20. This request uses the cookie, via the **-b** option, saved in the file during the authentication request. As per the response, CSRv lab1 and a folder named Folder1 exist under the root path.

Example 5-20 *API Request – List All Labs in Root Folder*

```
$ curl -b ~/cookie1 -X GET -H 'Content-type: application/json' http://34.170.93.121/
  api/folders/ | json_pp
{
  "code": 200,
  "status": "success",
  "message": "Successfully listed path (60007).",
  "data": {
    "folders": [
      {
        "name": "Folder1",
        "path": "/Folder1"
      }
    ],
    "labs": [
      {
        "file": "CSRv lab1.unl",
        "path": "/CSRv lab1.unl",
        "umtime": 1677319123,
        "mtime": "25 Feb 2023 10:58"
      }
    ]
  }
}
```

The nodes within CSRv lab1 can be listed by issuing the following API request:

```
$ curl -b ~/cookie1 -X GET -H 'Content-type: application/json'
http://34.170.93.121/api/labs/CSRv%20lab1.unl/nodes | json_pp
```

The response for this API lists all the nodes in this lab named CSRv lab1. The response contains all the details about the nodes, such as name, template, image, RAM, CPU, number of interfaces, status (represents the power state), and so on. Each node has a unique ID associated with it as well. A single node can be started by issuing the following API request, which starts the node with an ID of 2:

```
$ curl -b ~/cookie1 -X GET -H 'Content-type: application/json'
http://34.170.93.121/api/labs/CSRv%20lab1.unl/nodes/2/start | json_pp
```

To start all the nodes in the lab, use the following API request:

```
$ curl -b ~/cookie1 -X GET -H 'Content-type: application/json'
http://34.170.93.121/api/labs/CSRv%201ab1.unl/nodes/start | json_pp
```

All the nodes within CSR lab1 can be stopped using this API request:

```
$ curl -b ~/cookie1 -X GET -H 'Content-type: application/json'
http://34.170.93.121/api/labs/CSRv%201ab1.unl/nodes/stop | json_pp
```

This section provided information about some of the APIs available in EVE-NG and how they could be used in automation and the NetDevOps pipeline.

Alternatives

Products are available and used in the market that provide capabilities to simulate network topology and network devices. Like EVE-NG, these products provide features that can be used to emulate networking devices, create network topologies, and enable you to test simulated virtual network topologies along with connectivity to external physical network devices, virtual network devices, and other tools. GNS3 and Cisco Modeling Labs (CML) are two such options for creating virtual labs.

GNS3 is open-source software for network simulation. It is free to use by anyone, and it's developed and supported by the open-source community. GNS3's code is hosted on GitHub and allows the community members to contribute to development as well as provide support. Like EVE-NG, it also provides a GUI for designing network topologies. GNS3 has a client/server architecture. The GNS3 client provides the GUI, and the GNS3 server hosts the actual network devices that are simulated. The network topology is designed on the GUI provided by the GNS3 client. The client sends this information to the server, and the server uses this information to create the network devices and the connections between them. The client and server can be installed on a single platform such as Windows, macOS, Linux, VMware ESXi, and so on, or the server can be hosted separately from the client. The latter provides a scalable option. The server can also be installed as a VM in an on-premises or cloud environment. Like EVE-NG, GNS3 supports network device emulation using QEMU and Dynamips. Cisco and other vendors' devices can be emulated and used in GNS3 using QEMU images.

Cisco Modeling Labs (CML) provides the option to run virtual lab environments for on-premises environments. It can be installed as a virtual machine and bare metal on a server. CML as a VM can be installed on a variety of virtualization platforms, such as VMware Workstation, Fusion, ESXi, and so on. CML can simulate topologies for both Cisco and non-Cisco networking devices (using qcow2 files). Each device in a simulated network topology runs as a VM within CML. Cisco operating system versions (such as IOS, NX-OS, ASAv, and so on) and various open-source VM images for Linux distributions, WAN emulation, and so on are provided out of the box in CML. It provides a web UI for ease of use to create and manage network topologies. CML is offered as a commercial product by Cisco. Multiple types of licenses are offered to accommodate both single users and teams within an organization. At the time of writing, entry-level licensing (named Personal or Personal+) can simulate 20 or 40 network devices, respectively. The Enterprise edition is positioned for multiple users and for highly scalable networking simulation via the use of a clustering architecture. The Enterprise edition scales to simulation hundreds of network devices. This edition is also positioned for use in NetDevOps and allows integration with CI/CD pipelines. External IP connectivity from CML can be accomplished by using NAT or by bridging to the external network. Also, because it's offered commercially, CML provides Cisco TAC support as well.

Summary

This chapter covered in detail the use of EVE-NG for creating virtual network topologies by emulating a variety of network devices. Lack of a proper testing environment is one of the biggest hurdles in rolling out new network capabilities quickly. The use of virtual environments like EVE-NG for testing provides enhanced quality, reliability, and agility to configure changes on networks.

This chapter also covered the implementation of EVE-NG in the Google Cloud Platform. You got hands-on practice doing this.

Also, two use cases were provided. The first use case walked you through the capabilities of EVE-NG, the installation of network devices images, and the creation of network topologies. A second use case walked you through the steps to enable external connectivity for network devices within your virtual network topology. The REST APIs of EVE-NG were also explored. These capabilities are useful for NetDevOps use cases, where you want the ability to connect to your EVE-NG virtual network devices from outside the virtual topology and to interact with EVE-NG by using its APIs.

The next chapter will walk you through an end-to-end implementation of a NetDevOps environment, from inception to execution.

Review Questions

You can find the answers to these questions in Appendix A, "Answers to Review Questions."

1. EVE-NG can be installed as a virtual machine or bare metal on a physical server.
   a. True
   b. False

2. When EVE-NG is used as a virtual machine, what are its main considerations?
   a. Nested virtualization can cause performance issues.
   b. Only Cisco network devices can be emulated.

   c. Only non-Cisco network devices can be emulated.

   d. There are no performance impacts or considerations.

3. The Export CFG setting on EVE-NG is equivalent to which command on a Cisco router running IOS?

   a. copy running startup

   b. wr mem

   c. show running-config

   d. wr erase

4. All network devices in a newly created topology in a lab on EVE-NG are already powered.

   a. True

   b. False

5. Which ports must be accessible on EVE-NG for web administration, management, and access to network devices simulated within a virtual network topology?

   a. SSH, HTTPS, and telnet

   b. SCP, HTTP, and telnet

   c. SSH, HTTP, and telnet

   d. SCP, HTTPS, and telnet

6. What kind of bridges are automatically created on a Linux machine during installation of EVE-NG?

   a. Open Virtual Switch (OVS)

   b. Network bridge

   c. Linux virtual bridge

   d. Linux bridge

7. EVE-NG supports the emulation of devices using which technologies? (Select three.)

   a. Qemu

   b. IOL

   c. IOS

   d. Dynamips

8. QEMU images are not required to be stored with a specific directory name and path within EVE-NG.

   a. True

   b. False

9. Console access to each network device within a virtual network topology in EVE-NG is only possible using an application on a NetDevOps engineer's PC/workstation.

    a. True

    b. False

10. External IP connectivity of networking devices in a virtual topology requires which Linux kernel settings to be changed on the host machine? (Select two.)

    a. net.ipv4.ip_forward

    b. net.ipv4.conf.all.rp_filter

    c. can_ip_forward

    d. net.ipv4.conf.all.accept_redirects

## Chapter 6

How to Build Your Own NetDevOps Architecture

Congratulations, you made it this far and have learned about the different components of NetDevOps: source control, infrastructure as code (IaC), CI/CD, and test automation. You have also seen use cases where these practices excel, such as configuration and provisioning of networks, and a network simulation tool, EVE-NG, that you can use to build and experiment with test networks.

Throughout this book, you have access to code snippets, case studies, and examples. In this chapter, you will learn how to build an end-to-end NetDevOps architecture from scratch, putting to practice all you learned so far.

This chapter is divided into two use cases: the first uses git, Ansible, and Jenkins to orchestrate and automate configuration changes in a network. The second use case uses Slack, an instant messaging software, to verify configuration compliance of network devices, but it also makes use of git, Ansible, and Jenkins.

This is a practical chapter, so make sure you follow along and build the examples yourself.

Note This chapter's command syntax works in an Amazon Linux environment. It also works in a macOS environment. If you have a different environment, such as Windows or Ubuntu, your syntax might be slightly different. Likewise, version changes might introduce syntax changes, so depending on your setup, a little troubleshooting might be required.

Applying Configuration Changes

Network devices, and really most networking software, are text configuration driven, meaning these components expose a text-based configuration file that is parsed and reflects on the behavior of the component. Some are GUI driven, but this is a smaller percentage, and often this graphical layer just acts as a translation mechanism to text-based configurations.

As mentioned in Chapter 2, "Getting Started with NetDevOps," configuration is the most common use case for NetDevOps—and a quick win for the network teams—because it is a tedious and repetitive manual task for network operators.

At the end of this section, you will have a working automated network configuration pipeline that will ingest a configuration file from a source control repository and apply that configuration to a network device. It will also verify whether the configuration applied is working as expected.

> **Note**   Although the following sections do not have to be executed in a particular order, they are ordered by what usually works best.

Requirements

Before you start, there are some requirements you need to meet for this example:

- A GitHub account
- A Jenkins instance
- Automation tools, such as Ansible and Ansible modules

Creating a GitHub account is free. Using a different hosted git provider (for example, Gitlab or Bitbucket) will also work. However, the procedures to create and work with those repositories might be slightly different.

You can follow the instructions in Chapter 3, "How to Implement CI/CD Pipelines with Jenkins," to get your own Jenkins setup.

In this example, we will not use Docker containers. Therefore, you need to install Ansible directly on your worker nodes. You can do this by using the Ansible Jenkins plugin or by directly connecting to your worker nodes and use the operating system package manager (for example, apt or yum).

For Ansible modules, the ansible-galaxy tool provides an easy way to install any module. For example, to install the Cisco NX-OS collection, which provides a set of Ansible modules, plugins, and roles that you can use to automate the configuration of Cisco Nexus switches running NX-OS (which we use later in this chapter), you execute the following command:

```
$ ansible-galaxy collection install cisco.nxos
```

Target Network Devices

To make this example easier to follow along, we are using Cisco's Open NX-OS devices. They are virtual Cisco Nexus devices that are always up and available at https://sandbox-nxos-1.cisco.com/. They have open connections on port 22 for SSH, port 830 for

NETCONF, ports 80 and 443 for NXAPI, and port 443 for RESTCONF. The credentials are **admin** for the username and **Admin_1234!** for the password.

> **Tip**   You can use these devices to test anything you need outside this example. Also, other Cisco sandboxes are available that cover operating systems other than NX-OS.

Alternatively, you can create your own test network with EVE-NG following the instructions in Chapter 5, "How to Implement Virtual Networks with EVE-NG." Or you can use your own network equipment.

To target your specific devices, you need to change the Ansible inventory file as shown Example 6-1. You can build more advanced inventory files and then separate device types by groups. For more details on the Ansible inventory file structure, refer back to Chapter 1, "Why Do We Need NetDevOps?"

For simplicity, we have the device credentials (username and password) directly as variables in the inventory file. This is not recommended; for production, you should have them as environment variables on the worker nodes or use a secret management tool. You should *never* commit secrets to source control.

Example 6-1   *Ansible Inventory File with Cisco Open NX-OS Device*

```
[all:vars]
ansible_connection = ansible.netcommon.network_cli
ansible_network_os = cisco.nxos.nxos
ansible_user=admin
ansible_password=Admin_1234!
ansible_command_timeout=180
gather_facts=no
ansible_ssh_common_args='-o StrictHostKeyChecking=no'
[all]
sandbox-nxos-1.cisco.com
```

Setting Up Source Control

The first step when developing a new automation project is to set up source control. Depending on the tool you are using, the process might be slightly different.

In GitHub, after you log in with your credentials, on the top left, you'll see a plus sign (+). Click it, and the **New repository** option appears, as shown in Figure 6-1. Click it as well.

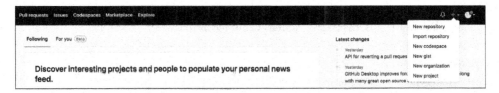

Figure 6-1 *GitHub New Repository Menu*

Now, you should see several open fields, as shown in Figure 6-2. You only need to fill in the repository name; all other fields are optional. Name your repository something descriptive (for example, nxos_configuration).

In this form, you can make your repository private, which is the recommended setting. The public repository can be accessed by anyone on the Internet. Private repositories require users and applications to be authenticated before access is allowed. In this use case, for the sake of simplicity, you can use a public repository.

Create a new repository

A repository contains all project files, including the revision history. Already have a project repository elsewhere? Import a repository.

Owner *   **Repository name ***

IvoP1 ▾   /

Great repository names are short and memorable. Need inspiration? How about legendary-fortnight?

Description (optional)

◉ 🖥 **Public**
     Anyone on the internet can see this repository. You choose who can commit.

○ 🔒 **Private**
     You choose who can see and commit to this repository.

Initialize this repository with:
Skip this step if you're importing an existing repository.

☐ **Add a README file**
     This is where you can write a long description for your project. Learn more.

Add .gitignore
Choose which files not to track from a list of templates. Learn more.

.gitignore template: None ▾

Choose a license
A license tells others what they can and can't do with your code. Learn more.

License: None ▾

ⓘ You are creating a public repository in your personal account.

Create repository

Figure 6-2 *GitHub New Repository Form*

When you click **Create repository**, you see the new repository URL. For HTTPS access, it's in the form https://github.com/[username]/[repository_name].git (for example, https://github.com/IvoP1/nxos_configuration.git). For SSH access, it's in the form git@github.com:[username]/[repository_name].git.

You'll also see instructions on how to use this URL.

Create a folder in your local workstation named network_automation using the **mkdir** command:

```
$ mkdir network_automation
```

Navigate to your newly created folder, add a README.md file, set up this folder as a git repository, and push your changes to the remote repository, as shown in Example 6-2.

This example assumes you have git installed and configured in your workstation, including git parameters such as username and email.

Example 6-2   *Creating a Git Repository from a Folder*

```
$ cd network_automation
$ git init
Initialized empty Git repository in /home/ec2-user/network_automation/.git/$ echo
  "This will configure NXOS devices" >> README.md
$ git add README.md
$ git commit -m "Added README"[main (root-commit) 6c6f9c1] Added README
 Committer: EC2 Default User <ec2-user@ip-10-0-0-1.eu-west-3.compute.internal>
Your name and email address were configured automatically based
on your username and hostname. Please check that they are accurate.
You can suppress this message by setting them explicitly. Run the
following command and follow the instructions in your editor to edit
your configuration file:

    git config --global --edit

After doing this, you may fix the identity used for this commit with:

    git commit --amend --reset-author

 1 file changed, 1 insertion(+)
 create mode 100644 README.md
$ git branch -M main
$ git remote add origin git@github.com:IvoP1/nxos_configuration.git
$ git push -u origin main
Enumerating objects: 3, done.
Counting objects: 100% (3/3), done.
Writing objects: 100% (3/3), 280 bytes | 280.00 KiB/s, done.
```

```
Total 3 (delta 0), reused 0 (delta 0), pack-reused 0
To github.com:IvoP1/nxos_configuration.git
 * [new branch]      main -> main
branch 'main' set up to track 'origin/main'.
```

If you navigate to your repository URL, you will find your README.md file there. You can find the detailed meaning of each of the previous **git** commands in the section "Source Control" of Chapter 1, as well as details on how to set up your local environment.

Note   By the time you read this book, the GitHub repository shown in this chapter's examples will no longer exist. This is on purpose; you need to create your own repository and follow the steps throughout this chapter. NetDevOps is a learn-by-doing culture.

You will use this local folder and remote the git repository throughout this part of the chapter. Any reference to changes, code, or directories is intended to be executed in this environment.

Developing Infrastructure as Code

Now that you have a code repository, it's time to structure it for an Ansible project. Ansible is the most used tool for network configuration changes, as mentioned in previous chapters.

You need to create two placeholder YAML files: conf.yml and verify.yml. Typically, as discussed in Chapter 2, a configuration use case has two major tasks: verification and configuration. Here's how to create the two YAML files:

```
$ touch conf.yml
$ touch verify.yml
```

On top of that, Ansible requires an inventory file to know which devices to connect to, and how. Create that file too:

```
$ touch hosts
```

In Chapter 4, "How to Implement NetDevOps Pipelines with Jenkins," you learned that an easy way to target two different environments in Ansible, such as development and production, is to have two different inventory files. Create a second file and rename the previously created inventory file to something more descriptive, like so:

```
$ touch hosts_dev
$ mv hosts hosts_prod
```

At this point you could organize this repository into folders, but to simplify thing, don't. Your repository should look like the one shown in Example 6-3.

Example 6-3 *Repository Structure Tree View*

```
$ tree
.
├── README.md
├── conf.yml
├── hosts_dev
├── hosts_prod
└── verify.yml
```

Open an inventory file (either of the two) and populate it with your device information. You can copy the one from Example 6-1. It's publicly available and connects to a virtual Nexus 9300 running NX-OS version 9.3(3).

The focus of this exercise is NetDevOps components, not advanced networking. Because of that, for the network configuration, you will focus on a core networking operation—configuring new VLANs.

This was one of the first examples in this book (refer to Chapter 1). However, now you are more experienced. As an exercise, edit the conf.yml file to read from a vlans.txt file and configure those VLANs on your target network devices.

Example 6-4 represents an Ansible playbook that uses the Cisco NX-OS module together with the **with_lines** Ansible plugin to configure a list of VLANs from a file on a NX-OS device. This playbook loops over the VLANs defined in the file and executes the config module once per item. This is just one of the many types of loops Ansible offers; for others, you can refer to their official documentation or a book dedicated to network automation with Ansible such as *Network Automation Made Easy* (Cisco Press, 2022).

Example 6-4 *Ansible Playbook to Configure VLANs on an NX-OS Device*

```
---
# Playbook to create VLANs on Cisco Nexus switches from file
  - name: create new VLANs
    hosts: all

    tasks:
      - name: provision VLAN
        cisco.nxos.nxos_vlans:
          config:
            - vlan_id: "{{item}}"
              state: active
        with_lines: cat "vlans.txt"
```

In order for this to work, you also need to create the vlans.txt file and populate it with VLAN numbers. Each VLAN number should be separated by a new line, like so:

```
$ echo "123\n124\n125\n" > vlans.txt
```

Do the same for verify.yml. Create an Ansible playbook that verifies the VLANs were successfully created and are present on the expected ports. Example 6-5 shows an Ansible playbook that retrieves VLAN information from the device and prints it. Then it verifies whether all the configured VLANs are present on port-channel 2. In this example, port-channel 2 is an interface with all VLANs enabled. Your case will be different, so modify the playbook accordingly.

Example 6-5 *Ansible Playbook to Verify VLANs Are Present on Trunk Port on an NX-OS Device*

```
---
# Playbook for the verification of VLANs on Cisco Nexus switches
  - name: Verify VLANs
    hosts: all

    tasks:
      - name: Gather vlans facts from the device using nxos_vlans
        cisco.nxos.nxos_vlans:
          state: gathered
        register: vlans

      - name: Print gathered VLAN information
        debug: var=vlans.gathered

      - name: Run show vlan id to see if the Vlan is on the port-channel 2
        cisco.nxos.nxos_command:
          commands: show vlan id {{item}}
          wait_for: result[0] contains Po2
        with_lines: cat vlans.txt
```

In a production scenario, you can have multiple and more advanced verifications. The same applies for the configuration playbook. You can even replace the entire network device configuration using the **nxos_config** Ansible module, instead of configuring a specific feature such as a VLAN.

Play around with Ansible locally before moving into CI/CD. You can execute these playbooks from your workstation as long as you have Ansible installed. This is the best way to test the playbooks and make sure they work as intended.

> **Tip** It is likely you will have to disable Ansible's **host_key_checking** option if you are working with devices that have untrusted certificates.

Example 6-6 shows a local execution of the "Verify VLANs" playbook from Example 6-5, after the "Configure VLANs" playbook executed successfully.

Example 6-6 *Verify VLANs Ansible Playbook Execution Output*

```
$ ansible-playbook verify.yml -i hosts_prod


PLAY [create new VLANs] ********************************************************
*********

TASK [Gathering Facts] ********************************************************
*********
ok: [sandbox-nxos-1.cisco.com]


TASK [Gather vlans facts from the device using nxos_vlans] *********************
***********************************************
ok: [sandbox-nxos-1.cisco.com]


TASK [Print gathered VLAN information] ****************************************
************************
ok: [sandbox-nxos-1.cisco.com] => {
    "vlans.gathered": [
        {
            "enabled": true,
            "mode": "ce",
            "name": "default",
            "state": "active",
            "vlan_id": 1
        },
        {
            "enabled": true,
            "mode": "ce",
            "name": "mgmt",
            "state": "active",
            "vlan_id": 100
        },
        {
            "enabled": true,
            "mode": "ce",
            "name": "dev",
            "state": "active",
```

```
                "vlan_id": 102
        },
        {
                "enabled": true,
                "mode": "ce",
                "name": "test",
                "state": "active",
                "vlan_id": 103
        },
        {
                "enabled": true,
                "mode": "ce",
                "state": "active",
                "vlan_id": 110
        },
        {
                "enabled": true,
                "mode": "ce",
                "state": "active",
                "vlan_id": 123
        },
        {
                "enabled": true,
                "mode": "ce",
                "state": "active",
                "vlan_id": 124
        },
        {
                "enabled": true,
                "mode": "ce",
                "state": "active",
                "vlan_id": 125
        }
    ]
}

TASK [Run show vlan id to check if the Vlan is on the port-channel 2] *************
*********************************************
ok: [sandbox-nxos-1.cisco.com] => (item=123)
ok: [sandbox-nxos-1.cisco.com] => (item=124)
ok: [sandbox-nxos-1.cisco.com] => (item=125)


PLAY RECAP ***************************************************************************
sandbox-nxos-1.cisco.com   : ok=4      changed=0    unreachable=0    failed=0
   skipped=0     rescued=0     ignored=0
```

Your execution output might be different, even if you're using the same Cisco public NX-OS device, because people can have configured other VLANs at the time of your execution. In this execution, you can see eight VLANs configured, including our three (IDs 123, 124, and 125).

To verify an error scenario, change the Verify playbook to check for a port-channel where the VLAN will not exist. Example 6-7 shows an execution of this playbook where the last task expects the VLANs to be present in port-channel 6. Because port-channel 6 does not exist, the task fails.

Example 6-7 *Verify VLANs Ansible Playbook Execution Failure Output*

```
$ ansible-playbook verify.yml -i hosts_prod

PLAY [create new VLANs] *************************************************
**********

TASK [Gathering Facts] *************************************************
*********
ok: [sandbox-nxos-1.cisco.com]


TASK [Gather vlans facts from the device using nxos_vlans] ************************
************************************************
ok: [sandbox-nxos-1.cisco.com]


TASK [Print gathered VLAN information] ***********************************************
************************
ok: [sandbox-nxos-1.cisco.com] => {
    "vlans.gathered": [
        {
            "enabled": true,
            "mode": "ce",
            "name": "default",
            "state": "active",
            "vlan_id": 1
        },
        {
            "enabled": true,
            "mode": "ce",
            "name": "mgmt",
            "state": "active",
            "vlan_id": 100
        },
        {
```

```
             "enabled": true,
             "mode": "ce",
             "name": "dev",
             "state": "active",
             "vlan_id": 102
         },
         {
             "enabled": true,
             "mode": "ce",
             "name": "test",
             "state": "active",
             "vlan_id": 103
         },
         {
             "enabled": true,
             "mode": "ce",
             "state": "active",
             "vlan_id": 110
         },
         {
             "enabled": true,
             "mode": "ce",
             "state": "active",
             "vlan_id": 123
         },
         {
             "enabled": true,
             "mode": "ce",
             "state": "active",
             "vlan_id": 124
         },
         {
             "enabled": true,
             "mode": "ce",
             "state": "active",
             "vlan_id": 125
         }
     ]
}

TASK [Run show vlan id to check if the Vlan is on the port-channel 6] **************
************************************************************
failed: [sandbox-nxos-1.cisco.com] (item=123) => {"ansible_loop_var": "item",
    "changed": false, "failed_conditions": ["result[0] contains Po6"], "item": "123",
    "msg": "One or more conditional statements have not been satisfied"}
```

```
failed: [sandbox-nxos-1.cisco.com] (item=124) => {"ansible_loop_var": "item",
"changed": false, "failed_conditions": ["result[0] contains Po6"], "item": "124",
"msg": "One or more conditional statements have not been satisfied"}
failed: [sandbox-nxos-1.cisco.com] (item=125) => {"ansible_loop_var": "item",
"changed": false, "failed_conditions": ["result[0] contains Po6"], "item": "125",
"msg": "One or more conditional statements have not been satisfied"}


PLAY RECAP ***********************************************************************
sandbox-nxos-1.cisco.com    : ok=3    changed=0    unreachable=0    failed=1
  skipped=0    rescued=0    ignored=0
```

Use what you learned in Chapter 4 and verify whether the Ansible playbook exit code is different in a successful execution and a failed execution.

Notice the **Gathering Facts** task in both execution outputs, even though your playbook does not have one defined. Ansible automatically gathers information from the devices it connects to. This behavior can be disabled, but it is enabled by default. You can use it to make your playbook more versatile.

Network devices' command syntax changes per platform. Example 6-8 shows an Ansible playbook that uses the gathered operating system, **ansible_net_system**, to apply the correct command syntax to each device type. It uses the module **nxos_vlans** for NX-OS devices and **ios_vlans** for IOS devices.

Example 6-8   *Ansible Playbook to Configure VLANs on NX-OS and IOS Devices*

```
---
# Playbook to create VLANs on Cisco switches from a file
  - name: create new VLANs
    hosts: all

    tasks:
      - name: provision NXOS VLAN
        cisco.nxos.nxos_vlans:
          config:
            - vlan_id: "{{item}}"
              state: active
        with_lines: cat "vlans.txt"
        when: ansible_net_system == 'nxos'

      - name: provision IOS VLAN
        cisco.ios.ios_vlans:
          config:
            - vlan_id: "{{item}}"
              state: active
        with_lines: cat "vlans.txt"
        when: ansible_net_system == 'ios'
```

Only execute this playbook on NX-OS devices, and you will see an output similar to the one in Example 6-9. Ansible skips the task if the **when** statement is false.

Example 6-9 *Multiple Device Types Ansible Playbook Execution Output*

```
$ ansible-playbook conf.yml -i hosts_prod

PLAY [create new VLANs] *********************************************************
**********

TASK [Gathering Facts] **********************************************************
*********
ok: [sandbox-nxos-1.cisco.com]

TASK [provision NXOS VLAN] ******************************************************
*************
ok: [sandbox-nxos-1.cisco.com] => (item=123)
ok: [sandbox-nxos-1.cisco.com] => (item=124)
ok: [sandbox-nxos-1.cisco.com] => (item=125)

TASK [provision IOS VLAN] *******************************************************
************
skipping: [sandbox-nxos-1.cisco.com] => (item=123)
skipping: [sandbox-nxos-1.cisco.com] => (item=124)
skipping: [sandbox-nxos-1.cisco.com] => (item=125)

PLAY RECAP **********************************************************************
sandbox-nxos-1.cisco.com   : ok=2    changed=0    unreachable=0    failed=0
   skipped=1    rescued=0    ignored=0
```

Alter your inventory file and add more network devices to it. Add devices that are neither IOS nor NX-OS and document what happens.

You are done with automation for now. Push all your changes to your remote code repository in GitHub.

Setting Up CI/CD

By now, you have a repository with Ansible automation scripts that configure and validate the creation of VLANs for Cisco IOS and NX-OS network devices. This is better than performing configuration tasks manually, but as you learned in Chapter 1, you can achieve even more with orchestration.

Create a new file in your folder and name it **Jenkinsfile**, like so:

```
$ touch Jenkinsfile
```

In this file, define, in a declarative way, the orchestration instructions. Refer to Figure 2-3 in Chapter 2 for a configuration pipeline architecture. Out of those stages, start by using the following three: retrieving the code (Code), configuring the device (Deploy to Dev/Prod), and verifying the configuration (Testing). Repeat them twice—once for the development environment and, if successful, once for the production environment.

You can reuse parts of the code in Example 4-24. Your final product should look like the snippet in Example 6-10. Notice the use of two different Ansible inventory files to target each environment. If you have a different directory structure that makes use of folders to store the playbooks and inventory files, adjust your shell instructions accordingly.

Example 6-10   *Simple Configuration Pipeline Jenskinsfile*

```
pipeline {
    agent any


    stages {
        stage('Clone repository') {
            steps {
                git (branch: 'main',
                url:       'https://github.com/IvoP1/nxos_configuration.git')
            }
        }
        stage('Deploy New Configurations - Dev') {
            steps {
                sh "ansible-playbook conf.yml -i hosts_dev"
            }
        }
        stage('Retrieve and validate show commands - Dev') {
            steps {
                sh "ansible-playbook verify.yml -i hosts_dev"
            }
        }
        stage('Deploy New Configurations - Prod') {
            steps {
                sh "ansible-playbook conf.yml -i hosts_prod"
            }
        }
        stage('Retrieve and validate show commands - Prod') {
            steps {
                sh "ansible-playbook verify.yml -i hosts_prod"
            }
        }
    }
}
```

```
post {
    always {
        cleanWs(cleanWhenNotBuilt: false,
                deleteDirs: true,
                disableDeferredWipeout: true,
                notFailBuild: true)
    }
}
}
```

Push your newly created Jenkinsfile to your remote GitHub repository, where the other files are.

Navigate to your Jenkins UI and create your pipeline. Follow these steps:

Step 1.   Click **New Item** in the top-left corner.

Step 2.   Give the item any name you like, select **Pipeline**, and click **OK**.

Step 3.   Scroll down until you find the section **Pipeline**.

Step 4.   In the **Definition** sub-section, select **Pipeline Script** from SCM.

Step 5.   In the **SCM** sub-section, select **Git**.

Step 6.   In the **Repository URL** field, enter your HTTPS repository URL.

Step 7.   (Optional) If you defined credentials when you created your GitHub repository, use the **Credentials** field to apply those.

Step 8.   In the **Branch Specifier** (blank for "any") field, enter */**main**.

Step 9.   Click **Save** at the end of the page.

Congratulations, you now have an automated pipeline that configures and verifies network devices. Time to execute it. On the same page you land on after creating a pipeline, click **Build Now**. If you navigated away from this page, you can find your newly created pipeline in the Jenkins main menu with the name you gave it in Step 2.

Figure 6-3 shows a successful execution. If any of your stages are not successful, and show in a color other than green, you can drill down into the execution logs to find the reason.

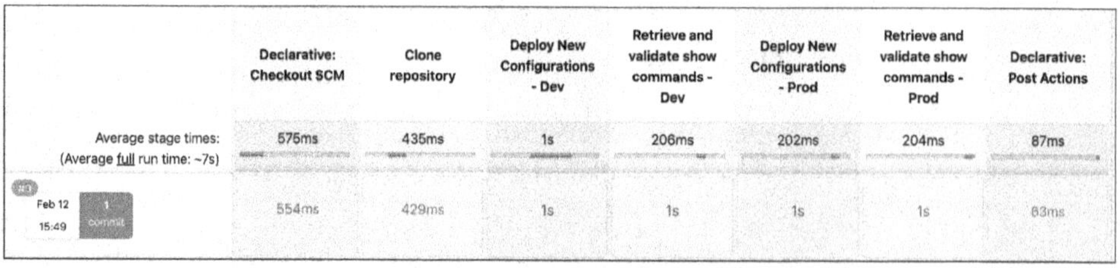

	Declarative: Checkout SCM	Clone repository	Deploy New Configurations - Dev	Retrieve and validate show commands - Dev	Deploy New Configurations - Prod	Retrieve and validate show commands - Prod	Declarative: Post Actions
Average stage times: (Average full run time: ~7s)	575ms	435ms	1s	206ms	202ms	204ms	87ms
Feb 12 15:49	554ms	429ms	1s	1s	1s	1s	83ms

Figure 6-3   *Successful Jenkins Pipeline Build*

Note A common error is missing the required Ansible modules (for example, **cisco.nxos**) in Jenkins worker nodes. If you missed this prerequisite, this could be why your build failed.

Now that you have a working configuration pipeline, it's time to improve it. Before a networking device configuration change, it's common to retrieve the device's configuration. This step was also represented in Figure 2-3 and its implementation in Example 4-24. You can reuse the configuration playbook or create a new one. Using a separate playbook is preferred. Create a new file for the playbook in the same directory:

```
$ touch save_config.yml
```

In this playbook, you want to accomplish two tasks: save the running configuration to the startup configuration and then retrieve the current configuration to a file locally. In Example 6-11, you can see an implementation of these tasks using the **nxos_command** and **copy** modules. We need two Ansible tasks to achieve the goal of retrieving the configuration and saving it to a file because there is no single module that does both.

Example 6-11 *Ansible Playbook to Save and Retrieve the Running Configuration for NX-OS*

```
---
# Playbook to retrieve and save the running-config on Cisco NX-OS switches
- name: Retrieve running-config and save it
  hosts: all

  tasks:
    - name: Retrieve the running-config
      nxos_command:
        commands:
          - term len 0
          - show running-config | begin ^version
      register: cli_results

    - name: Save the running config locally
      copy:
        content: "{{ cli_results.stdout[1] }}"
        dest: "configs/{{ inventory_hostname }}.cfg"

    - name: Save the running-config in the startup-config
      nxos_command:
        commands:
          - copy running-config startup-config
```

The running configuration is saved to the **configs** folder. Create it using the **mkdir** command if it does not exist:

```
$ mkdir configs
```

Like you did with the configuration playbook, you can make this playbook use the gathered facts of Ansible to apply the correct command syntax to both IOS and NX-OS devices. In Example 6-12, you can see the use of the **when** condition together with the **block** keyword to correctly map the command syntax to the operating system.

Example 6-12 *Ansible Playbook to Save and Retrieve the Running Configuration for NX-OS and IOS*

```
---
# Playbook to retrieve and save the running-config on Cisco switches
  - name: Retrieve running-config and save it
    hosts: all

    tasks:
      - name: NX-OS block
        block:
          - name: Retrieve the running-config NX-OS
            nxos_command:
              commands:
                - term len 0
                - show running-config | begin ^version
            register: cli_results

          - name: Save the running config locally
            copy:
              content: "{{ cli_results.stdout[1] }}"
              dest: "configs/{{ inventory_hostname }}.cfg"

          - name: Save the running-config in the startup-config NXOS
            nxos_command:
              commands:
                - copy running-config startup-config
        when: ansible_net_system == 'nxos'

      - name: IOS block
        block:
          - name: Retrieve the running-config IOS
            ios_command:
              commands:
```

```
                - term len 0
                - show running-config | exclude ^ntp.clock-period|Last.configura-
        tion.change|NVRAM.config.last.updated|Current.configuration.*bytes
            register: cli_results


        - name: Save the running config locally
          copy:
            content: "{{ cli_results.stdout[1] }}"
            dest: "configs/{{ inventory_hostname }}.cfg"


        - name: Save the running-config in the startup-config IOS
          ios_command:
            commands:
              - copy running-config startup-config
          when: ansible_net_system == 'ios'
```

Execute this playbook in your workstation. The result is saved in a file named with the
device's hostname, as shown in Example 6-13. The Ansible task's status (for example, ok,
changed, or skipping) can be different between the example output and your output. It
depends on the difference between the status of the device and what the playbook tries
to do.

Example 6-13 *Saving the Running Configuration Ansible Playbook Execution*

```
$ ansible-playbook save_config.yml -i hosts_dev

PLAY [Retrieve running-config and save it] *****************************************
****************************

TASK [Gathering Facts] ************************************************************
*********
ok: [sandbox-nxos-1.cisco.com]


TASK [Retrieve the running-config NX-OS] *****************************************
****************************
ok: [sandbox-nxos-1.cisco.com]


TASK [Save the running config locally] *******************************************
************************
ok: [sandbox-nxos-1.cisco.com]


TASK [Save the running-config in the startup-config NXOS] *************************
*********************************
ok: [sandbox-nxos-1.cisco.com]
```

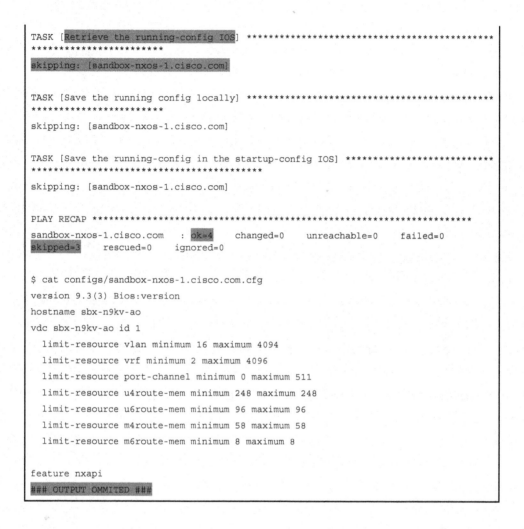

```
TASK [Retrieve the running-config IOS] ***********************************************
************************
skipping: [sandbox-nxos-1.cisco.com]

TASK [Save the running config locally] ***********************************************
************************
skipping: [sandbox-nxos-1.cisco.com]

TASK [Save the running-config in the startup-config IOS] ***************************
*******************************************
skipping: [sandbox-nxos-1.cisco.com]


PLAY RECAP ****************************************************************************
sandbox-nxos-1.cisco.com   : ok=4     changed=0    unreachable=0    failed=0
skipped=3    rescued=0    ignored=0


$ cat configs/sandbox-nxos-1.cisco.com.cfg
version 9.3(3) Bios:version
hostname sbx-n9kv-ao
vdc sbx-n9kv-ao id 1
  limit-resource vlan minimum 16 maximum 4094
  limit-resource vrf minimum 2 maximum 4096
  limit-resource port-channel minimum 0 maximum 511
  limit-resource u4route-mem minimum 248 maximum 248
  limit-resource u6route-mem minimum 96 maximum 96
  limit-resource m4route-mem minimum 58 maximum 58
  limit-resource m6route-mem minimum 8 maximum 8


feature nxapi
### OUTPUT OMMITED ###
```

When you execute this playbook in Jenkins, the local copy of the configuration is in your Jenkins worker node. Find a central repository to store these items; it can be anything, such as a virtual machine running Linux. Optionally, enhance this playbook to transfer the local copy of the configuration to the central repository. FTP and SCP are common tools used to implement this functionality.

Add a new stage to your Jenkinsfile, before the "configuration changes" stage, that executes your newly created playbook. Do this for both environments, as shown in Example 6-14.

Example 6-14 *Enhanced Configuration Pipeline Jenskinsfile*

```
pipeline {
    agent any


    stages {
        stage('Clone repository') {
            steps {
                git (branch: 'main',
                url: 'https://github.com/IvoP1/nxos_configuration.git')
            }
        }
        stage('Save running-configuration - Dev') {
            steps {
                sh "ansible-playbook save_config.yml -i hosts_dev"
            }
        }
        stage('Deploy New Configurations - Dev') {
            steps {
                sh "ansible-playbook conf.yml -i hosts_dev"
            }
        }
        stage('Retrieve and validate show commands - Dev') {
            steps {
                sh "ansible-playbook verify.yml -i hosts_dev"
            }
        }
        stage('Save running-configuration - Prod') {
            steps {
                sh "ansible-playbook save_config.yml -i hosts_prod"
            }
        }
        stage('Deploy New Configurations - Prod') {
            steps {
                sh "ansible-playbook conf.yml -i hosts_prod"
            }
        }
        stage('Retrieve and validate show commands - Prod') {
            steps {
                sh "ansible-playbook verify.yml -i hosts_prod"
            }
        }
    }
```

```
post {
    always {
        cleanWs(cleanWhenNotBuilt: false,
                deleteDirs: true,
                disableDeferredWipeout: true,
                notFailBuild: true)
    }
}
}
```

Your pipeline is now complete. Push all the changes you have made to your source control repository.

Execute your Jenkins instance and verify that your new pipeline retrieves and saves the configuration of the device and then configures and verifies some VLANs. It should do this for both your development and production environment.

At this phase, you can also add a stage that saves the new configuration, only present in the running configuration, to the startup configuration. This is a common procedure after performing configuration changes. Simply reuse the previous playbook in a new stage after the verifications are performed. This is the benefit of having playbooks separated by functionality.

Although this is a simple configuration use case (adding VLANs), the same pipeline architecture applies for any other configuration task. So, what happens if after configuring the VLANs you find that they are not present on the interface? Currently, the pipeline stops, and no other stage is executed. If this happens in your development environment, it won't affect your production environment. However, what if it works in the development environment but fails after configuring the new VLANs in production? Currently, those VLANs would remain configured on the network device.

Alter your verification stage to clean up the device. There are many ways to approach this, including replacing the running configuration with a known-good one and using the negative form of the previously applied configuration commands. The **cisco.nxos** Ansible module uses the second option.

Duplicate your **conf.yml** playbook as **clean.yml** to serve as the basis to your cleanup playbook:

```
$ cp conf.yml clean.yml
```

Change the playbook and task names. Change the stage variable from **active** to **deleted** and align it to the **config** keyword instead of to **vlan_id**. Example 6-15 shows the complete playbook and its execution.

Example 6-15 *Ansible Playbook to Delete VLANs and Example Execution*

```
$ cat clean.yml
---
# Playbook to delete VLANs on Cisco Nexus switches from file
  - name: Delete new VLANs
    hosts: all

    tasks:
      - name: Delete NXOS VLAN
        cisco.nxos.nxos_vlans:
          config:
            - vlan_id: "{{item}}"
          state: deleted
        with_lines: cat "vlans.txt"
        when: ansible_net_system == 'nxos'

      - name: Delete IOS VLAN
        cisco.ios.ios_vlans:
          config:
            - vlan_id: "{{item}}"
          state: deleted
        with_lines: cat "vlans.txt"
        when: ansible_net_system == 'ios'



$ ansible-playbook clean.yml -i hosts_dev

PLAY [Delete new VLANs] ************************************************
**********

TASK [Gathering Facts] ************************************************
*********
ok: [sandbox-nxos-1.cisco.com]

TASK [Delete NXOS VLAN] ************************************************
**********
changed: [sandbox-nxos-1.cisco.com] => (item=123)
changed: [sandbox-nxos-1.cisco.com] => (item=124)
changed: [sandbox-nxos-1.cisco.com] => (item=125)


TASK [Delete IOS VLAN] ************************************************
*********
skipping: [sandbox-nxos-1.cisco.com] => (item=123)
skipping: [sandbox-nxos-1.cisco.com] => (item=124)
```

```
skipping: [sandbox-nxos-1.cisco.com] => (item=125)
skipping: [sandbox-nxos-1.cisco.com]


PLAY RECAP **********************************************************************
sandbox-nxos-1.cisco.com   : ok=2       changed=1    unreachable=0    failed=0
skipped=1      rescued=0    ignored=0
```

This Ansible playbook should only be executed when the behavior verifications fail.
Modify your Jenkinsfile to incorporate a **post** section in the verification stage, as shown
in Example 6-16. Notice, in this example, the extra stage after the verifications. It saves
the running configuration to the startup configuration. This makes the configuration
changes durable, if successful, even in the case of device reload.

Example 6-16   *Final Configuration Pipeline Jenskinsfile*

```
pipeline {
    agent any



    stages {
        stage('Clone repository') {
            steps {
                git (branch: 'main',
                url: 'https://github.com/IvoP1/nxos_configuration.git')
            }
        }
        stage('Save running-configuration - pre-changes - Dev') {
            steps {
                sh "ansible-playbook save_config.yml -i hosts_dev"
            }
        }
        stage('Deploy New Configurations - Dev') {
            steps {
                sh "ansible-playbook conf.yml -i hosts_dev"
            }
        }
        stage('Retrieve and validate show commands - Dev') {
            steps {
                sh "ansible-playbook verify.yml -i hosts_dev"
            }
            post {
                failure {
```

```
                    sh "ansible-playbook clean.yml -i hosts_dev"
                }
            }
        }
        stage('Save running-configuration - post-changes - Dev') {
            steps {
                sh "ansible-playbook save_config.yml -i hosts_dev"
            }
        }
        stage('Save running-configuration - pre-changes - Prod') {
            steps {
                sh "ansible-playbook save_config.yml -i hosts_prod"
            }
        }
        stage('Deploy New Configurations - Prod') {
            steps {
                sh "ansible-playbook conf.yml -i hosts_prod"
            }
        }
        stage('Retrieve and validate show commands - Prod') {
            steps {
                sh "ansible-playbook verify.yml -i hosts_prod"
            }
            post {
                failure {
                    sh "ansible-playbook clean.yml -i hosts_prod"
                }
            }
        }
        stage('Save running-configuration - post-changes - Prod') {
            steps {
                sh "ansible-playbook save_config.yml -i hosts_prod"
            }
        }
    }

    post {
        always {
            cleanWs(cleanWhenNotBuilt: false,
                    deleteDirs: true,
                    disableDeferredWipeout: true,
                    notFailBuild: true)
        }
    }
}
```

Commit your changes and push them to your GitHub repository. You can modify your verifications playbook, as before, to simulate a failure and test your rollback mechanism.

Your Jenkins pipeline now has many stages. These files can grow quite large over time. If you continue to add functionalities to yours, it is worthwhile to go back to Chapter 4 and review the "Chaining Pipelines" section.

That's it. You now have a working NetDevOps pipeline. You can continue adding functionality to it (for example, an initial stage that verifies whether the changes being made are allowed, an input pause before making changes to the production environment, or an automated trigger such as a new GitHub commit). Adapt this pipeline to your needs.

Verifying Security Compliance Using ChatOps

ChatOps is a new field, also known as conversation-driven DevOps—but for you, conversation-driven NetDevOps. It consists of the use of chat client applications to trigger or facilitate DevOps actions. It can also be used to receive notifications instead of triggering actions.

In a ChatOps setup, an operator writes her intention in a chat application, such as Slack, and through a push mechanism this intention is executed. For example, the operator writes "configure VLAN 10," which triggers an Ansible playbook that configures VLAN 10 in a specific device.

The opposite can also happen. Instead of an operator asking for an action, the operator is notified that some action happened. For example, the user Joe connects to device NXOS01. The operator receives a chat message in a chat application notifying her of this access.

ChatOps is exciting because, oftentimes, notifications by email or management systems are ignored or acted upon late. Most companies already have a chat application that collaborators use to communicate among themselves. Incorporating functionality into it, especially using natural language, makes notifications more visible and real time.

This field is still young but is advancing rapidly. Currently, receiving notifications is the most adopted feature. However, triggering actions is quickly catching up. Still, many tools are not integrated natively and require custom scripts.

In this section, you will build a ChatOps system using Slack to verify the security configurations of your network devices. You will also configure a mechanism to receive status change notifications for your CI/CD pipelines.

Requirements

Before you start, there are some requirements you need to meet:

- A GitHub account
- A Jenkins instance with SSL configured

- Automation tools such as Ansible and Ansible modules
- A Slack account with administrator rights to a channel

As described previously in this chapter, creating a GitHub account is free. If you use a different hosted git provider, such as Gitlab or Bitbucket, it will also work. The procedures to create and work with those repositories might be slightly different.

For this section, your Jenkins instance must have SSL configured. It can use a self-signed certificate, but the connection must be HTTPS-enabled. The procedure to enable SSL on a Jenkins instance is beyond the scope of this book. Refer to the previous "Requirements" section in this chapter to learn how to configure Jenkins with Ansible.

Creating a Slack directory, account, and channel is free. In this section, you will use a Slack channel inside your directory where you will add two Slack applications. This procedure requires administrator-level permissions.

Setting Up Source Control

Create a new GitHub repository following the instructions in the previous "Setting Up Source Control" section of this chapter. Give the repository a different name, such as **compliance_verification.**

Move to the next section only when you have a new GitHub repository URL.

Developing Infrastructure as Code

To verify security compliance, you need a set of rules that you want to check for. In this example, we will use a simplified set of rules, but you can use any number of rules.

Python or Ansible is suitable for this task. Create an Ansible playbook and name it **compliance,** like so:

```
$ touch compliance.yml
```

There are many different ways to verify compliance. The easiest way is to verify whether a set of golden rules is configured. You can also add verifications of **show** commands.

Example 6-17 shows an Ansible playbook that retrieves the configuration of the device and verifies that the device is running NX-OS version 9.3(3). The playbook also verifies that NTP is configured according to a set of golden rules using the **nxos_config** module result. The playbook uses the Ansible built-in assert function to compare the actual to expected outcomes.

Although this playbook retrieves the configuration automatically using Ansible-gathered facts, you can have an explicit task for it. This is especially useful if you want to save the configuration in a central repository or exclude certain parts from it (for example, secrets).

Example 6-17 *Ansible Playbook to Verify Security Compliance*

```
---
# Playbook to verify configuration compliance on Cisco Nexus switches
  - name: Verify golden configuration compliance
    hosts: all

    tasks:
      - name: Version is 9.3(3)
        ansible.builtin.assert:
          that:
            - "ansible_net_version == '9.3(3)'"
          msg: "Current version is {{ ansible_net_version }}"

      - name: Check gold config status
        nxos_config:
          lines:
            - ntp server 172.16.0.1 use-vrf default
            - ntp source-interface mgmt0
            - ntp authenticate
          register: compliance_status

      - name: Golden rules are not there
        ansible.builtin.assert:
          that:
            - "compliance_status.changed == false"
```

Create an Ansible inventory file, or multiple files if you have several environments. Add these to the same directory in which your compliance playbook exists. You can refer to the previous section, "Target Network Devices," if you don't remember how to.

Test your playbook locally. Use the Ansible **--check** flag to make sure no changes are committed to your devices; only verifications should be made. Example 6-18 shows two Example 6-15 playbook executions: one where the device is compliant, followed by a second execution where changes are required. For the second execution to fail, you can change the expected configuration to a value that is different from the one configured on the device.

Example 6-18 *Ansible Playbook to Verify Security Compliance Execution*

```
$ ansible-playbook compliance.yml -i hosts_dev --check -v

PLAY [Verify golden configuration compliance] ***********************************

TASK [Gathering Facts] **********************************************************
*********
```

```
ok: [sandbox-nxos-1.cisco.com]

TASK [Version is 9.3(3)] ************************************************
***********
ok: [sandbox-nxos-1.cisco.com] => {
    "changed": false,
    "msg": "All assertions passed"
}


TASK [Check gold config status] ****************************************
*****************
ok: [sandbox-nxos-1.cisco.com] => {"changed": false}

TASK [Golden rules are not there] **************************************
*******************
ok: [sandbox-nxos-1.cisco.com] => {
    "changed": false,
    "msg": "All assertions passed"
}


PLAY RECAP *************************************************************
sandbox-nxos-1.cisco.com   : ok=4     changed=0    unreachable=0    failed=0
skipped=0    rescued=0    ignored=0


$ ansible-playbook compliance.yml -i hosts_dev --check -v


PLAY [Verify golden configuration compliance] *************************************


TASK [Gathering Facts] ************************************************
*********
ok: [sandbox-nxos-1.cisco.com]


TASK [Version is 9.3(3)] ***********************************************
***********
ok: [sandbox-nxos-1.cisco.com] => {
    "changed": false,
    "msg": "All assertions passed"
}


TASK [Check gold config status] ***************************************
*****************
changed: [sandbox-nxos-1.cisco.com] => {"changed": true, "commands": ["ntp server
172.16.0.3 use-vrf default"], "updates": ["ntp server 172.16.0.3 use-vrf default"]}
```

```
TASK [Golden rules are not there] ******************************************************
*******************
fatal: [sandbox-nxos-1.cisco.com]: FAILED! => {
    "assertion": "compliance_status.changed == false",
    "changed": false,
    "evaluated_to": false,
    "msg": "Assertion failed"
}


PLAY RECAP **************************************************************************
sandbox-nxos-1.cisco.com   : ok=3    changed=1    unreachable=0    failed=1
  skipped=0    rescued=0    ignored=0
```

Commit your changes to your GitHub repository. You will pull them from your CI/CD server in the next section.

Setting Up CI/CD

To start, create a Jenkinsfile. This will be a very simple pipeline compared to the previous configuration one. Then configure two stages: one to pull the repository and one to execute the compliance playbook. Example 6-19 shows a declarative implementation with an optional cleanup stage at the end.

Example 6-19 *Compliance Pipeline Jenkinsfile*

```
pipeline {
    agent any


    stages {
        stage('Clone repository') {
            steps {
                git (branch: 'main',
                url: 'https://github.com/IvoP1/nxos_configuration.git')
            }
        }
        stage('Verify Golden rules compliance') {
            steps {
                sh "ansible-playbook compliance.yml -i hosts_dev --check"
            }
        }
    }
```

```
post {
    always {
        cleanWs(cleanWhenNotBuilt: false,
                deleteDirs: true,
                disableDeferredWipeout: true,
                notFailBuild: true)
    }
}
}
```

Now, commit your Jenkinsfile to Github and create a pipeline from it. Refer to the previous section for the detailed steps on how to create a pipeline in Jenkins from a source control repository.

You will want to trigger this pipeline in a special way later, and for that you must create a special trigger. Go back to your Jenkins UI, select the pipeline you created, and click **Configure** on the left side. In the **Build Triggers** section, select **Trigger builds remotely (e.g., from scripts)** and then, on the **Authentication Token** field, enter **verysecretstuff**. Save the URL that is shown. Lastly, click **Save** at the end.

Often, compliance verification automations take a very long time—some because of the lengthy comparisons they do, and others because they fail to connect to the devices but must wait for the configured timeout periods. One way to speed this up is to have a first stage that verifies whether the devices are reachable. Create a freestyle project in Jenkins that pings the device by following these steps:

Step 1.   Click **New Item** in the top-left corner.

Step 2.   Give the item any name you like, select **Freestyle project,** and click **OK.**

Step 3.   Scroll down until you find the section **Build Steps.**

Step 4.   Click **Add built step** and select **Execute shell.**

Step 5.   In the **Command** section, write a connectivity check such as **ping -c 1** 10.0.0.1.

Step 6.   Click **Save** at the end of the page.

There are other ways you could accomplish this, but using a freestyle project is an interesting way to run simple commands.

Edit your Jenkinsfile to execute this project before performing any compliance verifications, as shown in Example 6-20. If the **Verify reachability** stage fails, the compliance playbook is not executed.

Example 6-20   *Enhanced Compliance Pipeline Jenkinsfile*

```
pipeline {
    agent any


    stages {
        stage('Clone repository') {
            steps {
                git (branch: 'main',
                url: 'https://github.com/IvoP1/nxos_configuration.git')
                }
            }
        stage('Verify reachability') {
            steps {
                build(job: 'reachability check')
                }
            }
        stage('Verify Golden rules compliance') {
            steps {
                sh "ansible-playbook compliance.yml -i hosts_dev --check"
                }
            }
        }


    post {
        always {
            cleanWs(cleanWhenNotBuilt: false,
                    deleteDirs: true,
                    disableDeferredWipeout: true,
                    notFailBuild: true)
            }
        }
    }
```

In Chapter 4, in the "Compliance and Reporting" section, you learned that you can also address uncompliant configurations in the same pipeline. Remediation playbooks are often complex, with commands in the negative form. However, if you are using a configuration playbook with Ansible's **--check** flag to verify compliance, to apply mitigations you only need to remove the **--check** flag. This execution applies the identified changes between the current state and the desired state. Example 6-21 shows a compliance Jenkinsfile with a remediation step using the same playbook.

Example 6-21   *Compliance Pipeline Jenkinsfile with a Remediation Step*

```
pipeline {
    agent any


    stages {
        stage('Clone repository') {
            steps {
                git (branch: 'main',
                url: 'https://github.com/IvoP1/nxos_configuration.git')
            }
        }
        stage('Verify reachability') {
            steps {
                build(job: 'reachability check')
            }
        }
        stage('Verify Golden rules compliance') {
            steps {
                sh "ansible-playbook compliance.yml -i hosts_dev --check"
            }
            post {
                failure {
                    sh "ansible-playbook compliance.yml -i hosts_dev"
                }
            }
        }
    }


    post {
        always {
            cleanWs(cleanWhenNotBuilt: false,
                    deleteDirs: true,
                    disableDeferredWipeout: true,
                    notFailBuild: true)
        }
    }
}
```

Before moving to the next section, commit the changes to your GitHub repository. You are now ready to set up your ChatOps integration.

Setting Up the Chat Interface

Open your Slack application, select a channel, and type the following:

```
/app
```

From the drop-down, select **Add apps to this channel**. In the top right, select **View App Directory**. A browser window pops up. In the search bar, type **Slash Commands** and select that application when it shows in the search results.

In the application menu, click **Add to Slack**. Type **/compliance** in the **Choose a Command** field and then click **Add Slash Command Integration**.

In the **URL** field, add the URL you copied from your Jenkins job prepended with your credentials and then replace it with the token you created, **verysecretstuff**. For example, if your credentials are **netdevops** for both the username and the password, the URL would look like the following:

```
https://netdevops:netdevops@JENKINS_URL/job/SampleJob/
build?token=verysecretstuff
```

Note   This step only works if your Jenkins URL is SSL-enabled. Otherwise, when you execute the command in Slack, it will show the following error:

```
/compliance failed with the error "dispatch_failed".
```

In the **Method** field, select **GET** from the drop-down. Scroll to the bottom of the page and click **Save Integration.**

The application is ready to use. Go back to your Slack application, in the same channel you started, and type **/compliance**. Verify the Jenkins job for which you created the trigger URL starts.

At this stage, you can trigger Jenkins actions from your chat application, Slack. This is possible with other types of chat applications, such as Cisco Webex Teams and Microsoft Teams. However, the configuration procedure will be different.

Besides triggering actions, receiving notifications is also common in ChatOps. Actually, it is the most common functionality because of the ease of this integration versus the benefits it provides. To configure it for your freestyle project, open your Slack application, select a channel, and type the following:

```
/app
```

From the drop-down, select **Add apps to this channel**. In the top right, select **View App Directory**. A browser window pops up. In the search bar, type **Jenkins CI** and select that application when it shows on the search results.

In the application menu, click **Add to Slack**. In the **Post to Channel** drop-down, select the channel you wish to receive the notifications on. Finally, click **Add Jenkins CI**

Integration. You are redirected to a new page. In a notepad, save these two values: Team Subdomain and Integration Token Credential ID. These are different for everyone; you will use them afterward in your Jenkins Job configuration.

Go back to your Jenkins UI, select the freestyle project you previously created, and click **Configure** on the left side of the page. Scroll to the bottom of the page to the **Post-build Actions** section. Click **Add post-build action** and select **Slack Notifications.** From the list, select all the notifications types you want to receive. Common ones are Notify Build Start, Notify Build Success, Notify Every Failure, and Notify Aborted. Click **Advanced** and then enter your previously saved team subdomain in the **Workspace** field.

For the **Credential** field, click **Add.** In the **Kind** field, select **Secret text** from the drop-down. Enter your previously saved integration token credential ID in the **Secret** field and then click **Add** at the bottom.

Click **Save** at the end. Your Jenkins job is now integrated with Slack notifications. Trigger this job, and verify you receive a notification.

Figure 6-4 shows a successful build notification for the PCI Compliance pipeline that took 2.2 seconds to finish.

jenkins APP 10:41 AM
PCI Compliance - #27 Started by user netdevops (Open)

PCI Compliance - #27 Success after 2.2 sec (Open)

Figure 6-4   *Slack Jenkins CI App*

You can also configure Slack notifications for your declarative pipelines. Example 6-22 shows the syntax. The message and credentials parameters are mandatory. You can tailor the message to your needs, adding variables from the build itself, as shown, or just text. The **slackSend** function is most commonly used in the **post** section of a pipeline.

Example 6-22   *Declarative Jenkins Syntax for Slack Notifications*

```
slackSend channel: 'jenkins', teamDomain: 'ivossede', tokenCredentialId: 'slack',
message: "${env.JOB_NAME} #${env.BUILD_NUMBER} ${currentBuild.currentResult}:
after ${env.BUILD_DURATION} \n"
```

Modify your declarative compliance pipeline to send Slack notifications after every execution.

At this point, you can trigger and receive status notifications of your networking activities using Slack. You can use both of these Slack integrations to configure different commands for different pipelines, and you can even pass variables at execution time. They are very flexible.

Summary

You have reached the end of this book. This last chapter consolidated what you learned from previous chapters into an end-to-end implementation and testing of a configuration NetDevOps pipeline. You used GitHub as a source control repository, created multiple Ansible playbooks as an infrastructure as code (IaC) tool as well as used Jenkins as a CI/CD orchestrator. You saw first-hand how all the pieces fit together.

You were introduced to ChatOps, a conversation-driven DevOps technique. In this chapter, you implemented it using Slack, a chat application, to trigger Jenkins pipelines and receive progress and status notifications of your networking tasks.

Although NetDevOps is more than just technologies and tools, you got hands-on practice, and you now have a working project that you can use to show your colleagues and leadership the benefits of NetDevOps.

This is not the end of your NetDevOps journey—it's only the beginning. Alter and improve this chapter's examples to fit your own networking environment and start taking advantage of automation and orchestration in your own networks. If you are needing inspiration, revisit Chapter 2 and implement one of those use cases.

Review Questions

You can find answers to these questions in Appendix A, "Answers to Review Questions."

1. Which Ansible module can be used to read all individual lines from a file?
    a. with_items
    b. with_lines
    c. lookup
    d. lineinfile

2. Which item type do you select in Jenkins for a declarative pipeline from SCM?
    a. Freestyle project
    b. Pipeline
    c. Folder
    d. SCM

3. What is the easiest way to install Ansible modules using the CLI?
    a. ansible-galaxy
    b. wget
    c. pip install
    d. curl

4. Which Ansible function allows you to verify if a certain condition is true?

   a. assert

   b. find

   c. expect

   d. when

5. Which type of build trigger do you need to configure in a Jenkins pipeline to be able to trigger it from Slack?

   a. Poll SCM

   b. Build after other projects are built

   c. Trigger builds remotely

   d. Build periodically

6. What Slack application can be used to trigger remote Jenkins jobs?

   a. Jenkins CI

   b. TriggerCMD

   c. Slash Commands

   d. Pullflow

7. Which of the following is not a benefit of ChatOps?

   a. Near real-time feedback loops

   b. Natural language support

   c. Single management interface

   d. Easy integrations

8. Which Ansible flag is used to not apply the changes?

   a. verbose

   b. check

   c. diff

   d. syntax-check

9. What are the mandatory parameters of the **slackSend** Jenkins function? (Select two.)

   a. message

   b. tokenCredentialId

   c. channel

   d. teamDomain

10. Do you need to explicitly gather facts using the **nxos_facts** module or can Ansible automatically gather device information for you?

    a. Yes, you need to explicitly do so.

    b. No, Ansible gathers device information for you.

Answers to Chapter Review Questions

Chapter 1

1. E. All of the above.

2. A. Continuous integration/continuous delivery/deployment.

3. C. It is an agentless and idempotent tool. Ansible does not require agents or other software on target devices, and the control node does require Python and other packages.

4. A. git clone, git add, git commit, and git push. The remote repository is cloned first. Next, any modifications to the file(s) are added and committed to the local repository and then pushed to the remote repository.

5. C. resources. The resources block in the configuration file defines the actual state of the infrastructure.

6. D. Jenkins. This is the tool for release management and implementing pipelines.

7. A. Cisco pyATS. This Python-based automation test suite has extensive coverage of networking devices—routers, switches, firewalls, and so on—and is one of the options for testing automation.

8. B. Streaming telemetry. This allows you to retrieve as much data as possible, as quickly as possible, and with minimal impact to the CPU processing on networking products.

9. B. False. Only Terraform builds the current state of the infrastructure that it provisions.

10. B. False. Not all the networking products offer virtualization capabilities. Also, there may be restrictions on the features and data flows supported on virtual network devices.

Chapter 2

1. B. Ansible.

2. A. Code. All NetDevOps pipelines start by checking out source code from a code repository. However, this is one of the fundamental components.

3. D. Automatic on a schedule. Most data collection jobs run continuously and are triggered on a schedule. However, you can still run them on an ad hoc basis, if required.

4. D. Unlimited. You can trigger any number of actions from an alarm—from notifications to calling other pipelines.

5. B. Retry. Idempotent actions produce the same result when executed once or multiple times. If a stage has a probability to fail but is idempotent, there is no risk in retrying the stage multiple times.

6. A. Inference stage. In machine learning, inference is the process of running live data in a machine learning algorithm to calculate an output (that is, make a prediction).

7. B. Acquiring new skills. Upskilling your current workforce or hiring additional folks to cover the missing skills is often the biggest investment a company has to make when adopting NetDevOps practices.

8. C. Solving current challenges. Solving your organization's challenges is the most important item. This should be your number-one priority when starting your NetDevOps journey.

9. D. Cloud. The cloud is not a type of tool; rather, it is a model where your tools can be hosted (that is, a hosting model). The other option is "on-premises" (that is, in your own infrastructure).

10. B. No. Although network device virtualization has improved a lot in the past few years, there is network device software that is either not available in virtual form or not fully featured. This more commonly happens with proprietary solutions.

Chapter 3

1. C. Self-managed (on-premises or cloud).

2. A. Declarative and scripted pipelines.

3. A. Distributed architecture with a controller and agents.

4. A. Yes.

5. A. True.

6. D. Webhook on GitHub.

7. A. Trigger builds remotely.

8. B. False.

9. A. Integrate Jenkins with GitHub using plugins. Create a pipeline in the Jenkinsfile and save this file in the GitHub repository.

10. C. Jenkins integrations with such tools can be done using plugins.

Chapter 4

1. A. input

2. C. GPG key

3. A. build

4. B. fixed

5. B. 0. Jenkins treats any nonzero exit code as an error.

6. C. tfsec

7. A. You would use **error(")**.

8. A, D. You can use the **options** directive for the whole pipeline or for specific stages.

9. A. The correct expression is **cron('H/30 * * * *')**.

10. B. No, you need to use a plugin such as Workspace Cleanup.

Chapter 5

1. A. True. Both VM and bare-metal installations of EVE-NG are supported.

2. A. Nested virtualization can cause performance issues.

3. C. show running-config.

4. B. False. By default, all devices are powered off (that is, stop).

5. C. SSH, HTTP, and telnet.

6. D. Linux bridge.

7. A, B, D. QEMU, IOL, and Dynamips.

8. B. False. The folder and the names of the QEMU images must follow a specific format and path.

9. B. False. Console access to network devices is possible using an application on a PC and via the web administration page using HTML5 console access.

10. A, B. **net.ipv4.ip_forward** and **net.ipv4.conf.all.rp_filter**.

Chapter 6

1. B. with_lines.

2. B. Pipeline.

3. A. ansible-galaxy.

4. A. assert.

5. C. Trigger builds remotely.

6. C. Slash Commands.

7. D. Easy integrations. Many of the tools, like Jenkins, do not yet have a native integration. Custom integrations are troublesome.

8. B. --check or -c.

9. A, B. message and tokenCredentialId.

10. B. No, Ansible gathers device information for you. If gather_facts is not disabled in your playbook, Ansible automatically gathers some device information.

Index

X-Y-Z

Register your product at **ciscopress.com/register** to unlock additional benefits:

- Save 35%* on your next purchase with an exclusive discount code
- Find companion files, errata, and product updates if available
- Sign up to receive special offers on new editions and related titles

Get more when you shop at **ciscopress.com**:

- Everyday discounts on books, eBooks, video courses, and more
- Free U.S. shipping on all orders
- Multi-format eBooks to read on your preferred device
- Print and eBook Best Value Packs

Cisco Press